Cherishing Zion

Cherishing Zion

Coping with the Death of a Child and Other Challenges of Life

Paul and Ruth Manwaring

To Adam, Moriah, Nyal,
Samuel, and Jacob

"...Thou art in thy youth, and therefore, I beseech of thee that thou wilt hear my words and learn of me; for I do know that whosoever shall put their trust in God shall be supported in their trials, and their troubles, and their afflictions, and shall be lifted up at the last day."

ALMA 36:3

"...The Lord Gave,
and The Lord Hath Taken Away;
Blessed be the Name of the Lord."

JOB 1:21

Contents

Acknowledgements

We are extremely grateful to many who have provided assistance to what Ruth and I have tried to create with the telling of our story.

We have been encouraged by others for years to write this story, and we even felt it was something we had a divine obligation to fulfill. Life can thrust things at us that deter us from our goals. We are grateful to Jason and Maxine West (Ruth's sister and our brother-in-law) for insisting we attend a book writer's workshop with them that gave us the vision and motivation to finally begin in earnest. We also thank Michelle Prince, who conducted the workshop, for her encouragement, her expertise, and her resources in bringing this work to publication.

Thank you to Rebecca Packard for her review of the manuscript and the corrections and content observations offered; to Jen Keller, who lost a daughter and has given wonderful feedback from her unique perspective. Thank you, Shelby Ward, for a serendipitous meeting that eventually led to your reading and offering a thumbs up to our attempt to approach a multi-cultural, religiously-diverse audience.

I am grateful for Joanne Johanson, my secretary, my administrative assistant, and my friend, who, on her own time, has read the manuscript more than once, offering her insights and suggestions. They have been of great value, as well as have the many discussions regarding this work.

My brothers Richard and Steve Manwaring have contributed their skills in writing, editing, and graphic design. Richard, thank you for your careful editing, but also for your suggestions on how to approach complicated ideas and delicate subjects, for which you have a wonderful talent. Steve, as a graphic artist you have a

Cherishing Zion

wonderful feel for aesthetics and visual composition. The cover of this book is mostly Steve's creation.

Ruth and I owe our lives and our faith to our parents who brought us into this world and gave us wonderful homes. They raised us, stood by us, and have supported us throughout our lives. Max and Lois Hanks have been our exemplars and cheerleaders. They are the salt of the earth. Shirley Manwaring is an amazing woman, a virtual saint. She has been a wonderful sounding board as we have often discussed elements of this work.

We are grateful to our children, Adam, Moriah, Nyal, Samuel, and Jacob, who are participants in this story. It is a family story. They have contributed in many ways, including one chapter of their own personal observations and experiences.

Introduction

The purpose of this book is to offer help and hope to our fellow men who are going through difficulties that seem too heavy to bear. Our story deals with the loss of a child and all the associated pains, questions, and trials we experienced and that perhaps you and others might experience in similar circumstances.

When my wife and I first became parents and were about to go home with Adam, our newborn son, the nurse handed me our baby, and I placed him in his car seat. We were about to leave the security of the hospital and do something on our own for which we had no prior experience. I wanted to ask, "Is there a manual you can give us to go with this infant, so we can know how to take care of this baby?" We received no manual on that occasion, but I am grateful for the "manuals" for living that have been provided by the gracious efforts of those who have experienced life and shared the lessons they learned by writing them down. During times of difficulty in my life when I was looking for answers, I have often turned to reading to gain knowledge and insights. My path has been illuminated, and I have been encouraged by the personal experiences of the authors. I have vicariously gained much through their wisdom, and it has carried me through many of my trials. They were all written by normal people who cared enough to take the time to share their stories in an article or a book. I am so grateful for their efforts. We all have times when we are in need and faced with seemingly insurmountable trials and overwhelming afflictions. Perhaps our story will give hope to those with little hope. It is my desire that this story will give answers to questions we all ask during times of great difficulty: Why me? Why did God let this happen? How do I survive this trial?

The greatest lesson I have learned in handling the toughest challenges of my life is to trust in God to help me. When other sources fail, He is always there. He can see everything we cannot, and He knows the best path for us to follow to come off conqueror of our circumstances. The following words of scripture sum up a fundamental principle of this book: "...I beseech of thee that thou wilt hear my words and learn of me; for I do know that whosoever shall put their trust in God shall be supported in their trials, and their troubles, and their afflictions, and shall be lifted up at the last day." (Alma 36:3)

God has a plan for us. He wants us to grow and develop strength as we go through life. He wants us to become like Him in character and deed. In so doing, we will ultimately find our greatest joy. He will not force us against our will, though He will encourage and try to inspire us in multiple ways. Paths of growth often take us through wonderful experiences, but usually the greatest periods of growth come through our most difficult trials. These are opportunities not to be squandered. Some of these trials are unique and rare and may never come again. It would be sad to waste, or to not gain, as much growth as we possibly can from these adversities.

I once heard the following quote: "Life is like an old-time rail journey—delays, sidetracks, smoke, dust, cinders, and jolts, interspersed only occasionally by beautiful vistas and thrilling bursts of speed. The trick is to thank the Lord for letting you have the ride" ("Big Rock Candy Mountains," *Deseret News,* 12 June 1973, A4).

This book is written for all people and all faiths, or even to those of no faith persuasion at all. It is written from my perspective, my personal experience, and my religious background as a Christian. I was initially concerned about how to write this book and who my audience would be. Should it be to only those of my faith or to a much broader audience? As my wife and I discussed it, she pointed out to me that this story is much bigger than just one limited group of people or just those of our faith. For example, you don't have to be a Jew to appreciate the story of Viktor Frankl in his book *Man's Search for Meaning*. He was an inmate in Auschwitz, a Nazi concentration camp for Jews. I am not a Jew, but I still benefited from his experiences and the lessons of life he learned and shared.

We attended a book writers conference, and I had the opportunity to share some basics about the story you are about to read. People of diverse backgrounds were there, many for the specific purpose of writing to promote their business, some for the purpose of writing a novel, etc. I was hesitant to share a faith-based personal story in this audience, not knowing how it would be received and not wanting to offend anyone or have them feel like I was somehow pushing religion on them. I finally took the risk to share our story after watching another woman openly and unashamedly talk about how her faith in God led her to write her story about working with special needs children. I saw how her openness and sharing was well received. After I had shared the basics of our story, numerous people approached me and told me this was a story that needed to be told. Some were deeply touched, even to tears. The responses and the depth of their sincerity surprised me. I was encouraged by how a brief synopsis of our story deeply affected them.

At the end of my presentation, I said, "I don't know exactly who my audience should be, but if nothing else, this story needs to be written for my children and my posterity." One man, a doctor, came up to me later and said that I was thinking way too small; this story needed to be made available to people in similar circumstances to what we went through. He handed me a note he had written: "Contact St. Jude's Children's Hospital, maybe a list of support groups, so you can get your book into the hands of as many people as possible who need your message and thereby have the greatest impact. Pediatric cardiologists, etc." Another woman wrote a brief note to me, "I love your story. My parents never recovered from the loss of my sister – and lived a horrible life! They never recovered! God will use you and your story in a big and beautiful way! Trust Him!" All of this broadened my thinking. As my wife Ruth and I talked about it, she said, "People will understand because this is a story that crosses over all barriers of faith and enters the personal struggles of life we all deal with." I trust her faith and judgment.

The events and experiences related in this book are all true and deeply personal. It is written as we have lived them.

PAUL A. MANWARING

Preface

This is a story about love. This is a story about faith and trust in God. This is a story about trial, courage, heartache, and resolve. This is a story about gratitude to God for knowing what we need and loving us enough to let us go through the pain and adversity we would never choose ourselves, in order to obtain His designs for us.

All stories of any significance have a beginning – perhaps many beginnings. I choose to start this true tale of the heart with an incident that took place during an ordinary night in the Manwaring home in Twin Falls, Idaho, sometime early in the year 2002.

CHAPTER 1

Cherish, Cherish, Cherish

I became aware of a warm body in the bed next to me, but it was not my wife. I realized it was one of my children, which was not uncommon, but it had been a while since one of them had crawled into bed with us in the middle of the night. I assumed it was one of the younger boys and went back to sleep. It wasn't until after I woke up that I realized it was my only daughter, Moriah, who was then ten years old. It had been years since she last crept into our bed in the night. Moriah and I were both awake before anyone else in the house, so I took the opportunity in the quiet of that early morning hour to ask her why she had climbed in bed next to me. She then shared a very unusual experience.

She related how she had gotten up in the middle of the night to go to the bathroom and had just climbed back in her bed when she heard a voice in her bedroom, a female voice, coming from the other side of the room next to Jacob's toddler bed. Jacob was our youngest child, and he shared a room with his sister. The voice startled her because it came from an unknown, unseen source. She said, "Daddy,

1

it kept saying the same thing over and over." I asked her what she heard. She replied, "The lady kept saying 'Cherish, cherish, cherish.'" Moriah said she hid under her blanket and closed her eyes because she was afraid. She then prayed to Heavenly Father to make it stop. When the voice ceased, she was still nervous, so she came into our room and climbed into bed next to me. After explaining all of this to me, she asked, "Daddy, what was that? What happened in my room last night?"

I initially wondered if it was all a dream, but knowing Moriah and the manner in which she spoke of these events, I felt this was a real experience for her. I then found myself thinking maybe the adversary, the devil, was trying to scare her, but my immediate reaction to that thought was "No, that does not fit Moriah." Now it needs to be understood that Moriah is a very good and pure girl. She was young, but she had already exhibited a great capacity to be obedient and loving toward her Heavenly Father and others. It just didn't feel right to even suggest it to her.

I thought for a moment and expressed an idea. "Maybe it was a spirit or an angel from Heavenly Father giving you a message that you need to cherish your little brother Jacob."

Moriah then replied, "What does 'cherish' mean?" It was then that I fully realized this experience was nothing she dreamed up or imagined. I explained, "Cherish means to treasure, to prize, or to hold dear."

Perhaps the suggestion regarding cherishing her younger brother Jacob came to me because it reminded me of a story my own mother shared when she herself was a little girl. My mother had a dear great aunt who had become old and was ill. There was a new child on its way to my mother's family that this great aunt did not live long enough to see come into the world. My mother's little sister, Carol, was born not long after her great aunt passed away. My mother was only seven years old. The death and funeral of her aunt was a sad event for my mother as she experienced for the first time the permanent separation from someone she loved. As my mother describes it, there was an alcove in her small bedroom adjacent to her bed where the bassinet was placed for Carol to sleep in during the night. One night as my mother was about to go to sleep, she lay there in her bed with a clear view of her little sister. She looked over, and to her shock and surprise, she saw her great aunt leaning over the bassinet, admiring her infant sister. My mother was very young but understood the concept of death. She had seen her great aunt's lifeless body at the viewing before the funeral. She knew her dear aunt was "gone to heaven," so she was confused and surprised to see her again. My mother became frightened and pulled the cover up over her head. Eventually, she ventured to pull the covers down again to see the same scene. This time her aunt looked over at her and smiled lovingly. A calm came over my mother. She continued to watch as her aunt returned to admiring baby Carol. My mother said, "I gradually fell asleep watching this loving and peaceful scene."

I was a little boy when my mother first told me this story. It became one of the building blocks in my development of faith in God and a belief that the veil between this life and the next can be thin at times. I also realized there is a continued interest in family relationships that extends beyond the bounds of this mortal sphere.

My suggestion to Moriah came from the context of my mother's experience. Perhaps this was a repetition of a heavenly visitation a generation later?

Then another thought impressed itself upon my mind. I said, "Or maybe it is the spirit of someone who wants to come and join our family, to be born into our family." To this, she said simply, "But Dad, then that should have happened to you or Mom, not me."

She had a good point there. But Moriah didn't know her mother's perspective and decision—she was finished having children. The last couple of attempts to have children had been very difficult for my wife, Ruth. She had been hoping for another girl to be born into our family. Ruth's patriarchal blessing[1] stated that she would be "privileged to provide mortal tabernacles for her spirit brothers and sisters." The "brothers" part was already well fulfilled with four boys in our family. The "sisters" part was still lacking one girl. Moriah was our only girl. She had been preceded in birth by her older brother Adam, and then came her younger brothers, Nyal, Samuel, and Jacob. After Jacob had been born, Ruth had felt so exhausted, she told me, "I think I am done." She asked me if that was okay. I had always felt that it was more her place to determine when she felt she had had enough children, so I replied, "If you feel we are done, I will support you." For my part, I had always wondered and felt there might be another child, but I did not know if it was just a personal quirk that I like even numbers, my interest in having a large family, or whatever else. I did not want to pressure Ruth into having more children, so I supported her in her decision. But now, with what had happened with Moriah, I began to wonder. I began to rethink our position. Something felt right about the simple suggestion or explanation I had made to my daughter of another spirit waiting to join our family.

Later that day, Ruth asked me why Moriah had climbed into our bed the night before. I related the conversation of earlier that morning. I shared my answers to Moriah without giving Ruth my impressions about them. It was later, after Ruth had pondered what I had shared, that she said she wanted to discuss the issue further. She had been thinking about what Moriah had experienced and "realized there must be a purpose for it. What was it? Should we consider having another child?" Ruth struggled because she felt that with the birth of Jacob, we were done growing our family, and she had felt relieved. On the other hand, she also recognized we had plenty of resources to bring another child into the world, and we also had the

---

1. A patriarchal blessing is a blessing that is given by a patriarch, a man of faith and wisdom, who holds the priesthood and who is in tune with God. The blessing given by a patriarch is specifically for the person receiving it. It contains counsel and specific promises from God to the individual, based on their worthiness and faithfulness.

health to do so. She wondered whether she needed to reconsider the issue. We talked about it for a while, and I shared with her some of my thoughts. I knew I needed to allow her the freedom to make her own decision. I suggested we consider fasting and praying about it. We decided to do so.

The decision-making process took a couple of months. We did not receive any definite answer about the question as to whether we ought to try again, at least not any overpowering feeling. For me, it just felt right. For Ruth, it was a struggle, and understandably so. It would be a much greater investment personally of her time and effort, a sacrifice of much greater proportions both physically and mentally. It would mean giving up some of the personal freedom she was beginning to experience with our family growing up.

Ruth weighed the pros and the cons of this matter. The cons included a list of things that concerned her, some trivial, others more serious. There were some reasons for considering the possibility of having another child. Again, her patriarchal blessing became an issue to reconsider. Moriah's experience with "cherish" played on her mind.

Ruth fasted and prayed about the decision on more than one occasion. She also went to the temple in Boise[2] as part of the process to receive inspiration. On May 16, 2002, Ruth recorded the following in her journal:

> *I came fasting. It sure would be nice to get a strong manifestation of some sort. But as I told Paul, my experience has always been to make the decision with prayer, praying to do the right thing – the Lord's will – decide – act, then receive confirmation at the end. ...But as I keep telling Paul – having another baby affects more than just me. If I had the decision,*

---

2. A temple is a church for special occasions and purposes. There are regular churches that are open to the general public for daily worship, but a temple is an even holier sanctuary for very private worship. A temple is the most sacred place of worship on earth—it is the house of the Lord. It is a place set apart from the rest of the world where faithful people can draw closer to God. The temple in Boise was nearest to us at that time.

I wouldn't – I was done. Obviously. If not, we'd have had a baby last year. But I'd made my choice and Paul had supported me and I enjoyed Jacob. I was through. I gave most of my maternity/baby stuff away, but I don't want any regrets. I don't want to wonder. I won't understand if this next child is not a girl. I have fasted with more sincerity, more frequently about this question than probably anything else. I am hugely terrified of having a baby with a disability. That's always been a concern, but I'm really concerned now.

...I have enjoyed this spring, to feel like I'm in control – I can do many projects myself instead of feeling frustrated waiting for someone else. I like having the Mendes' baby [helping care for a friend's baby], because I can give her back & sleep through the night. I wonder how the kids will do when we can't give the baby back to someone else.

I can't complain – we have the means. It will be fun to see what the Lord has in store – because obviously, it's not what I thought. I don't feel overwhelmed. A little sad about the continued struggle to get back in shape. I've had two years and I'm sadly not there – not close – not near. What's a baby going to do to this older body?

As you can see, eventually she came to the conclusion we ought to try to have another child, to exercise faith and put it into the Lord's hands and see how it would go. Before long, we found out we were expecting. Ruth's doctor was concerned because of her age, making her a higher risk of having a child with Down syndrome or other problems. He didn't realize he was playing on one of her greatest fears, having a handicapped child. She also had another great fear, the fear of losing a child. Her own mother had suffered the loss of a child, Ruth's older brother Nyal, who drowned in a canal near their home, where he was playing when he broke through the ice as a three-year-old. Ruth was not old enough to remember it herself, but she grew up witnessing the anguish and heartache her mother exhibited on many

occasions. It was a devastating experience, which completely incapac-
itated her mother for weeks after her son's death. It severely tested her
mother's faith. She shared with Ruth how she had to begin building
her faith again, brick by brick after her Nyal's death.

We had already experienced several miscarriages during the
first couple of years of our marriage. Ruth had gone through the difficulty back then of having others know that she was pregnant, and
then having it end in a miscarriage. After those first experiences,
she preferred not letting people know she was carrying a child until
it was obvious. Because of these experiences, we didn't even tell the
children, knowing they would be the least likely to keep the secret,
especially the younger ones. As time passed and Ruth's stomach
began to swell, I am sure there were a few who wondered if we were
going to have another child, but no one had yet asked about it when
something significant happened.

It was late in November 2002. Many of Ruth's family had come
to our house for Thanksgiving dinner. Ruth was busy getting things
ready when she started to bleed. She called the doctor. He told her
to take it easy, lie down as much as possible, and to come see him
the next day.

The next day, Ruth called me from the doctor's office. She was
distraught. The doctor could find no heartbeat. At the midpoint
of her pregnancy, she was being told the baby had died within her
womb. We were both heartbroken. I rushed to the hospital to be
with her. They were about to go into surgery to do a dilation and
curettage (a D&C) procedure to take the baby. We were heartsick.

Reflecting on what happened next, Ruth recorded the following:

*Even though I've miscarried before, and it should be easier
now because I have 5 kids surrounding me – it's so different
having a D&C. I get choked up whenever I think of the actual
surgery. I am ok when I remember the lack of heartbeat, I
accepted seeing the ultrasound – the body, the legs, the head*

and no heartbeat. But when I think that they literally sucked the fetus to pieces to get it out "through the smallest opening possible," I cry. I can't imagine viewing or performing the process. I feel bad my baby had to experience that (not that the spirit was there). Or to think that anyone would choose that as an option. What a horrid world we live in! A "missed abortion," the doctor called it. The only solace was that the baby had stopped developing days before. I don't even think about how the tissue had begun to decay, etc. It really did need to come out. I hadn't given up hope til there was no sound on the Doppler.

There were complications with the procedure, and Ruth lost a lot of blood. They were concerned about her and wanted to keep her in the hospital overnight for observation and to possibly give her a blood transfusion. When they told Ruth she might need a transfusion, she looked at me and said, "If I need a transfusion, then I want your blood." I asked her later why she wanted my blood, and she said simply, "I know your lifestyle, I know how healthy you are, and I know your blood is clean."

As I pondered this later, I saw an important lesson. As a believer in Christ, I rely on Him for the strength I need to be clean and pure in this world. My personal belief is that His blood is different than any other blood, in that it was sacrificed for all of us so we too might be clean and one day live again after this life is over. We would do well to acknowledge that need and say, "I want your blood. I recognize, desire, and absolutely need the blessings which come from your sacrifice on our behalf."

As it turned out, a transfusion was not needed. While she still lay in the hospital bed recovering, she looked at me, exhausted and heartbroken, and said, "I can't do this anymore. I hope you are okay with it, but I just can't do this anymore. I'm done." I didn't want to see her go through any more pain and heartache and readily agreed to her decision. We had tried, and it just didn't pan out. The doctor wanted tests to be done to find out why the baby had died. We also requested tests be done to find out what the gender was. I struggled to understand the significance of what had happened. Did this fall into the category of a stillborn child – who is not considered in medical terms as a "birth," but we can still keep a record of it in our personal journals or family record? Was the statement in Ruth's patriarchal blessing only a generic phrase … "brothers and sisters" … or should it be considered literal? What about the baby blessing[3] I had given Adam when I stated that he would be an example for his younger brothers and sisters? I had felt inspired to say that, but was it also a generic phrase?

When the tests came back, there was no conclusive evidence for exactly what caused the baby's death, but they did establish a gender. It was a girl. Ruth had already picked out a name for a little girl many years before. The name was Zion.

When she was pregnant with our fourth child, she had wanted to even out the genders at two boys and two girls. She had a girl's name picked out – Zion – but didn't even think of a boy's name. She woke up in the middle of the night with one name emblazoned on her mind like a neon sign – "Samuel." She said out loud, "But I don't want a Samuel," (meaning "I don't want a boy," plus she didn't care for the name). She later told me about the experience. I said, "Well, I guess we'll just have to wait and see. If it is a boy, then it will be Samuel."

Another interesting anecdote – it was maybe a week or so after this nighttime experience that we were babysitting a boy and trying to get all of the kids loaded up in our van to take them to soccer practice when this boy came running through the kitchen. He suddenly stopped and looked at Ruth's stomach, looked up at her, and said,

---

3. In our church and tradition, a baby is given a name and a blessing shortly after birth. Generally, this is done by the father of the child. He seeks the inspiration of heaven for the words he should speak in the blessings pronounced upon his baby.

"I think you should name this baby Samuel." He then ran on out to the car. It left Ruth and me standing there gaping at each other. She asked me if I had said anything to anyone. I replied, "No, not anyone." She said, "Neither have I." We told the boy's family about what he said, and they replied, "That's strange. He doesn't even know a Samuel." Out of the mouth of babes?

Well, that baby turned out to be a Samuel, and the next one was a Jacob. Was this last one finally a Zion? Could we count her as the second sister?

Time progressed with all the usual things to keep a family busy. Three years passed before we knew it. Our kids were very active in sports, music, church, school, and family events. With five children, there was always much to do. Adam and Moriah progressed into junior high school. Nyal, Samuel, and Jacob were all enrolled in elementary school, and Ruth kept constantly involved in worthwhile projects and just being a mom. Jacob was in kindergarten. Her days were different now because there were no more children at home during the day. It was a new phase of life, a phase she was beginning to enjoy.

CHAPTER 2

"I Didn't Warn You"

Our world began to turn upside down with an accident that took place on the night of Thursday, December 1, 2005. The first heavy snowfall of the season came that day in Twin Falls, Idaho. It was a wet snow – nearly two feet of it. I cranked up the snow blower that evening and went to work clearing our very long driveway and the walkway to our front door. The neighbors were out doing similar activities while kids were playing up and down the street. Mine were making snow forts and caves in a huge pile of snow one neighbor had pushed up into a great hill with his tractor as he plowed the private rural street we lived on. It was an evening full of happy and productive sounds, the kind of evening you could envision later ending with the family gathered around a cozy fire, each child nursing a mug of hot chocolate before bed. It was the perfect start of the Christmas season. In fact, earlier in the day, Samuel and I had taken a couple of our Christmas nativity scenes (crèches) to a community Crèche Festival to be set up for display along with scores of others temporarily donated for the purpose of celebrating the birth of Jesus

11

Christ during the Christmas season.

Since the snow was a heavy wet snow, periodically it would set-tle in the exit chute of the snow blower and form a plug that needed to be loosened up. I would shut off the augers and the blower by releasing a spring-loaded handle. I had a long screwdriver that I kept in my back pocket to break up the packed snow. After I had done so, I was able to continue for a while longer before having to repeat the process.

The kids were playing, and it was a great evening overall. The driveway was long and very wide, and it took time to get the whole thing cleared off. I finally got the job done, stopping at least a dozen times to clear the snow that had settled in the chute. I had just put the snow removal equipment away when I noticed my elderly neigh-bors' walkway covered in snow. I thought of how they weren't feeling very well and decided to clear their walkway for them. I revved up the snow blower again and headed over to their property and then up their walk. When I got to the front door, Jim and Ella May heard the machine and came out to thank me for doing their walk, and we exchanged pleasantries for a few minutes. When I turned back to the snow blower to continue, the chute was clogged again. I thought, "Well, I'll just clear this chute real fast," released the handle, and reached in my back pocket for the tool. But it wasn't there. I hadn't brought it with me. I thought, "I don't want to go all the way back home for the tool, and besides, I haven't had a problem all night clearing it out, I'll just scoop out the snow in the top of this chute with my hand and be on my way."

I reached my hand into the chute to clear out the top layer of snow. What happened next changed me forever. A tremendous pain shot through my hand. I screamed in reaction to the unseen trauma, knowing only that something had just happened to cause me severe pain. Ella May asked if I was all right. It was then that I looked at my hand, which I had been shaking because of the pain. What I saw was a sight no one would ever want to see on another human being, let alone on one's own person. It was truly a gruesome sight. I'm sure I must have looked dumbfounded as I stood there staring at my right hand, shielded from their view. In shock and disbelief, I numbly replied, "I have just lost all four of my fingers." All that remained were mangled remnants and bloody stumps.

Jim was a take-charge kind of guy. He and his wife quickly moved into action to provide me with a towel for the bleeding and to call an ambulance. They made me sit down on a bench on their porch. Another neighbor, Todd Coates, came running when he heard my scream and took on the gruesome task of looking in the snow blower and snow for my missing fingers.

I was immersed in shock and disbelief. My first thought was, "Hold on! Stop! Let's go back and try that again!" I wanted to hit the rewind or reset button. I could not grasp that this was really happening to me. But within moments I realized this was for real, and my next thought was simply, "This is permanent."

In psychology, I have studied the steps a person goes through following a significant loss, such as the death of a loved one, but it can apply to any loss. What happened for me was a classic example of progression through those steps of loss and grief, but what amazes me is that it all took place within a couple of minutes, a process that can take months or even years to complete.

Denial was the first stage, followed by anger. I became so angry. I chastised myself, "How could you be so stupid? You know better than that. How could you have put your hand into a running machine? What could you have been thinking?"

Perhaps I sensed the futility of such a course, or perhaps the next stage came quickly because of the compelling nature of the circumstance – but grief and despair were my next emotions. I realized I was facing the prospect of a handicap for the rest of my life. I am right-handed, and this was my right hand that was injured and maimed. I knew this would leave me unable to perform many tasks with the ease I had always enjoyed. My thoughts were full of despondency, "What am I going to do? What will become of me? How will I get along?"

In the midst of my hopelessness, I found myself directing my thoughts toward heaven in a pleading prayer based on faith, trust, and testimony. "Why wasn't I warned? Why was there no warning?" You see, I have had many experiences where God has warned me about impending danger.

One summer I was leading a group of friends, including a couple of my brothers, on a hike/scramble/climb up Deertrap Mountain in Zion National Park, where I worked for three summers while going through college. We were almost to the top, after ascending over two thousand vertical feet. Our trek brought us to a narrow ridge. There was a sheer drop-off of two thousand feet on one side and hundreds of feet of steep drop-off on the other side. We had only a final twelve-foot cliff to scale to reach the top. As we contemplated how to climb this small cliff safely, I had the impression that we should not go on. The alternative was to turn around and go back, all the way back down the way we had come – a precarious descent. If we scaled this last twelve feet, we would reach the rim trail, and it would be a safe and leisurely walk off the mountain via another route, an established trail. The warning, however, was clear. I could not shake it. So we went back, despite the great inconvenience. It took at least twice, maybe three times longer to retrace our route than it would have to have continued. But everyone returned safely. I still feel confident that the outcome would have been tragic, even fatal, had I made a different choice.

On another occasion in Zion National Park, some of us had decided to explore a narrow canyon, Pine Creek Canyon, near the Great Arch. Before we had reached the mouth of the canyon, there was a summer cloudburst that brought a nice cleansing rainfall. It forced us to take shelter under a ledge. After the storm, a downpour of forty-five minutes, I volunteered to go ahead and explore the canyon while the others went to get some gear we had stored back down the trail.

As I walked along the floor of this canyon, I admired the beauty of the canyon walls towering above me two hundred feet on each side, though only about twenty feet apart. It was serene and gorgeous. The sun filtered down the red canyon walls causing a kaleidoscope of colors. I wished I had a camera with me to preserve the beauty. In the midst of this quiet moment, I had an interesting impression that I should turn around and go back. I simply obeyed the thought, not thinking much about it. After a short time, I had another thought impress itself upon my mind, and with this thought came an unmistakable sense of urgency. HURRY! I picked up my pace from a leisurely walk to a brisk one. I wondered as I strode along, why the hurry?

This continued only for a short time. What happened next, I will never forget. I heard a voice, and whether it was an external audible voice or internal, it was as real as anything I have ever heard. But this time the message came with great urgency, volume, and pitch, and was literally shouted at me: RUN!!! Its suddenness and power startled me into action. I immediately began to run at full speed, a full-out sprint toward the canyon entrance, probably about 150 yards away. As soon as I cleared the canyon mouth, I scrambled to higher ground and stopped, sucking in air to catch my breath, trying to comprehend what was going on, having no idea why I had been commanded to run.

Within ten seconds after exiting the narrow canyon, I heard a roar like a thunderstorm, but there was no sign of rain. At that moment, a wall of muddy water and churning debris about ten feet high exploded from the canyon mouth I had just exited like it was shot out of a fire hose. The torrent, churning just a few steps below me, continued another 30-40 yards before going over the edge of a 120-foot cliff. This was a flash flood. I have never been so close to such a powerful, dangerous display of nature. The volume of water grew, and I watched as a cottonwood tree was ripped from the bank opposite me and sucked into the flood, where it snapped like a toothpick. I grew weak with the humble realization and sure knowledge that this was nothing I would have survived without that warning. I had no suspicion of any danger present, but the Lord knew what was coming. He warned me and preserved my life. There is no other explanation for me. And I have ever been grateful to Him for His kindness. I gained a sure testimony that day that He can indeed warn us of impending dangers if we will listen and obey. The list of experiences goes on and on throughout my life, though this last one was the most dramatic. So many times, my life, health, and happiness have been preserved by whisperings or warnings from the Spirit. Thus, the question, "Why was there no warning?"

In that moment of my great despair, standing there with my bloody and mangled hand, I heard a quiet and clear answer to my plea, almost like an audible voice, and certainly just as clear to understand. It said simply, "I didn't warn you." But with that answer came a peace and a comfort I will always appreciate. Instead of reacting with further anger or despair, brought on by a feeling of abandonment, my thoughts were, "So this accident is okay with you. You knew I would do this." Along with those thoughts and feelings came a trust that He would stand by my side and everything would be all right. I felt an assurance that somehow He would also see me through it to the end.

From that moment on, I knew everything was going to be all right. I knew I would be able to adjust, and I would be able to handle whatever might be a part of the healing and the handling of problems associated with this accident in the future. It is still a matter of gratitude and amazement to me that I have never looked back with regret, and I have never felt a reason to be angry at the situation or myself, or to despair since that moment. There would still be challenges ahead, but these were all manageable from this point on. All of this took place in only a couple of minutes as I sat there on the porch while my neighbors were frantically doing damage control.

I share this because it plays into the future of this story. It serves as preparation for events to come. Often one trial or adversity prepares us for others in our future.

It was my neighbor who discovered later while putting away the snow blower for us that the spring-loaded handle had stuck that one time. As I had tried to clear the snow with my hand, I thought only the engine was running, but in fact, the auger and blower were also fully engaged.

I remember the ambulance taking so long that I just about got up and went to my car to drive myself to the hospital. My only wish was to get medical attention and get things on their way to healing. The protests of my neighbor Jim kept me there waiting. The ambulance finally arrived and transported me to the emergency room. En route, I was able to talk to my wife via the EMT's cell phone and asked her to do two things: Please call President Kent J. Allen, our Stake President (a church leader)[1] who was also a doctor (dentist) and ask him who he might recommend as a good orthopedic surgeon. I also asked her to call our Bishop and my friend, Todd Clark, to come and give me a blessing. My neighbor Todd Coates had given me my fingers (or remnants thereof) which he had packed in a snowball and placed in a baggie. I handed it to the EMT. He asked me what it was, and I replied, "My fingers are in there." His comment on that is also a point of instruction. He said, "You never put damaged tissue directly on ice. It can freeze the tissue so it begins to die and become useless for reattachment."

Ruth followed us to the hospital and showed up not too long after I arrived. It was the first time we had seen each other since before the accident. Bishop Clark arrived right after.

I have to say that up to this point I had been able to maintain a healthy attitude about what had just happened to me. I had already decided to be positive about the experience and to accept the unfortunate circumstances of what had happened. I found myself in

---

1. A Stake President is a church leader that has responsibility over several congregations within his stewardship (a Stake). These congregations that comprise a Stake are called Wards, which are each overseen by a Bishop. These men are asked to serve for a period (years) without any compensation. This they do in addition to their regular occupation.

a good frame of mind. It was a good thing the Bishop was there, too. Bishop Clark has a cool head and a great sense of humor. He joked with me about the whole experience, which was right in line with my disposition at that point in time. We both knew the value of being able to joke about serious matters to relieve anxiety. He helped turn an obvious tragedy into a normal life event to be joked about on the spot – not having to wait two or three months for such an attitude to develop. While we talked, he stood at the foot of the gurney I was lying on, and he tied my shoelaces together. He made jokes about my being a little "short handed." I still use that quip and many others from that evening in the ER.

Having gotten a call at the end of a dinner date, Presidents Allen and Browning (a counselor in the Stake presidency) arrived shortly thereafter with their wives. I was grateful they were all allowed into the emergency unit. Bart Browning is another jokester, and there was further humor and laughter. I remember asking what they had for dinner, and he quipped, "Oh, not much, just some finger food." He might/might not have meant it as a joke, but we all saw the connection, and then the humor of it, and laughed together over the unintentional (?) pun. The nurses and hospital personnel must have wondered what the mirth was all about, but it was just what I needed. In fact, later when the surgeon eventually arrived and came into the curtained emergency room, he said, "From the laughter I heard before coming in, I thought this was the wrong room. It sounds like we are having a party in here."

At one point, things turned a little more serious, and I said, "I would like a blessing[2] to help with the surgery and the road ahead." I recorded the following in my journal a couple of days later (typing with my left hand) on Dec. 3, 2005:

2. Blessings will be mentioned often in this volume. Blessings can be given by those who hold the priesthood. They lay their hands on the head of the person being blessed and speak the words they feel inspired to express. These blessings are given for both healing and comfort. In James 5:14-15 of the New Testament it states, "Is any sick among you? Let him call for the elders of the church; and let them pray over him, anointing him with oil in the name of the Lord; and the prayer of faith shall save the sick, and the Lord shall raise him up."

Bishop Todd Clark anointed my head with oil and Pres. Kent Allen sealed the anointing with a blessing. I don't remember everything that was said, but I do remember being told the doctor would be blessed in the operating procedure and my hand would heal well, and that with the physical healing would also come an emotional healing; that I would be able to accept my circumstance and have a positive attitude about it. I felt greatly comforted by this blessing. I felt very comforted by the presence of these good brethren. I was grateful Ruth was there and how she tried so hard to be strong. She fell in step with the positive attitude that was present. The only time I cried was when I looked over after the blessing and saw Ruth in tears. It was a cry on both of our parts born of mutual love and caring. I felt a deep tenderness also for my brethren in this great and powerful fraternity of the priesthood. I remember taking Pres. Allen, as he came to give me a hug, and in a very natural way pulling his face next to mine and giving him a kiss on the cheek. I did the same with the Bishop who has been such a good friend.

Their love and concern were apparent just by their presence. In the days ahead, I learned how important and significant it is when someone pays a visit to another person who is going through a difficulty or a challenge in their life. Sometimes, that is all that is needed, just to show up. I know it was good for my wife for them to be there also and for the comfort she felt with dear friends supporting her. I didn't realize it at the time, but she was dealing with her own anxiety and fears behind a mask of calm.

Dr. Retmier was the surgeon on call, and we had been informed by our sources that he was very good. When he arrived, he examined my hand and gave me some wonderful counsel, which confirmed everything that was in my mind. It was just good to hear it audibly expressed. He said, "Don't second guess yourself over what could have been done differently. Don't worry about the coulda, woulda, or shouldas. It won't do you any good." (For example: I could've done such and such differently or I wish I would've simply not helped my neighbor, etc.) He continued, "Just move on and concentrate on getting better. You'll be okay. Life will be fine. You'll adjust and be able to do much of what you have always been able to do."

I can't tell you how much I appreciated his advice. It was full of hope and the perspective of moving forward. Finally, after two hours in the emergency room, I bid farewell to my wife and friends as I was wheeled into surgery. The following paragraph is part of my journal entry from December 3, 2005, and explains what happened next:

> *I was then put under general anesthesia for the operation. …After the surgery was completed, Dr. Retmier visited with Ruth and told her that he was pleased he was able to save as much of my index finger as he was. The middle two fingers are lost, basically below or about the middle knuckle. The index finger that remains is somewhere between the middle and the end knuckle. The surgery took a couple of hours. I remember coming out of the fog and the very comfortable sleep I was in and asking the time and asking with very slurred speech for Ruth. She stayed with me till I was settled in my room about 2:45 AM before she finally went home. I had another great sleep and was up in the morning about 6:30. I felt like I wanted to get up and get going. I was allowed to walk around and did some visiting with folks I met to see if I could serve anyone and cheer them up. I spent a good while with EJ Morgan and his wife. He had a hip replacement. He was the father of our former Bishop - Paul Morgan.*

I have discovered that serving others is a good strategy in dealing with those things that usually drive us to self-pity and self-focus. It felt good to serve someone else and to turn the focus away from myself. My wife was able to bring the children to see me before they went to school that day, a Friday. They had such concern on their faces. Their love and concern was very tender and a great comfort to me. I was also able to joke with them, reassure them, and help them understand that this was not a terrible tragedy, and that everything would be okay. I knew that if others sensed I was okay with what was happening, they could be okay with it as well. "Besides," I said, "I have had fifty good years with those fingers. I can manage for the next fifty without them. Plus, I will get them back in the Resurrection anyway."

My journal entry continued:

...They allowed me to be released from the hospital around 9-9:30 AM. I had a lot of visitors and callers yesterday at home. When we arrived at home, Bishop Morgan (our former Bishop and now 2nd counselor in the stake presidency) & his wife were waiting for us. We had a nice visit. He said that Pres. Allen had something he wanted to share with me, an impression he had during the blessing he gave me."

Pres. Allen did come by later in the day to see how I was doing. He said he wanted to share a thought that had come to him, a comparison that although not perfect seemed appropriate. He told me, "You were wounded and received scars in your hand while helping a neighbor. Jesus too received wounds in His hands while helping His brothers and sisters." Then he said, "Whenever you look at your hand, remember that you share this with Him. The Savior sustained wounds in His hands from the great good He did for all of us with the atonement. Someday your hand will be fully restored because of the power of Christ through the Resurrection." I like those thoughts.

I have since used my hand to participate in sacred ordinances, and I have been grateful that He left me enough of a right hand that I can participate fully in those ordinances – in the temple and in partaking of the sacrament. The right hand has often been considered the covenant hand. I recorded the following on December 4, 2005:

It has caused me to ponder further, especially as I was tired last night and found my positive outlook being tested and slipping into discouragement – that this is to be my covenant hand, and to be used in doing good. It needs to have some things connected to it, like a compassionate heart. I realized too that this is my escape from despair – namely – service to others. I will not raise this hand in anger, but only in compassion and giving. I pray I can ever be true to this concept.

Over the next few days, I had many visitors and condolences expressed in cards and phone calls. One friend, Will Kezele, came by with his wife Robyn and asked if he could do something for me. I could not think of anything right off. Then he had an idea. He knew I wore a tie each day to work. He asked if I could bring him five of my favorite ties, which I did. As we talked, he tied a tie around his neck, then loosened it and slipped it off his head. He proceeded to the next tie until all were ready for my use. All I had to do was slip it over my head and tighten it up. I was also touched by Samuel, my seven-year-old son, who wanted to do something for me. He insisted on being my scribe when I needed to write things down.

Each visit felt like the hand of God reaching out to me or putting a loving arm around me. It is hard to explain how that was for me, but it is a lesson I will never forget. I literally felt God's love and reassurance in every kind expression of love and concern from everyone who approached me in any form. I don't think they realized how personally they were working with God on His behalf. I pray I can always be such an instrument in His hands and remember that it is worth the sacrifice of a minute or two to participate in the transference of His love to one of His children in need.

My way of dealing with this injury was different than my wife's way. She wanted me to stay down after the surgery, but the doctor had said that I could resume life as I normally live it. My wife quipped, "Yes, but you don't know how Paul *normally* lives his life."

I stayed down that Friday, but by the end of the day, I felt like I had to be doing something. The next morning (Saturday the 3rd) was a temple trip with the ward (our local church congregation), and the Bishop had asked if I would like to go. I thought, "What could be better right now for me than to draw closer to my Heavenly Father?" It was a wonderful trip. It was also a long trip, one hour and forty-five minutes each way to Boise and back, plus the two hours spent in the temple. The next day (Sunday), I arranged to be picked up and driven to my early morning High Council meeting. When I later saw Ruth at church, she was furious with me. I couldn't understand it at first, but then it dawned on me that she was scared. This is how her anxiety came out. This was a new and scary thing. She also reminded me that the doctor had said there was a possibility that the repair on my index finger or little finger might not take, and I could lose them. She feared that my overdoing things might result in such loss. I reassured her everything would be all right, and then I complied with her wishes and took it easy.

I read of a couple where the husband had been diagnosed with pancreatic cancer, a fatal disease. In the article, his wife was asked how they dealt with the difficulties, if they ever argued. She replied, "As far as our classic arguments, yeah here and there. I'd get all pissed off because I thought he'd acted badly, but he had a good reason. He had cancer. During one of our arguments, he brought up the C word, which really upset me. Not so calmly, I said back to him, 'This is happening to me, too.' The look on his face was so heartbreaking. It stopped everything in its tracks right there, and he actually never pulled out that card again." (Lisa Niemi, widow of Patrick Swayze). I share this because I understand even better now that when you care about someone, when they are going through a difficult life-changing experience, you too are going through it with them.

I will never forget the day we went in to have the bandages removed for the first time after surgery. Ruth was with me, and I really wanted to protect her from the scene she would be exposed to. At least I had already seen what it looked like after the accident. She had not. In the emergency room, my hand had been wrapped in a towel. We were given the option of either coming in every day to have a nurse change the dressings, or Ruth could be shown how to do it. I seriously thought she would go for the first option, so I was quite surprised when she said she would do it. She has always deferred any bleeding wounds to me when our children have suffered injury because it makes her too queasy. But here she was, willing to learn how to take care of me and change my dressings.

When they removed the bandages that first time after surgery, it was quite a sight. I was not expecting to see what I saw. It made me feel weak. I tried to have a good sense of humor and put on a show of strength, but it was hard to do, staring at the ghastly sight of sewn flesh and the absence of what had once been there. I then began to worry about Ruth. She got a bit nauseous at one point, but she hung in there. About this and subsequent events I wrote:

> *I have been trying to joke and put on a good attitude about the whole thing – however I must admit, the toughest part is when I see my hand – my altered hand, my modified hand, and the state it is now in. It isn't pretty – but the doctor says that it looks healthy and that there is no infection. For this, we are grateful. Ruth has been a true blessing to me. She has been strong at these moments when the dressing is changed and doesn't seem too bothered by the scene. It helps me to maintain my positive view even in private. I truly do believe all will be alright. I guess reality checks are a good balance. It is truly an altered existence. It will be nice when this slow healing process is much further along.*

I cannot express my gratitude sufficiently for her care and her sensitivity to my needs over the next few weeks. More than once, I told her that I could go through this on my own if I really had to

– but I was glad I didn't have to. It was such a comfort to have her there doing what no one else would want to do. I asked how she was able to handle it so well. She replied, "Because someone has to do it." I know it was more than that. Love and care give us strength beyond our current abilities.

Healing takes time. In retrospect, some aspects of the healing process seemed to go quickly, while others dragged on and on. As I went through physical therapy, I was hoping to have normal feeling in what was left of my fingers, but even now, they continue to feel swollen and stiff much of the time (more than twelve years have now passed). I constantly must work out the stiffness, and an hour later, I can do it all over again. There is nothing better than to have someone rub my hand. I could have someone do it all day long, and it still wouldn't be enough. The only thing that would cause me to say "stop" would be guilt for making someone use up so much of their time and energy on me. Once while in a church meeting, singing "I need thee every hour," I realized that my hand was a lesson in that regard. It reminds me that I do need Him every hour, that in nothing can we receive His help once and then not need Him anymore. I wrote on December 21, 2005:

> *I am beginning to realize something of the long haul as this healing process is making itself evident as a long continual process. The doctor told me it would be a year before I really know what I have in terms of a functional hand. It has been easy in some ways to be positive the past while. I can see how that can be challenged over time. I intend to be a marathoner with this – to persevere and maintain a positive outlook over time. I will simply make the best of what I have to work with. I will try to not get too discouraged. Some things will take longer, and some will require creative solutions – require me to develop new skills. Every once in a while, I have reality checks about the things I will and will not be able to do. Bowling. I*

saw a bowling ball the other day in a thrift store. Two of the three holes would remain empty with my new situation. How can I solve this? Well, I suppose that I could have a ball drilled for my index and my little finger – or – I could learn to bowl left handed.

On that last note, I have learned to bowl left-handed.

I have had to learn to write holding a pen/pencil between my thumb and the remainder of my index finger. What is also amazing to me is that my handwriting for the most part has not changed much. It appears that handwriting is more a part of the personality and the person, rather than just the physical appendage that expresses it. This makes sense to me because I still am the same person I always was. I must accept that some people view me differently when they see my hand, but that doesn't change who I am, what I believe, and how I treat others.

I remember walking with my wife in the mall after I had the cumbersome wad of bandages from surgery removed, when each finger stub was wrapped individually, and my loss was clearly evident to all. I remember feeling self-conscious and wanting to hide my hand. I did not want others to have to pity me, feel sorry for me, or avoid me. Then as I thought about it further, I realized others would be comfortable with me if I was comfortable with myself. I made a decision on that day that I would not let it bother me, and I would behave around others in a manner that they would know it didn't bother me. That was the right decision, a good decision, a significant life-altering decision. I have seen the benefits of it many times.

There have been other adjustments as well. I had to learn a new way of typing. Even now as I "write," I use the new modified method that began when my hand was bandaged. Only my thumb was available during those first few weeks. I continued to use my left hand with all the normal keys, and then did the "hunt and peck" method with my right hand (thumb). I have gotten faster, but I will undoubtedly never be typing at about a hundred words a minute like I used to. I have also learned to adjust to other things that a right-handed person would normally do, and I have become somewhat ambidextrous. I always try first with my right hand, and if I cannot do what I am attempting to do, then I switch to the left. I have found I can still do most things with the right hand. My wife says it is because I am stubborn and persistent. I suppose she is right, but I just like to know my limitations. And I also try to eliminate all the limitations that I can. Most can be overcome with effort.

Recently, my sister-in-law Paula asked if I could share my thoughts about staying cheerful during difficult times. She was going to teach a lesson on the subject and wondered what I could share from my experiences. My letter to her includes much of what I have just shared, plus some things I want to make sure are mentioned:

Dear Paula,

I am happy to respond to your request. I hope I can capsulize this in just a few short concepts. I have actually been thinking about this a lot lately.

Being able to be cheerful during great difficulty? It really starts with and ends with Faith.

When I lost my fingers, the ability to handle that incident did not begin at the doorstep of my neighbors. In the months previous I feel like I had been prepared. I had been trying hard to be in tune with God by doing the normal little things we all are supposed to do. As I look back on it, I think I was prepared in a number of ways, months in advance, without knowing I was being prepared for anything. It started with a goal I set during the previous summer to be more submissive to whatever difficult circumstances or inconveniences might come my way - like a flat tire, an untimely stoplight, someone getting in my face about something, or whatever. I remember too that a book had just come out I had heard about and felt like I ought to read: Between a Rock and a Hard Place by Aaron Ralston (he had a hiking accident and had to cut off his own arm to survive). I kept putting off going to the bookstore to find it, but one day, saw it in Costco – so I snagged it up and read it. It totally changed my thinking about losing a limb and gave me the perspective that it does not have to change the person or the quality of life. I finished the book only a week before my accident.

I had come to trust God over the years, and that there is often a purpose to the challenges we experience. I also had faith and trust that He can guide us away from unnecessary hardships by giving us warnings from the Spirit. Difficulties must be viewed from a more eternal perspective.

Paula, I think what happened on my neighbor's doorstep was really a culmination of the preparations that had gone before. When I looked down and saw the mess my hand had become plus the accompanying despondency I felt ... it was now a natural trigger for me to turn immediately to my Heavenly Father with one pleading question: "Why wasn't I warned?" I just knew if I had been warned I would have held back. I would have responded to a feeling of restraint. I was confident I was in a position to hear ... but then I did hear. An answer came immediately, "I did not warn you." I think that months earlier I would have been a bit angry with the Lord with that answer. I would have felt like He did not care, but there, in that moment, I had such a trust and faith in my Heavenly Father that I submitted to my situation, even as I had been practicing daily, almost hourly, for some time. ...I did not feel like I needed to know the purpose, it was enough to realize He was aware of me and my plight. I also knew right then and there that He would help me through whatever difficulties and adjustments may lay ahead. It was a "knowing" that came with the feelings of comfort from the Spirit.

It still amazes me in a way that that moment changed everything. My whole attitude switched from being despondent to being more upbeat. I can honestly say I have never felt like I needed to look back.

...I share the experience with my fingers because it is a quicker one to share to make some of the points I wanted to make. But the same principles applied with what would take place over the next few months following the loss of my fingers. Maybe the fingers accident was another preparation for our next trial. ...But our next experience was more intense and a whole new level of stress and difficulty. We had to keep coming back to trust and faith with each new bump and turn in the road, of which there were many. Each time faith proved to be the answer to each new situation. He provided what we needed when we needed it. There were also tender mercies all along the way – as you know. I think those tender mercies are always there for each one of us, if we will just look for them. They are reassurances that He is aware of us and that He loves us and cares about our feelings. He is constantly watching over us. This alone can give us great cause to be joyful.

I hope this helps in some way.

Love,
Paul

The great point of the preceding letter is that in hindsight I can see with clarity that I was being prepared without realizing it. I believe all of us are being prepared for the challenges we have yet to face, if we are willing to respond to our present circumstances with faith. As we try to handle the smaller challenges, they prepare us in ways that are imperceptible at the time, for unseen trials and adversities around the next bend. Perhaps our story can be for someone else what Aaron Ralston's book was for me: a needed preparation for something that might otherwise become a challenge beyond one's capacity to endure. Our experience will not be yours just as Aaron's was not mine, but perhaps the principles and similarities will be a blessing. I once heard it said, "If you approach everyone you meet as if they are currently going through some type of crisis in their life, you will be right about half the time." Perhaps there are things in this book that will speak directly to someone who is in the middle of a crisis and pleading for hope and help.

It was sometime in the next couple of months, during the healing process of my hand, that Ruth made one of the most shocking discoveries of her life. Another journal entry from March 26, 2006, provides a bridge that ties this last experience to the next significant part of our story:

> *...Lately I have noticed things about Ruth and her demeanor that have left me wondering about something, especially when it seemed that she was late with her period this month. I started to put it all together and it made sense that the unthinkable may be happening. Is Ruth pregnant? I pondered this for a couple of days before I finally asked her about it yesterday. She said that she is having all the symptoms of pregnancy (unless it is menopause). I asked how that is even possible, to which she replied, "I don't know." We have been very cautious and have not been careless about this matter. It is a bit scary at this point. My first thought has been – "I'm 50 years old. I have no business having a baby at this age. I will be well past retirement when this baby is old enough to leave home. I had wanted to go on service missions with Ruth right after we retire (and retire early if possible)." Then, I thought*

*of Ruth – she is really going to be impacted by all of this even
more than me. She is on the brink of having her days to herself
– with Jacob going into first grade next year.*

Ruth initially suspected – and then feared – and then had confirmed – that she was again expecting a child. To say this was
unexpected would be a gross understatement. It simply should not
have happened. I repeat: It just should not have happened.

CHAPTER 3

A Partner with the Great Creator

Our reactions to what was happening were quite different. Ruth was despondent and shocked. Her whole world was rocked and shaken. All her plans were being drastically altered by events beyond her control. She was into a new stage of life, and her daytime hours were her own. Jacob was now in kindergarten for half of the school day and next year would be in school all day long with his siblings. Ruth had the freedom to serve and help others and get the things done she had been putting off for some time. I could understand her feelings, but my thoughts were in a different direction. They made it hard to totally empathize with her.

My first reaction was – "This is from God. This is not even supposed to be happening. The only way it could happen is if His hand is in it." I also *knew* immediately this was the little girl promised to us, the fulfillment of Ruth's patriarchal blessing. It was a knowing built totally on faith, but I sensed it was true. I knew I had to carefully nurse Ruth along, but it was not easy. Underlying her fears of having to give up a portion of freedom in her life was something much deeper, something neither she nor I would understand for some time to come – something that would shape the purpose of this whole story and reshape our future, our family, and our faith.

It is somewhat ironic that here she was struggling with the thoughts of having a baby when the story had been very different seventeen years earlier, right after we first got married (1989). We were both Brigham Young University students, and Ruth was working at the Missionary Training Center as a teacher, having returned from the California Ventura Mission only a short time before we met and started dating. I was a graduate student working on a PhD and teaching some classes at BYU. We decided we were both far enough along in life that we would start our family as soon as we were married and let the Lord determine when our first child would be born. As it turned out, it happened right away. Ruth became pregnant, and we were both excited about the news.

We looked at books that tracked the development of the embryo and fetus, and we read about what to do and what not to do. We wanted to be good, responsible parents, even as the baby developed in the womb. As time progressed, it was hard to keep it a secret. In fact, we had no reason to keep this a secret, so our family and friends became aware very early on that we were expecting. Ruth was surprised she did not feel the morning sickness many young mothers-to-be endure, so this started out as a pleasant and exciting experience all around.

Then one day, a Friday in early May, I got a phone call from Ruth while I was at my office on campus. She had gone in for a checkup because of some abdominal discomfort she was experiencing. The doctor was concerned, and he had ordered an ultrasound at the hospital. He told her he was not sure but thought it could be a tubal pregnancy. Ruth was alarmed. This was terrible news. She understood that if this was a tubal (ectopic) pregnancy, the pregnancy would have to be terminated, and she would also lose the fallopian tube that was home to this fetus, this developing baby of about two and a half months. The situation was even worse than that. This was the only fallopian tube she had, due to something that had happened as she prepared to serve a mission. Ruth explains:

> *Part of the mission application process included a compre-*
> *hensive medical exam, so at age 20 I had my first physical.*
> *As thorough and embarrassing as that initial exam was, the*
> *doctor was concerned with a mass he felt in my abdomen, so*
> *he sent me to another doctor to affirm his concern. They both*
> *suggested I have an ultrasound done. The ultrasound verified*
> *that I had a mass the size of a grapefruit, and I was scheduled*
> *for surgery to remove a dermoid cyst. It was situated and had*
> *so grown that it required removal of the ovary nearest it. I*
> *was left to heal and wonder how the surgery would affect my*
> *ability to have children in the future.*

So, with one ovary removed, she had only one ovary remaining. If that was taken too, then she would never have her own children. Having children and a family was of paramount importance to her. It was her great goal and desire in life.

I met her at home, and we had a prayer together. In that prayer, we pleaded with the Lord that everything would be all right, that he would spare her the results we feared. I also committed to Heavenly Father that we would concede to His will and trust that everything would be all right. It was a hurried prayer because we barely had time to make our appointment.

The nurse who did the ultrasound explained what she was doing, and at one point, she pointed to a little white light pulsating on the screen and asked, "Do you know what that is?" We answered, "No." She replied, "That is your baby's heart beating."

I have never had the feeling that I experienced with that news. I felt a rush of emotions that was profound. It was a feeling that flooded over and through me like nothing ever had. This was a new life we had created! And there on that screen, we could see the evidence of it inside Ruth! It was an amazing feeling for me as a father.

I felt I was in the company of the great creator of all life, and indeed was a partner with Him. It was a feeling of sacredness filled with humility, gratitude, and awe.

As the nurse proceeded with the examination, we waited silently. Finally, after checking and double-checking, she said this was a "viable pregnancy." I wanted to be sure what that meant, and I asked her for clarification. She said that the pregnancy was in the right place, and we should not have any problems. We were so relieved and left the hospital stress-free.

The relief did not last long, however. Later that evening, Ruth began to bleed a little bit, and she called the doctor. He said she was threatening miscarriage and needed to stay down, getting up only to go to the bathroom, and that the next twenty-four hours were important. She followed the doctor's instructions faithfully. I tended to her and brought her whatever she needed. The next day was a Saturday, and she was able to rest without worrying about school or her job responsibilities. Later in the afternoon, she sent me out to run some errands. When I returned, she was not on the couch where I had left her. There was a trail of blood from the couch to the bathroom, where I found her in tears. She had already called the doctor, who informed her that she needed to get to the hospital. She was having a miscarriage and would need to complete the process there with medical attention.

We spent a long time in the emergency room. We were finally ushered to an examination room to wait. There were others in more urgent need of the staff than we were. While we waited, Ruth experienced the pain of a complete miscarriage without the assistance of medical staff before they were able to come and help us. The process took place naturally. Once this was confirmed, the doctor completed what he needed to do. The doctor who saw to her needs was a good man. He tried to offer Ruth encouragement. He said, "I know this is most difficult right now, but these things happen because there is often something not quite right with the development of the baby. It is a blessing that the pregnancy does not continue." However true those words may be, they can offer only so much comfort at a time like this. A miscarriage is not just the loss of a baby, which is tremendous in its own right, but it is the loss of the possibility of what might have been. The hopes and dreams that naturally accompany the anticipation of the birth and growth of a child are suddenly crushed and gone. The devastation is tremendous.

It was midnight before we got home, tired, physically exhausted, and heartbroken. Ruth was indeed devastated. I tried to comfort her, encourage her, but couldn't seem to find the words that would penetrate her solemn mood of numbed silence. She was not to be consoled. I tried to reassure her that everything would be all right, and we would yet have children – but the attempt fell on deaf ears and a broken heart.

The next morning, she felt up to going to church, and perhaps hoped to find there some comfort and solace. We did not count on what would await us there. It just happened that this Sunday was Mother's Day. As she put it: "I was twice wounded in my heart ... all the talks and songs were praising motherhood, and I winced at all the happy smiles that were lit up around me." The talks, the songs, the theme – all reminded her of what she was not to be.

Our congregation had a tradition of recognizing the mothers by giving each of them a flower at the end of the service. Certain mothers were singled out. They had the oldest mother stand to be recognized, and she received a flower. They had the mother of the most children stand, the newest mother, and then they asked for the newest expectant mother. Others looked to Ruth, not knowing what had just happened the night before, thinking she was the person who should stand and accept the honor. She was horrified and wanted to flee the church. She did not want a flower. She did not want to be there. She wanted desperately to go home and begged me, "Please take me home now." We left. She felt exhausted and emotionally overwhelmed. I tried once again to console her. I asked her how I could help. I asked her to tell me what she was feeling, to talk about it, to help me understand what she needed, but she would not talk. I felt frustrated. I felt useless and inept. She just wanted to sleep.

As she fell asleep, I felt like I needed to go for a drive. I am the kind of guy who wants to fix things, to make them better, and I was failing most miserably with trying to help my wife. I didn't know what to do. I could see how devastated she was. I wanted to talk to God, alone. I drove and wound up at a place I had been to many times – the trailhead to the Y on "Y Mountain." I began to hike and found myself finally near the top of the Y, a huge block letter displayed on the side of the mountain, standing for BYU. I was in seclusion, and I prayed for a long time. As I prayed, I asked for help. I asked what was wrong with Ruth. Why couldn't she have the faith that everything would be okay? What could I do to help her? The heavens seemed sealed. I could not get any kind of solace, any insight to a solution. I finally began to feel like enough time had passed that she would be awake, and I needed to go home. I was discouraged.

As I trudged down the mountain trail, I asked a question I had not yet asked. I don't know if it was the words I used, or the sincere caring behind the words, or what may have been different, but I asked simply, "What is Ruth feeling?" With that question came one of the most insightful answers I have ever received to a prayer. I heard in my mind words, words not my own nor recognizable as such. They were in Ruth's voice, and they said, "I have lost the baby." But it was more than words. I also heard inflection laden with emotion: "*I* have lost the baby!!" And with those words, I felt her feelings. I felt them as real as if they were my own. They were feelings of guilt, feelings of self-castigation, and thoughts of self-condemnation. She was blaming herself for what had happened, that she had done something that had brought this about, that she was somehow to blame.

It was the most amazing thing. It was as if I was inside of her mind and body, and I knew exactly what she was feeling. I also knew exactly what to say and do. I wanted to fly from the mountain to her side and speak those words she needed to hear from me. I couldn't get there soon enough. She was just waking as I entered the room. I knelt by her bedside, took her in my arms, and told her through tears that it wasn't her fault. I testified to her that I had watched how carefully she had taken care of herself and the baby. It was not her fault in any way; she need not feel guilty. Together, we grieved the loss of our baby.

There is a scripture that states the following: "And he shall go forth, suffering pains and afflictions and temptations of every kind; and this that the word might be fulfilled which saith he will take upon him the pains and sicknesses of his people. And he will take upon him their infirmities, that his bowels may be filled with mercy, according to the flesh, that he may know how to succor his people according to their infirmities."[1]

I learned something about the atonement of Jesus Christ that day on Y Mountain. I don't know how Christ is able to do it, but I know He truly does have the ability to take upon himself our pains, and our infirmities, our sicknesses, and all that troubles us. He completely understands what we are going through. It is more than sympathy. It is even more than empathy that He experiences. He was, and is, able to actually experience what we feel, our very own personal feelings. I know this because He allowed me to experience that as a proxy that day. I know that whatever I am feeling or experiencing, He too somehow went through it, bridging time and space, in a garden and on a cross – half a world away, about two thousand years ago. I can never say to Him, "You don't understand. You don't know what I am going through!" None of us can say that. Because of what He did, He also knows exactly how to comfort us, to succor us. Jeffrey Holland, a modern-day apostle of Jesus Christ, once said that "succor means to hasten or run to the aid of another." Tad R. Callister states in his epic work, *The Infinite Atonement*:

> *The Savior voluntarily took upon himself not only the cumulative burden of all depression, all loneliness, all sorrow, all*

---

1. Alma 7:11-12.

mental, emotional, and physical hurt, and all weakness of every kind that afflicts mankind. He knows the depth of sorrow that stems from death; he knows the widow's anguish. He understands the agonizing parental pain when children go astray; he has felt the striking pain of cancer and every other debilitating ailment heaped upon man. Impossible as it may seem, he has somehow taken upon himself those feelings of inadequacy, sometimes even utter hopelessness, that accompany our rejections and weaknesses. There is no mortal condition, however gruesome or ugly or hopeless it may seem, that has escaped his grasp or his suffering. No one will be able to say, "But you don't understand my particular plight." The scriptures are emphatic on this point – "he comprehended all things"[2] because "he descended below all things."[3] All these, Neal A. Maxwell explains, "were somehow, too, a part of the awful arithmetic of the atonement."[4]

For quite some time after this miscarriage, Ruth struggled to have the faith to believe she would ever be able to have children. It was a fear she had, probably not uncommon to women in general, at least those who truly desire children. It was compounded by the fact that over the next year, she had two or three more miscarriages as we continued to try to have a child. It was as if her body was simply rejecting motherhood. No wonder she struggled. It was a battle of discouragement for her. She wanted so badly to have children, but it just was not happening. And it wasn't getting any better. To hope was to set oneself up for another crushing disappointment and accompanying despair.

About this period, Ruth shares the following:

"The following months, it seemed all I heard about in the news were reports of babies being abandoned in trash bins, or

2. D&C 88:6.
3. D&C 122:8.
4. Tad R. Callister, *The Infinite Atonement* (Salt Lake City, Utah: Deseret Book, 2000), 111-112.

young children who were victims of abuse. It seemed so unfair to me that so many people were oblivious to the heartbreak of some, oblivious to the blessings they took for granted in healthy children and the unfairness that there were those who would abandon a babe while some were so desperately wanting to love and care for a baby. I thought it a cruel joke that God played on those who wished for and those who didn't want the same thing.

I remember going in for a follow-up with the doctor and he shrugged off my hurting heart, saying, "You come back after you have had seven children and tell me how concerned you are about getting pregnant again." I remember having to sit on my hands because I wanted to reach over that wide, wooden desk and punch him in the face. I couldn't believe his lack of concern or empathy. I was hurting then and didn't want to hear about hope or what seemed an impossible future. We spent the next year tracking my temperature and charting patterns all in the hope of optimizing our chances for getting pregnant again.

We were hopeful that I might be pregnant again a few months later, when during a hiking trip to the bottom of the Grand Canyon I lost another embryo. Time and again we would hope and then be disappointed. It seemed like time went by so slowly that first year of marriage.

One evening, I came home from school. Ruth had been at home alone with her thoughts. I readily saw a peace and a calm about her that I had not seen for some time. She had spent some time reading in the scriptures and then her patriarchal blessing. She saw what she had not been able to see with all the encouragement that I or anyone else had tried to give her. This time it came from God through the Spirit. She told me simply, "The Lord told me in my patriarchal blessing that I will be a mother in Israel, that I will provide mortal tabernacles for his spirit sons and daughters. It will happen."

It seemed that once she had found her faith again, the Lord blessed her quickly. Maybe that is the purpose of those trials. They stay with us until we learn to truly trust in Him and His promises and His timetable, until we learn the personal lesson He wants us to learn. She became pregnant, but there was something different about this one. She had morning sickness … and afternoon sickness … and evening sickness, for about six or seven months of her pregnancy. And that is how we have always known if Ruth has a truly "viable" pregnancy. Ruth reflects on this period saying:

> *I believe, looking in hindsight, that it was all right to have had those miscarriages. I was able to finish my college degree before the birth of our first child and it has given me empathy to understand those who have experienced similar losses. I have come to realize God does not want babies to be thrown away in dumpsters or for adults to hurt innocent children, but He does allow us to use our agency. I believe we will have to answer to Him for the choices we make throughout our lives at some point and I believe His judgment will be perfect.*

So, there she was in the early years of our marriage, hungering for a baby, being denied at every turn, plagued by the doubts it would never happen, sick to death that it might not, then finally finding peace and resolve. Now, years later, she was expecting our sixth baby, and she was troubled by the thought of it, sick to death that it was happening. Ironic, but an understandable irony.

My journal entry from March 26, 2006, expresses my thoughts at that time:

> *The timing for this could hardly be worse – yet I find the same acceptance for whatever may yet happen that I have always felt, even when that first pregnancy did not work out. It was difficult, but I was able to submit to God's will in the matter. I have found this to be the case with this matter as well. If this is truly*

a viable pregnancy, then I can't help but feel it is God's will, no matter how inconvenient it may be to our current plans. It also makes me think that maybe Ruth's patriarchal blessing may have an answer in this matter yet. I was comforted to know the last baby we lost was a girl. Ruth's blessing says she will provide earthly tabernacles for her spirit brothers and sisters. The plural part of that has always made me wonder. I have assumed that our last attempt fulfilled that qualification. Maybe it did. I guess we will see. At this point I can accept whatever God may have in store. I was honestly very comfortable with the thought that we have our family (except for that question). I was certainly not looking to tempt fate in any way. This is totally unplanned and unexpected. We'll see what happens now. I am inclined to apply my lesson from my accident. "This is what we have – let us make the best of it." I am inclined to be happy – because to be otherwise would be unproductive and make life miserable. Right now, Ruth is struggling. I hope I can be supportive without making her feel worse or guilty. I think she needs to be able to feel bad about what is happening. I think she will eventually be okay with this – but she needs some time to work through it all. I don't think she is very happy with me either ("somehow it must be his fault"). Certainly, I carry some blame, but I am inclined to think it is an accident, the kind which no one has control over, providential. It just happened, and now you deal with it. May the Lord bless us to handle this well. This is my prayer.

CHAPTER 4

"I Struggled with My Struggling"

It was indeed my feeling that this pregnancy was God-given, and I had sensed from the beginning everything would work out just fine. In an effort to help Ruth, I gave her a priesthood blessing. I felt impressed to tell her that everything would be all right with this baby. In my desire to console her, I told her my interpretation of those impressions, that the baby would be healthy. Eventually, we would all learn some very important lessons about the workings of the Spirit. The general impressions had been right on, that everything would be all right, but the personal spin I put on it of a completely healthy baby was not accurate at all.

As I mentioned at the end of the last chapter, Ruth struggled with concerns and fears. She feared there would be problems with this baby. The doctor had talked with her about the dangers of getting pregnant at her age. He spoke of the possibility of having a child with genetic problems like Down syndrome or other complications.

Most of this chapter is Ruth telling her story of this period after finding out about this pregnancy. It is a story of learning to submit to a kind and wise Heavenly Father, a father who will never force our submission to Him. It must be given willingly. She begins her narrative with our move to Twin Falls.

❧

Prior to the birth of our fifth child, we had been considering the utility of the home where we lived in southern California. It had been a wonderful starter home. Shortly after we bought it, our second child, Moriah, was born, and it became her first home. Three more children followed. We had filled up our small three-bedroom, one bath home with all these wonderful blessings from heaven. We had been talking with Paul's employer and looking at alternatives to expanding our living space. We were grateful to be offered the opportunity to move back to Idaho with Paul's work. Twin Falls, Idaho, was closer to family, but still in a community that would allow our children to grow their own testimonies of Heavenly Father and His goodness.

As we settled into our new home and community, we felt so blessed. We felt like we had found our "garden of Eden." We grew gardens, raised beef and chickens, the kids had paper routes, etc.

It was during this stage of our marriage that Paul and I found we had to make the hardest decision of our marriage to date—when to conclude inviting children to our family. We had been united in our desire to begin our family with our marriage union and didn't take lightly the decision to shut the door on expanding our family and focus on the spirits we had been entrusted with from God. I loved being at home with my five children. I was living my dream of being a mom and a wife.

Paul and I tried to counsel with the Lord about His (God's) desires and our wishes, and we never felt really directed in any decision. When we left California, Paul and I asked many times, "Should we have more children or not?" We talked, prayed, fasted, and pondered in the temple over the topic. I approached it from both directions

(Should we? Should we not?) at different times, seeking guidance.

A couple of years after moving to Twin Falls, we decided to go ahead and try to have another child. We found we were pregnant again, and before we made the announcement to family, we learned that the baby's heartbeat had again gone silent. That was the day after Thanksgiving. This time, the fetus was far enough along that a D&C was necessary. I was discouraged and saddened with that experience and felt like maybe it was God's way of giving us an answer to our difficult decision. I felt a degree of peace about that direction. So, I resolved that now it was time to shift gears from bearing children to raising them, and that's what we did. Our kids were old enough to be left with one another, the older ones babysitting the younger ones, when Paul and I both had meetings, etc. I had been involved in parent-led preschools (Joy School) and now felt to focus my time and energies on volunteering in the kid's classrooms. Jacob was getting ready to start kindergarten. He would be eighteen when Paul was ready to retire. It seemed all was determined, and we were decided in our life's path.

I felt to focus on our HUGE Primary (children's organization at church)[1], which I had been asked to lead as the president. I also enjoyed being able to get our kids involved with a couple of musical/instrumental groups (Jazz Band, "Strings Alive"). I was enjoying Jacob as he followed along in the wake of his siblings' paths. I enjoyed watching all the "finals": final diapers, final training pull-ups, giving away baby stuff, the last car seats, the last Joy School, the final kindergarten, etc. I enjoyed the freedom of yard work, shopping, etc. without having to stop and feed someone, change a diaper, etc.

On December 1, 2005, Paul had an accident with a snow blower that left his hand mangled and missing all or most of three fingers. We spent the next few months readjusting to our new normal. I was

---

1. Primary is the name of the organization for the children in our church. It is a Sunday School for children from ages one-and-a-half to eleven years old. Our primary at this time had about 120 children.

starting to feel settled with our life at that point, and then I started noticing hints that I might be pregnant. And so, thus began my "mighty wrestle" with the Lord.

As I struggled, I struggled with my struggling. How does that even make sense? I had wanted children. We had tried to obtain the Lord's direction. We wanted to be guided by God. We had prayed, and then when I had felt settled and was ready to begin the next phase in life—BOOM! I was pregnant again. I gained 15 pounds in the first three months. I had given away most of my maternity clothes and infant/baby items. We were transitioning to having teens and preteens. I was rocked with the news. I was concerned with my age and Paul's age. I was mad at God. How could He have waited so long? Why would He send us a child so late? We had been willing for years and had asked for His wisdom. Why would He do this now?

I struggled with my struggling. Why was I so upset? Babies are good things. Why was I so concerned? All my life, I had believed children were such an amazing blessing. Such a joy to look forward to, to have, to hold, to anticipate, to prepare for, and to desire. Why was I so upset to find myself in the condition I was at this time? Here I was being so negative, so distraught, so dismissive, and such a party pooper. At one point, I wrote the following: "Congratulations? No – this is condolences. A big punishment. A great embarrassment – the biggest of my life. Not a blessing, more of a travesty ... Why do I have to bear this burden? There is no hope for a happy ending." I did not like feeling that way, but I could not deny the dread and apprehension I felt. Then I would be upset for feeling angst. I instructed my husband we wouldn't be announcing my pregnancy until we were certain this would not also end in a miscarriage. I balked and went around with a dark cloud hanging over me. I felt like I was being punished by God.

Morning sickness and nausea started and became a constant companion. Ginger ale had been my lifesaver. I rationed it for when I had something pressing to do and needed to feel up to doing it. A pregnant relative mentioned something in passing that reminded me about taking prenatal vitamins/supplements, which helped the queasiness but not my attitude. I had a sense of dread, mourning, despondency, disappointment, disaster, etc., from the get-go.

As the months, weeks, and days kept rolling along, eventually it became obvious that I was swelling with new life, and people would congratulate me/us. Their good wishes were met with a grimace or a dismissive shake of my head. I would look at them through a pained smile. I tried to erase all the heavy, dark feelings that were my constant companions. I would stare back at people and keep most of my cynical/cryptic comments to myself as people would congratulate me/us on our new child. I could not get excited about having another baby. I felt guilty and so bad for feeling this way. I just could not get out from under my dark cloud. I tried to show a brave face to the family and to the world, but I felt like such a hypocrite.

As Paul and I discussed plans and arrangements, I would share some of my concerns and doubts with him, and he would just smile and try to reassure me that everything would be all right. I would retort and ask, "And what if it is not?" Again, he would smile and encourage me to have more faith. Paul was at peace and optimistic.

I had always been grateful to have healthy children and had silently feared having to leave the hospital without a newborn babe, of having empty arms, without the baby that had been carried and delivered. I didn't think I could have dealt with the recovery and hormones and milk coming in without the joy of having the infant in my arms afterwards. I had taken for granted the blessings that had been mine in the past.

The other thought that I often had was admiration for families and parents who raised children with a disability and feeling so unequal to that enduring task. It seemed that all my fears were being placed before me as a giant mountain to climb, and I didn't feel up to the task. My husband would lovingly put his arms around me and say everything was going to be all right if we just had enough faith, and then I would feel bad because I felt like my faith was lacking.

Besides Paul, the first to know was Aunt Maxine (my younger sister), because I had to swallow my pride and embarrassment and call her to ask her to bring maternity clothes over. Because of the weight I gained in the first three months, hardly anything fit. That provided some welcome relief. Thus began the re-accumulating. She also brought a bag of infant items.

The next person to know I was pregnant was Adria Sumsion (a friend and coworker from church). On June 14, a Sunday afternoon, as we were out making visits, she asked if I was pregnant. I didn't want to say anything if she was just guessing. I replied, "Why are you asking?" She told me she'd had a dream in which I had a child. I then confided the truth to her, and as we talked, I found myself opening up my heart and sharing with her all my concerns. Soon thereafter, she dropped off a pink receiving blanket. "Think Pink," the note said, "Heaven's Treasures are Yours." She gave me a black maternity dress that was to become my staple wardrobe.

We finally told the children. They were excited. Jacob exclaimed, "I can't believe we're gonna have a baby." As it became obvious I was expecting and I could no longer keep my secret, people responded in kind ways. A friend brought over a bag of toddler clothes with a few toys in it, and another friend asked if I'd like an infant mattress. Still, another friend left a big haul of a swing, a Sesame Street toy, and an infant sit-up chair. I had to swallow my pride again when Adria invited me to stop by the girls' garage sale – there were a lot of baby items. I purchased a stroller. She brought her car seat later when her baby grew out of it. Another friend loaned yet more maternity stuff.

As Ruth's story continues, she eventually began to take small steps in the direction of accepting her circumstances. The same day she talked with Adria, she recorded that she read something in the scriptures (Isaiah 51:2-3) that impressed her, a message of hope:

> *Look unto Abraham your father, and unto Sarah that bare you: for I called him alone, and blessed him, and increased him. For the Lord shall comfort Zion: he will comfort all her waste places; and he will make her wilderness like Eden, and her desert like the garden of the Lord; joy and gladness shall be found therein, thanksgiving, and the voice of melody.*

God can take our life that feels at times like a "waste place" and a "wilderness," and turn it into something like a garden full of joy and gladness. She also wryly commented, "It had better be a girl – no choice."

She was also impacted by verse seven of the same chapter – "Hearken unto me, ye that know righteousness, the people in whose heart is my law; fear not ye the reproach of men, neither be ye afraid of their revilings." She took from this a personal message and made a private resolve: "Don't worry about what others will say." In August, there was a lesson taught in church about Job from the Old Testament. She seemed to allow the lessons of his hard life find personal application for hers. A further resolve, "I just need to be quiet – be grateful and have faith. God doesn't punish us. He lets things happen according to His plan."

There were people placed along the path and experiences that helped her to feel like she could trust just enough to take that next step to the next stepping-stone.

CHAPTER 5

Problems Arise

Our situation began to change many months into the pregnancy when we realized our insurance would not allow our baby to be born closer to our home in the Twin Falls Regional Medical Center, where we preferred to deliver, unless we changed to a different primary care physician. We made the necessary change and felt good about the doctor we had chosen, Dr. Don Smith. I had worked with him in the church, and we knew him as a good man who was competent and caring.

Our first appointment with Dr. Smith was during the first week of September, only a few weeks before the due date. He wanted to get to know his patient and do an ultrasound to see how the pregnancy was coming along. At this point we were about thirty-one weeks, or a little over seven months, into the pregnancy. Initially he was pleased with what he was seeing. He asked us if we wanted to know the gender of the baby. It was customary for us not to know the gender of our children before they were born. We had always let it be a surprise. So we replied, "No." However, as you can imagine, this was the one time we *really* wanted to know ahead of time, considering the special circumstances of this particular birth.

Dr. Smith continued the ultrasound and then noticed something that caused him concern. He was looking at the heart of the baby. He changed the angle of what he was seeing and went back and forth. He then sent us to radiology for a more detailed look at the heart.

The Southern Cross

Dr. Smith said that something doctors look for in an ultrasound of a fetus is what they call the Southern Cross, a cross section of the heart that looks like a cross, which indicates the division of the chambers of a normal healthy heart developing in a baby. He did not see what he hoped to see. The next week, September 14, 2006 (week 32), he did an echocardiogram with a couple of doctors/specialists. They spent an hour prodding and looking. Finally, Dr. Smith and his colleague recommended we see a pediatric cardiologist who specialized in diagnosing in-utero heart problems. We did not have such a specialist in Twin Falls, Idaho, and would have to travel to Boise, two hours away. Dr. Smith was candid with us about the possibilities. He said, "It is not conclusive, but your baby might have heart problems that can potentially be very serious." This news caused us tremendous anxiety and concern. Who would not be concerned with such a potential crisis?

Boise Specialist

As it turned out, I had to go to Boise the next day for a meeting. We decided Ruth would accompany me. She wanted to take care of a few errands and go to the temple. I suggested we try to see a specialist. Along the way, I called another doctor acquaintance of ours, Reed Harris, a cardiologist in Twin Falls, and asked him for a recommendation of a specialist in Boise for the specific concern we had been alerted to. He gave us the name of someone he was confident would be excellent to consult with, a Dr. Michael S. Womack.

Ruth was insistent that seeing a specialist would be impossible on such short notice. She felt I was being too optimistic. She chided, "Doctors don't just have cancellations and take a patient off the street. Doctors just don't work like that." I said, "Well, that may be, but we won't know unless we ask." I think that Ruth was feeling like the world was toppling down on her. She had finally come to accept her pregnancy and the impending birth of our baby, and now this. It seemed like fate was turning against her, and she was struggling to have faith and to find the positive in a future that was taking on a darker and more ominous hue.

What happened next was a tender mercy from our Father in Heaven. Ruth recounts her version of the events of that day:

So, Paul called and left a message on the answering machine explaining our circumstances of being in Boise for the day and explaining that we would like a consultation, left his phone number, and hung up.

I dropped my husband off at his meeting, and I proceeded to go shopping on my way to the temple. While I was deep in the walls of a box store, my husband called, and through a series of lost calls and bad reception, I thought I was mistaken when he said the specialist doctor had called him back and said he could see us that day.

I was sure I hadn't heard him correctly. "Really?! When is he available? When does he want us to come in?" To which Paul replied, "Whenever it is convenient for us."

"No way," I thought. I didn't hear that right. Paul said, "I told him I finish my meetings after lunch, and we could come then." I was shocked. Not only could he visit with us this same day, but on our schedule! "Inconceivable!" (to quote an infamous Princess Bride *character).*

We went over to Dr. Womack's office for our consultation when Paul finished his morning meetings. Come to find out

Dr. Womack wasn't seeing patients that day. He was in the office by himself trying to get paperwork completed. He spent a good three hours with my husband and me. He did his own ultrasound and recorded it to send to colleagues for their opinions and evaluations.

He spent those hours trying to explain the complexities of the human heart to two strangers who had walked in off the street by drawing diagrams and simplifying terms for us and making sure we were understanding the intricacies he was describing. He kept asking, "Do you have any questions? Are you understanding? How can I explain this more clearly?"

Unheard of. I would never have believed it possible if I had not experienced this miracle.

Dr. Womack was certain of some things, and uncertain about other parts of his diagnosis. He explained the difficulty of examining a baby in utero with complete accuracy. One problem he was sure of was something he called Truncus Arteriosus, related to the inflow and outflow of blood. He could also see that there was indeed a problem with our baby's heart. The chambers of the heart had not formed properly. He believed that we were looking at a condition called Atrioventricular Septal Defect (AVSD), or Common AV Valve, or AV Canal. He said that it is common enough for one or the other of the two problems to be seen, but not together. This would be a real challenge. He explained that the baby would need to have immediate attention upon birth and that it would need to have open-heart surgery to survive. The level of care and expertise could not be provided at just any hospital in the intermountain west. It would have to be provided in either Boise or Salt Lake City, Utah. "We could deliver you here, but we don't have the follow-up intensive care that your child could require. I am not sure what exactly we are looking at here, but it would be wise to be prepared to be in the best facilities available."

Portland or Seattle were remote options, but upon learning we had family in Utah, his recommendation was to go to Primary Children's Hospital in Salt Lake City because their expertise in post-surgical care was the best.

This devastating news was presented by a doctor who took the time to fully explain everything to us in language we could understand. He took time to answer all our questions. He was a caring professional who understood the importance of people needing to have the truth, but to have it presented in a way that also gave them hope and solutions. He told us that such surgery on a baby by trained specialists was now possible, and this gave us hope. Ruth continues with her perspective of what happened next.

Dr. Womack gave us his email and phone number and encouraged us to get hold of him if we had any further questions.

As we counseled with him and each other, we began to consider going to Salt Lake even though it was twice as far from us as Boise. Dr. Womack sent us on our way with a referral for physician recommendations in Salt Lake City – and with a kindness I have never before or since experienced with a medical specialist.

To top it off, I was shocked when Dr. Womack called our home later to check on us and ask if we had any more follow-up questions.

As I look back on our experience, I describe my initial hesitancy with accepting my pregnancy like the scene from Indiana Jones and the Last Crusade movie. Indiana is looking across a deep and giant chasm that separates him from the Holy Grail, which will keep his father from dying. He can't see how it is possible, and yet, he knows he has to cross this void in order to get the help he seeks. Desperately and daunted, he steps out into the darkness, and lo and behold, his foot hits something solid where his eye sees only air and space. He should be plummeting into the abyss. In surprise, he reaches down and grabs a handful of pebbles and dirt and tosses them out into the air, and a natural narrow, perfectly camouflaged bridge becomes visible to his sight that he couldn't see before his timid step of faith.

I had not wanted to put my foot forward in this journey. I tried to deny the path I was on, and then one by one, I found a helping hand reaching out to me as I stepped from one stepping-stone to another.

This perspective didn't become clear to me until later as I looked back over the journey we had experienced, and I could see the stepping-stones and the many hands that had held ours along the way. Dr. Womack was one of those gentle, kind hands helping me travel this path.

I felt that was a tremendous day for me personally. This was helpful for me to accept that we were committed to having this baby and getting all the best medical care possible to fix any possible problem that may be made manifest in this developing infant.

The effect of that visit for Ruth was powerful. It was still a scary path with many unknowns ahead, but we were beginning to feel like God would stay with us on this path. Though we cannot see Him, He is there.

With this important new information, we decided we needed to be upfront with everyone about these recent developments. Ruth wrote, "We broke the news to our children and extended families. We tried to explain as best we could the doctors' concerns and guesstimates about what could be the possible heart conditions that may be included with this baby."

As we tried to decide the best course to take going forward, we had further communication with Dr. Womack. Because of insurance, proximity of family, and the advice of experts in the field we had been thrust into, the best option for the birth of our baby was indeed Primary Children's Hospital in Salt Lake City, Utah. This was a drive of about 3-1/2 to 4 hours from our home in Twin Falls. We had a contingency plan to go to Boise via *Life Flight* if an emergency dictated that necessity. I paid the dues to be a *Life Flight* member, which could potentially save us thousands of dollars. We began the process of connecting with the proper doctors and specialists in SLC to monitor the progress of the baby and for tests they felt were useful for diagnosing the situation.

Sometimes moments of hope can be short-lived because our thoughts often gravitate to the reality of the situation, and fears have a way of taking over again, especially when new problems are introduced. The process of exercising faith is often a roller coaster of emotions. It is so easy to focus on the fears and realities of what we see right in front of us, versus the unseen possibilities of what can be and the hope that somehow it will all turn out all right. A few days later, September 19, 2006, I recorded the following in my journal:

Ruth has handled it well enough until tonight. We have found out that one of the associated things that (sometimes) goes along with one of these conditions is Down syndrome. Ruth has feared that more than anything. I am not sure what her fear is exactly – she won't express it to me – but it is a major concern and always has been. As she says – it is colossal. I have tried to encourage her that everything will be okay – to trust in the Lord. Right now, that is a real stretch for her. We really do not know what the outcome of all of this will be. It may be that Downs is not a part of this. We do not know yet. She just does not feel like she can handle something like that. I believe the Lord can bless us to handle those things that overwhelm us. I pray He will bless her, because she needs it right now.

More potential bad news came a few days later. My journal entry from Saturday, September 23, 2006:

"As the events of this past week have unfolded, there are fur-
ther complications. We received an email from Dr. Womack on
Friday in which he suggested yet another possibility based on
the question of a doctor in Portland who reviewed the echocar-
diogram images. The question was brought up about a single
ventricle anomaly instead of the Atrioventricular Septal Defect
(AVSD). This is more serious and requires a series of surgeries.
The survival rate is not as high, and it leaves a person with more
limited ability. There are often other problems associated with
these kinds of combinations of problems. For example, Hetero-
taxy Syndrome includes a reversal of the internal organs (left
and right side), and that includes a whole new set of problems.
...These could be problems which would necessitate us having
to make a decision that, as the doctor put it – to decide – not
what we can do, but what we should do. As Dr. Smith said –
there are some things that are more difficult than death. A life
that may not make it anyway – a life that would be subjected
to multiple surgeries, and then still have problems with defects
and functioning, etc."

In talking with my mother as I was writing this book, she
recalled that earlier in this pregnancy, sometime during the summer, she and Ruth were at the pool with the children in St. George,
Utah. Ruth told her at that time, "I feel strongly there is something
wrong with this baby." She was so right.

CHAPTER 6

Preparations and Blessings

As we were faced with these new problems, I began to consider whether there might be other solutions to our dilemma. All my life I had been acquainted with the power of faith and the miracles that can result from the righteous exercise of faith. I began to wonder if there might be a miracle in the wings for our little baby and for our family. I knew that God can perform miracles, but I also knew that His knowledge of what we need for our growth and experience does not always fit perfectly with what we desire. I had learned already a very important and very hard lesson: that we need to put His will above our own. We need to trust that He knows what is best for us and that we need to be willing to submit our will to His. On the other hand, He wants us to express our desires to Him. He wants us to exercise and develop faith.

I recently sat next to a man on a plane with whom I had a most interesting conversation. I could tell he was a very good man, that he loved his family, and that he desired to help people around him and make the world a better place for his having lived in it. I immediately liked him. He is a biomechanical engineer with a PhD, a scientist, and a tenured professor at a noted East Coast university. As we talked about his life, he told me he is an atheist. I asked him to explain why and on what basis he rested his position. It was rather simple: He believes what he can see and experience with his senses. I understand that. It makes sense to me when people think that way. In the physical world, most of us think that way about most things. He then asked me why I believe in God and a higher power. What evidence do I have?

That was a good question. What evidence *do* I have? Have I exercised faith and received tangible results? Evidence? The answer is "Yes. I have." I would like to share just one sample of many from my life that has convinced me there is a God who loves us and who has the power and ability to bless us, even with miracles.

The Miracle of My Brother Mike

My family was living in Kitzingen, Germany, where my father was assigned for his first tour of duty in Europe while serving in the U.S. Army. Our family had grown to six children, all boys. I was about six years old and attending first grade. The rest of the boys were also in school at some level except for Mike and Steve. Steve was about three years old. Mike was about a year old, had just learned to walk, and was speaking his first words.

My mother had asked a friend to babysit the boys while she attended to the needs of another family whose mother had died. She was getting burial clothes for the deceased mother, and this required her to go to Wurzburg where there was another military installation, about thirty to forty minutes away. The boys were taking a nap, so the babysitter went across the street to her home to take care of something for a few minutes. While she was gone, my brothers woke up. Mike could say only a couple of words at this point, one of which was "baff," meaning bath. He loved to take baths. Steve, being a good brother, accommodated him by hauling him out of his crib and taking him into the bathroom. Steve began filling the tub with water and then put his little brother in the tub. He apparently put him in the end of the tub where the faucet was. Mike began to cry and then to scream. Steve couldn't understand why he was crying. My mother explained that someone had given Steve a coin two or three days earlier, and Steve carried this coin with him constantly everywhere he went and kept it clenched in his little fist. Steve had dropped the coin in the water in his effort to get his brother into the tub. When he reached for the coin to retrieve it, he realized the water was extremely hot when it burned his hand. It should be noted here that the water heater that fed our part of the apartment building was broken and the temperature was much hotter than normal. The water coming out of the tap was near boiling in temperature. Mike had boiling water pouring over him. Steve had the presence of mind to grab Mike and pull him from the tub, which probably saved his life. However, severe damage had already been done. The babysitter heard the tumult and came running to find the two little boys in the bathroom, Mike still screaming in pain. She immediately called an ambulance. It took Mike to the nearest military hospital in Wurzburg for emergency care.

When I came home from school, I was confronted with the aftermath and commotion stirred up by this incident. People were still grouped together discussing what had happened. We were all worried and heartsick.

My mother explains what happened next. People called around trying to locate her and to get word to her of what had happened. This was long before cell phones, when it was nearly impossible to get hold of someone if they were not near a landline. She was stopped by someone at the Post Exchange (PX), a military store in Wurzburg, who had just heard about the incident with Mike and who knew our family. She recognized our mother and told her the bad news. Mom went to the hospital immediately. She arrived shortly after Mike did in the ambulance. By this time, Mike was not in good shape. Blisters had formed and already burst, and Mike was losing a lot of fluid. A family friend from our church group was on the medical staff at the hospital and coincidentally happened to be in the ER when Mike arrived, prior to my mother's arrival. This was not his normal area of assignment. When he realized this was a Manwaring boy who had just come in with severe burns, he immediately began to notify others he knew about what had happened and to assist with Mike's care.

The doctors determined that Mike had suffered third degree burns from the waist down. They tried to put an IV in him, but he was so small that they were unable to find a vein large enough to do so. He was in desperate need of more body fluid and was going into shock. My mother describes the nursing staff as "battle-hardened women who had seen everything and seemed fairly callused to injury", but there was one nurse who took my mother aside and explained to her that her child would die if she did not do exactly what she told her to do. She put a gown and a mask on my mother and put a sterile sheet over her, covering her from the neck down and then placed my little brother in her arms and said, "You take care of this baby and love him as only a mother can. Calm him and get him to drink as much fluid as you can. His life depends on it. Just love him." This army nurse understood the power of love in the healing process. The sheet soon was soaked with the body fluid and blood dripping from Mike's wounds, but my mother continued to cradle, love, and care for her little boy. She was finally able to get him calm enough to drink, and he was eventually stabilized as she nurtured him through the night.

My father was miles away in "the field" on military maneuvers and was difficult to reach. It was not until late evening when he arrived at the hospital. He gave Mike a priesthood blessing with the assistance of another faithful brother. The doctors said that because of the amount of tissue damage, extensive plastic surgery would be needed. They did not think he would be able to walk again because of the damage to his feet and ankles. If he did walk, he would not be able to walk normally.

A few days later, we were allowed to go to the hospital to see our brother. It was an old hospital with large rooms, and Mike was in a room by himself on the first floor. They did not allow us to go into the room because everyone who went in had to be gowned and masked to prevent spreading infection. His room opened to a lawn on the back side of the hospital, and there were French doors that allowed us to look into his room and see him. There he lay on the bed on a sterile sheet with his hands tied, naked from the waist down. The whole lower half of his body was covered in black scabs. It was a terrible and disturbing sight for my young eyes, and my heart broke for my baby brother. I remember leaving my other four brothers at the French doors and going over by an ivy-covered wall or hedge and crying. I offered a prayer asking Heavenly Father to help my brother and heal him. My mother tells me that later that evening we all knelt down as a family to say our family prayers and to pray for Mike. She said that I did not want to pray. She asked me why, and I said, "Because God does not answer prayers." She asked why I would say that, to which I replied, "Because of the big black scabs and that God did not take them away." She explained that the scabs were a blessing at this point, and because of them, "Mike is able to heal better, they help to keep his body fluids in and protect the new skin that needs to grow underneath." I was looking for an *immediate* answer to my prayer. I understood then that Mike *was* being healed and God *was* answering our prayers. And indeed, the healing did continue. I can't help but think that God heard the prayer of a little six-year-old boy.

Mike was in the hospital for about a month. He made phenomenal progress. The doctors were baffled at the rapid pace of his healing, and they continually revised their prognosis to keep up with the unexpected changes. By the time he was released from the hospital, he did not need plastic surgery, nor did it appear that his mobility would be impaired in any way.

Mike continued to heal and made a full recovery. He has been very physically active all his life. He has participated in various sports and has not been hindered in the slightest. Two examples are worth mentioning. When Mike and I worked at Zion National Park one summer, we both ran together from the base of Angels Landing up to the top and back, 2 ½ miles each way, a 1,500 foot climb and descent. Mike recently posted on social media that he'd completed his 54th trip up Angels Landing. We also recently ran a marathon (26.2 miles) together. Just a few years ago, our families were water skiing together, and I looked at Mike 's bare legs and commented on the burns he had experienced as a baby. "Mike, where are the scars from your burns as a child?" He replied, "If you look really close, you can see a bit of a pattern here and there on my skin. But that is it." I did have to look hard to see any scarring. It was virtually unnoticeable.

Tender Mercies

As miraculous as this experience was, my mother points out something else that was part of her story. This has also become an important part of our story in this book. It was in the little things that happened after Mike's accident. They were also miraculous in a quiet, subtle way. The friend who happened to be in the emergency room when Mike arrived and assisted in his care; the person who ran into Mom at the PX in Wurzburg having just heard from someone about Mike; the life-saving nurse who knew exactly what to do in a critical moment. We call these small miracles "tender mercies." It is a term I have used already a couple of times.

David A. Bednar teaches us that the tender mercies of the Lord are from "a loving Savior sending ... a most personal and timely message of comfort and reassurance ... some may count ... as simply a nice coincidence, but I testify that the tender mercies of the Lord are real and that they do not occur randomly or merely by coincidence." [1] Tender mercies are "very personal and individualized blessings, strength, protection, assurances, loving kindnesses,

---

1. David A. Bednar, "Tender Mercies", *Ensign*, May 2005, 99.

consolation, support, and spiritual gifts received from and because of and through the Lord Jesus Christ."[2] Tender mercies are those quiet blessings that tell you God is there, He is watching over you, and that He cares. If we are not careful, we might not see them. But if we are looking and are aware, they will always be there – if we will have faith and trust in God.

Seeking a Miracle

My purpose in sharing this is so you can understand why I have a real belief and trust that God can perform miracles. I have seen them and experienced them. The previous example is only one of the many I have personally witnessed. It should not be surprising, therefore, that I began to wonder if there might not be a miracle of healing for our baby. Who wouldn't want such a miracle? Wouldn't it be wonderful if our child could be born whole and healthy and not have to go through the pain and difficulty of open-heart surgery? Wouldn't it be a great blessing to also involve my own children in such an exercise of faith that might sustain them in their own future as my experiences had been for me?

On September 20, 2006, I wrote the following:

> *As I sit here in my office praying about the impending crisis in our life of having a newborn that potentially has many heart complications along with the potential of having associated defects (syndromes) like Down, DiGeorge, Heterotaxy – I have been trying to understand what to pray for. I have faith that the Lord can cause a miracle to happen, and that this baby can be healed. I think others in the family have that faith, too. Sam and Jacob, Moriah all come to mind first. Perhaps all of us have that kind of faith. I am not sure this is the direction it will go – though I believe it can. What I find myself believing most is that God has a purpose in all of this.*

---

2. Ibid.

I trust Him completely. At this point, I am not so concerned for the inconvenience it may bring to my life/our lives. What I do feel as I am praying is – everything will be all right. It will be. In the scriptures, we find some instances of Christ healing others that are very instructive. For example, John 9:1-3:

[1]And as Jesus passed by, he saw a man which was blind from his birth.

[2]And his disciples asked him, saying, Master, who did sin, this man , or his parents, that he was born blind?

[3]Jesus answered, Neither hath this man sinned, nor his parents: but that the works of God should be made manifest in him.

He said it was that the works (or power) of God might be manifest. In other words, this person was born with this problem so the power of God might be shown at this moment – that others' faith might increase, that they might have greater faith in God – to show that God exists and is interested in us, His children, and that we can trust in Him. He will take care of us, bless us, and love us.

It was God's will that this person be healed, and that was His purpose before this person was even born. I don't think we change God's mind. I think we learn His mind and we submit to it – to His will – whatever it may be. My colleague Max Leavitt said it well. "You don't fast to change the Lord's mind, but to learn His will and bring your mind in accord with His."

I presented the idea to my wife, that I would like to seek a blessing of healing, a miracle, by having our family fast[3] and pray, and then to seek the blessing of our ecclesiastical leader and friend, Pres. Allen. I

---

3. In Isaiah 58:6, we read about one of the purposes of fasting - as the Lord instructs us, "Is not this the fast that I have chosen ..., to undo heavy burdens, and to let the oppressed go free, and that ye break every yoke?" Fasting from food humbles us and makes us more submissive. It helps put us in a correct frame of mind to petition God for desired blessings, and yet be willing to accept His will for us.

had worked closely with him and had confidence in him because he had the power and gift of healing. He had recently given a blessing to a young man who had come to him about an issue regarding his shoulder that would require surgery. The young man was told in the blessing that the Lord would make his shoulder whole. When this young man went back to the doctor and X-rays were taken to determine the best course for surgery, the doctors could find nothing wrong. Comparing the previous and current X-rays showed an incredible difference. The shoulder had been healed. I felt that if there was a miracle to be had, it could come in concert with our faith and with a blessing from this man.

Ruth was concerned, however, and for a good reason. She said, "What if it isn't the Lord's will that our baby is healed? What might this do to the faith of our children? How would they react and respond if they prayed for health and the baby was still sick or worse? You have to help them understand that sometimes God doesn't always answer our prayers the way we want." This is a very important point. It is a point on which the faith of many people has been crushed. I had already learned in my life that God knows best the course things should take in our life. We know He *can* do miracles, but miracles come in all shapes and sizes and even different time frames. It is all right with Him if we have desires for certain outcomes. In fact, we may find ourselves wanting something so badly and deeply that "our teeth ache", as my father used to say. But ultimately, we need to trust that He has heard our pleas and that His will *will* be done. We need to desire what He wants for us more than what we want for ourselves. We should never try to force a blessing from God. He is more than willing to bless us, but the blessing may often come in the form of a trial we would not prefer or expect. He may need us to go through a very painful experience in order to develop the knowledge and compassion to help someone else, another of his children, who can be blessed by what He gave us through that trial. We should never try to force His hand to accommodate our wishes, but we should seek His will and to align our will with His, even while expressing the desires of our heart.

We should also be careful to never think He does not care when we do not get what we want. This is another line of thinking that can potentially lead us away from God. Some people may choose to get angry with God because they feel like He is punishing them unjustly. They can't see beyond their intense desire for things to be a certain way. But God is truly an all-wise and all-loving parent. Every parent has had the experience of not giving a child something they wanted because it might be dangerous or harmful to the child in some way. If we could only magnify that concept many times and realize that what seems to be the very best course in our eyes may be far from it. We simply cannot see what He can see. It takes great trust and courage to deviate from a course that all our reasoning and sophistry says is best. It also takes great patience to have the kind of trust and faith that allows us to not push our own agenda but be willing to submit to His. Neal A. Maxwell wrote,

> *Patience is tied very closely to faith in our Heavenly Father. Actually, when we are unduly impatient, we are suggesting that we know what is best—better than does God. Or, at least, we are asserting that our timetable is better than His. We can grow in faith only if we are willing to wait patiently for God's purposes and patterns to unfold in our lives, on His timetable.*[4]

We presented the idea to the children and asked them if they would be interested in fasting as a family and praying to Heavenly Father for a miracle to heal our baby. We explained that what we sought was not just our desires for the baby, but more importantly, that Heavenly Father's will would be done. They all agreed. We determined to do a twenty-four hour fast and to arrange for Pres. Allen to give Ruth a blessing. At this point in time, in 2006, our children were the following ages: Adam, 15; Moriah, 14; Nyal,10; Samuel, 8;

4. Neal A. Maxwell, "Patience", *Ensign*, Oct. 1980, 28.

and Jacob, 6. All of them had fasted before, except for Jacob, but even he was willing to do so. Our purpose in fasting was to show our sincerity to God for our desires to be heard, to humble ourselves before Him, and to be able to accept His will, whatever that may be.

We began our fast on Saturday, September 23. The next day we went to church and then to our appointment with Pres. Allen at 1:30 PM. He was gracious and kind. As we came into his office with all our children, he greeted us warmly. He knew the desire of our hearts and the purpose of our coming. We had asked Bishop Clark if he could also be there. He and I assisted Pres. Allen as we laid our hands on Ruth's head and Pres. Allen began to speak. The blessing he gave Ruth was directed at both her and the baby. He spoke under the inspiration of heaven. Ruth later recorded some of the points of the blessing, which I chronicled in my journal as follows:

> *Pres. Allen said he struggled to be able to say what he wanted to say and what we wanted to hear. Finally, he said, "I feel constrained." He blessed Ruth with emotional peace, spiritual endurance, and physical strength. He gave counsel to delegate our church callings and responsibilities to others who are willing to carry our loads while we might be away. He blessed Ruth as a mother in Israel. He talked about the knowledge of the eternal nature of families and the truthfulness of the gospel. He blessed us as parents with clarity in thought as we are faced with decisions. We would have the opportunity to nurture and love this baby.*

Ruth asked the children what they remembered? Nyal remembered a phrase about the baby, "She would be exalted by others." He wondered what exalted meant. I wrote down my own remembrances of his words in the blessing.

> *Ruth, you are a woman of faith. Your children will call you blessed.*

It is a great privilege and honor to be a mother.
This child is a special child.
It is coming to earth to receive a body.
It will be exalted and held in high esteem.
The birth will not be without complications.
This child will have challenges.
I bless you to be able to accept God's will for you.
He will bless you with the strength and ability to cope with
the challenges that may come.
Paul will become a father again with the birth of this child.
This child will bring a special feeling of love to the family.

By the time he was done, it was apparent to all of us that a miraculous and instantaneous healing of our baby's heart was not part of God's plan for our family, but there were some wonderful things that had been said and great counsel was given. We felt like we now knew God's will and the direction we needed to concentrate our efforts and faith. We needed to prepare mentally and emotionally for all the challenges that could come with such a complicated birth and subsequent medical procedures. I recorded the following after the blessing:

...I am at peace with the outcome – I just know that it will be
God's will being done, just as Pres. Allen said in his blessing.
The journey there is not specifically laid out. This is where
the adventure lies. The adventure of faith. You know the end
result will be great (from the Lord's perspective). You just don't
know the middle of the story. What a concept! We may start
a book at the beginning, knowing the end already will be an
"all's-well-that-ends-well" ending, but you don't set the book
aside just because you know the ending. You read it because
there is so much to be gained in the reading, so much to feel,
so much to learn, so much to experience that is valuable and
wonderful, even exciting at times.

I need to add that although there was not the immediate miracle we had sought, in the end, there was a much greater miracle in store, one we could not anticipate from our limited perspective at that time. We need to let God choose the kind of miracle He wants to give us. Sometimes, the greatest miracles of all are the changes that take place within our own hearts and souls.

I share the following wisdom from a letter written by a young missionary in Africa (Spencer Segal) dated Feb. 13, 2017. It seems very appropriate for this discussion right now.

In this life, it is so easy to rely on what we can see, what we can perceive with our five senses. The concept of faith, the "substance of things hoped for, the evidence of things not seen" (Hebrews 11:1) has seemed to have fallen out of style. We doubt anything that is not seen, measured, catalogued by scientists or experts.

However, we sometimes forget that this same skepticism should be extended to cover our own ability to perceive. All that glitters, after all, is not gold. Even the best-designed experiment is flawed. Even the wisest human being is less than perfect. Sometimes, the only way to find an answer, to know if something is true or false, is to ask the only One who isn't imperfect: God Himself. In fact, He has promised us that He will answer any of our questions if we just ask Him with real intent, meaning that we are willing to act on His answer.

We felt like our prayers had been heard and our sacrifices accepted. Our little six-year-old Jacob made such a sacrifice of love that day in fasting. His experience was different than Nyal's and Samuel's who both said, "We have fasted twenty-four hours, and we aren't even hungry." As Ruth remembers:

"Jacob, my youngest, had never really fasted for a whole twenty-four hours. Bless his heart, he committed and

although he suffered greatly for lack of water and food during that time, he wanted to be included in our family's plea to God to "fix" the baby's heart. He lay in the van all the way home, then moved to the couch and lay down. His energy was spent. He valiantly came to the table and drank some water and ate some watermelon. When dinner was ready, he tried a bite or two and was just too tired to eat anymore. He finally lay down for a nap."

A Critical Conversation

The next thing I remember of major significance was a conversation Ruth and I had one evening as we were relaxing and talking together. It developed into a conversation that was very disturbing and concerning to me. We were trying to figure out our future and discussing the problems we could anticipate. We knew we would need to travel the 240 miles to Salt Lake City to have the baby. We were told that the baby would be born in the University of Utah Hospital and in a delivery room that would have an access window through which the baby would immediately be passed into the Newborn Intensive Care Unit (NICU) to stabilize the baby, allowing assessments to be made about what needed to happen post-delivery. As we discussed these things, Ruth made a comment that seemed to come out of the blue. "What if it is not the right thing to have surgery?" I wasn't sure that I had heard her right. "What do you mean?" I asked. "What if it is the best thing to *not* operate?" she repeated. I stuttered, "Do you know what you are saying? Without surgery, our baby will not survive. Of course, we have the surgery done. If there is any chance for life, we take it!" My mind was reeling, dumbfounded by the suggestion. Where did this come from? What was the thinking behind it? How could Ruth even entertain such a thought? Is the stress of everything we are going through finally getting to her? Does she just want to be done with all of this and get back to a normal life? Is the anticipation of all the problems that are sure to come with perhaps years of recurring surgeries and the prospect of a baby born with Down syndrome and the lifelong dependence on us too much to bear? I was concerned – deeply concerned – about Ruth.

Within a few days, I had the opportunity to speak privately with our OBGYN, Dr. Smith. He had the experience of many years of working with mothers throughout their pregnancies, childbirth, and postpartum issues. The whole enchilada. I approached him with my concern about Ruth and what she had suggested. I was open and frank about everything I was thinking. Was this normal? What should I make of it? How should I handle it? What should I do?

Dr. Smith looked at me, and I shall never forget what he told me next. He said, "I have been working in this field for a lot of years now. There is something I have learned that I do not fully understand, but I know it is real. Mothers have an intuition and inspiration that we men, fathers, do not have. It seems to be a God-given quality that is given to many mothers. I have seen it over and over again. All I can tell you is don't discount it. Listen to your wife. Listen to Ruth."

I was not expecting that answer at all. It really caused me to reevaluate. It began to change the direction of my thoughts and open my mind to the possibility that maybe she knew something or felt something that did not come out of any kind of desperation, but out of the inspiration of a good woman and mother who was in tune with God. That was one of the reasons why I had married her. She came from a good farming family, and she was raised on the concept that you take what life gives you, face it full on, and do what you need to do. She was not fleeing from challenges. That was not Ruth. In fact, one of her greatest fears in her life had always been the possibility of losing one of her own children. As mentioned, she had lost a brother just older than her. She watched how it had affected her mother and the heartache she had felt because of it. Even her mother's mother had suffered a similar loss. Ruth did not want to lose a child. She did not want a third-generation repeat of what her grandmother and her mother had gone through.

As I considered the possibility (and only the possibility, not probability, mind you) of it being God's will that there be no surgery, I was also scared. If it ever did come to a point of having to make a life and death decision like that, how can someone even do that? You would have to be so sure. How could I ever make such a decision on my own? I would have to know in my heart that it was the right thing, without question. I could never live with a good conscience the rest of my life without that assurance.

Personal Preparation

The question I asked myself was simple: If it comes down to having to make a life and death decision regarding our baby, what would I have to do to prepare to make the right decision?

I wrote down my thoughts:

1. *I will need to be as in tune with God as I have ever been in my life.*
2. *Consider the mental health of Ruth and her ability to deal with the situation.*
3. *Listen to Ruth and her intuition. Counsel together. Evaluate with her.*
4. *Consult with the physicians. I will need the best advice of competent medical doctors.*
5. *I will need the advice of trusted priesthood/religious leaders.*
6. *Study the literature. Be informed.*
7. *Make a decision that will be right with God so that you can stand before Him someday and have a clear conscience that you did the right thing.*

My path was clear. I needed to do my part and trust in God to do His part. I needed to trust God to do what I was not capable or qualified to do. I needed to follow the concept taught in the scripture:

"…we are saved by grace *after all we can do*."[5] Do all I can do and trust that He will do the rest.

The Picture Becomes Clearer

Ruth continued to see Dr. Smith. At week thirty-three, he determined that an amniocentesis ought to be done. But because the baby was too big, they felt that a specialist in Salt Lake City should do it. An appointment was set up for October 3. We were once again on the road. Another journal entry explains what happened next:

October 5, 2006

Ruth and I went to Salt Lake on Tuesday. (It is now a Thursday.) The purpose was to meet with doctors at Primary Children's and U of U Hospitals. We met first with Dr. Su, the pediatric cardiologist at Primary. He did another echocardiogram. His diagnosis was a bit different than what we have had so far. It accounted for the others and the confusion or question of what they were seeing. He believes that what we are looking at with this baby's heart is an AV Canal and a Hypo-Plastic Aorta. The basic problem is that the aorta artery that takes the blood to the body is not functioning properly because it has not properly developed. It is too small. That is, it is constricted and will not allow much blood to pass through it. The valve is also small, in proportion to the diameter of the artery. In addition, the ventricles did not fully separate, and so there is in effect only one ventricle. The big problem comes when the baby starts to breath and the oxygen needs to get to the body. The heart mixes the oxygenated blood and the oxygen-poor blood. There are a lot of complicated parts to this problem, and I think I understand most of it, but the bottom line is – without intervention, this baby will die. It will need to have some major surgery soon after birth in order to survive. This

---

5. 2 Nephi 25:22.

surgery is one of the most difficult to perform on a newborn. I somehow felt comforted to know this information. It felt like we finally had a firmer grip on the problem we are facing. There have been so many questions, and the "not knowing" is a little anxiety producing. I still reserve a hope that they might find something less complicated when the baby is actually born. I do not rule out the possibility of more intervention on God's part. I believe He can do whatever is needed to meet His desires and purposes for this child.

We then went to the perinatologist – Dr. Michael Draper. He impresses me as a very good man as well as a caring doctor. His specialty is in dealing with high risk pregnancies.

Dr. Draper did an amniocentesis and conducted a FISH test to see if there were any chromosome abnormalities. He also did a level two ultrasound. He said he could not see anything wrong and felt that this baby would be normal except for the heart problems. This was good news, but I found myself a little torn as to how to accept it. I didn't want to bank on this news just yet because I didn't want to be let down later by more conclusive test results. We were able to visit the maternity ward and saw where Ruth would give birth. We set a date of October 30 for her to be induced. We had been at the hospitals for about six hours with all of the testing and consultations. It was time to gather up our pieces of the puzzle and our feelings and head back to Twin Falls. The day had worn us out, more emotionally and mentally than physically. As Ruth stated, "I was concentrating so hard to understand everything going on that I feel worn out mentally." Before we left Salt Lake, we decided to go to the temple. It was good to be there. We were able to sit in the celestial room for a few minutes as well. I was glad for that part of the day. We finally arrived home at 12:45 AM.

A few days later, on October 8, we saw Dr. Smith at church. He asked us, "Did Dr. Draper call yet with the amnio results?"

"No."

"Well, you ought to know that the results show that the baby does have Downs."

The FISH test verified what was suspected. Ruth wrote simply, "I was disappointed, but not surprised." This was another letdown in this emotional roller coaster ride we were on, but at least we knew one more thing we had to plan and account for.

On the subject of children with Down syndrome, this is a condition many people fear, like any abnormality they have had little experience with. Most people would naturally be initially devastated with this kind of news. It conjures up all kinds of visions of challenge and inconvenience, feelings of inadequacy as to how to handle all the unknowns associated with such a condition. But this kind of reaction is not universal. When I told my youngest brother Jeff about the diagnosis, his immediate and exuberant response was "Lucky!" I knew immediately where his enthusiasm came from. His wife's nephew, Joey, has Down syndrome. Joey has been a delight to their entire family. There may be a handicap, both mental and physical, but a great quality that you see in a Downs person is an innate ability to love others with a love that is pure and unconditional. Of course, there are real challenges with raising any child with a handicap, but the compensating blessings are perfectly known by those with firsthand experience.

Dr. Smith also reassured us on this occasion about the path ahead of us. "It will be very clear. The doctors will explain and help you all along the way." He was so right.

Getting Ready
Something we learned through this whole experience was that it was good for us to try to take care of anything we could do ourselves, to plan and prepare for any foreseeable contingencies. There was peace in having a plan and feeling like we had some semblance of control in our lives. Some of the decisions we needed to make included

where we were going to stay. We had family in Salt Lake and the vicinity that we might impose on, but there was also the potential for an extended stay with the surgery and recovery. Doctors said that it could be two or three months. Ruth discovered they had a place for parking a trailer on the hospital property, and she favored the idea of having a place close to the hospital where we, but principally she, could stay, as I still had work and the care of family to consider.

We also knew we would need help with all the things that need to happen with the lives of our children: getting them to their various activities, meals to prepare, clothes washed, and so on. We knew we could count on the children to help with some things, and we could also count on our mothers to help with anything else that was needed. Ruth's sister was about an hour and fifteen minutes away in Pocatello and could also help from time to time.

At some point in our research and conversations, we heard of the Ronald McDonald House and realized this was another option. I will speak more about this later. What a marvelous and absolutely wonderful blessing that charitable service is to so many people!

One thing I feel to mention is a conversation we had with Dr. Su. As we sat and talked with him, he laid out clearly the problems he was seeing, as well as future potential problems. He did not paint a very positive picture of what the future might hold for us. He gave us the real options we had before us. Of course, there was the option to have the baby and have surgery or not have surgery, plus there was the option to terminate the pregnancy. He said he was legally obligated to share that option. I have to say we were a bit shocked at the last choice because this was something we had not considered in all of the trials we had gone through with all of our pregnancies.

The issue of terminating a pregnancy has been debated in the halls of justice, in courtrooms, and in the public and private settings of people's lives. It is something that is very complicated because of the many reasons why people might seek a termination of a pregnancy. I won't get into a discussion of all those issues, but I will share some thoughts about the importance of having a reverence for life. We know statistically that most abortions are done for reasons of convenience (or inconvenience). Only a very small percentage fall into the category that prompted Dr. Su to share with us the option of termination.

Life is sacred. Very sacred. I read an excellent article by a God-fearing, world-renowned heart surgeon on the reverence of life. Dr. Russell M. Nelson shared the following:

Another contention raised is that a woman is free to choose what she does with her own body. To a certain extent, this is true for all of us. We are free to think. We are free to plan. And then we are free to do. But once an action has been taken, we are never free from its consequences. Those considering abortion have already exercised certain choices.

To clarify this concept, we can learn from the astronaut. Any time during the selection process, planning, and preparation, he is free to withdraw. But once the powerful rocket fuel is ignited, he is no longer free to choose. Now he is bound by the consequences of his choice. Even if difficulties develop and he might wish otherwise, the choice made was sealed by action.

So it is with those who would tamper with the God-given power of procreation. They are free to think and plan otherwise, but their choice is sealed by action. The woman's choice for her own body does not validate choice for the body of another. The expression "terminate the pregnancy" applies literally only to the woman. The consequence of terminating the fetus therein involves the body and very life of another. These two individuals have separate brains, separate hearts, and separate circulatory systems. To pretend that there is no child and no life there is to deny reality.

It is not a question of when "meaningful life" begins or when the spirit "quickens" the body. In the biological sciences, it is known that life begins when two germ cells unite to become one cell, bringing together twenty-three chromosomes from both the father and from the mother. These chromosomes contain thousands of genes. In a marvelous process involving a combination of genetic coding by which all the basic human characteristics of the unborn person are established, a new DNA complex is formed. A continuum of growth results in a new human being. The onset of life is not a debatable issue, but a fact of science.

Approximately twenty-two days after the two cells have united, a little heart begins to beat. At twenty-six days, the circulation of blood begins.

Scripture declares that the "life of the flesh is in the blood" (Lev. 17:11). Abortion sheds that innocent blood.[6]

One more quote is appropriate. This comes from another man of God and a lawyer, D. Todd Christofferson:

I now turn to … the sacred nature of our physical bodies. As God and Christ are deserving of our reverence, so their works are deserving of our respect and reverence. That of course includes the marvelous creation that is this earth. And yet as wonderful as this earth is, it is not the greatest of God's creations. Greater still is this marvelous physical body. It is in the very likeness of the person of God. It is essential to our earthly experience and key to our everlasting glory. It has been my blessing to be present at the moment of the birth of each of our five children. In each instance, I felt that it was a sacred experience. Clearly something divine and miraculous was taking place. … Certainly, there is plenty of what we might call

---

6. Russell M. Nelson, "Reverence for Life," *Ensign*, May 1985.

"real-world experience" associated with birth. To all mothers everywhere I readily admit that I didn't share your pain, and I don't pretend to understand. But, speaking seriously, does not a woman's suffering in the creation of a physical body add to the holiness of that creation and of the woman herself? Her sacrifice further sanctifies something already holy.[7]

It is my heartfelt belief and testimony that each life is sacred to God. Each birth is the entrance of one of his beloved children into mortality. We all come into different circumstances, with different challenges, but this does not ever diminish the sacredness of each life – the life of a pure, completely innocent, and even holy child of God.

Ruth with Samuel as a newborn

---

7. D. Todd Christofferson, "A Sense of the Sacred," *Ensign*, Nov. 2004.

CHAPTER 7

A Child Is Born

Ruth's due date was November 7, but the doctors wanted to schedule the birth with induced labor a week earlier (October 30) so there was little chance for unexpected complications. This day was now swiftly approaching. We had tried to prepare in every way we could think of. The plan was for the baby to go almost full-term to give it more strength and the greatest chance of survival.

Ruth recorded the following about this period of waiting and anticipation:

In the last few weeks of my pregnancy after making another long trip to SLC, I was concerned about being able to make it to SLC when I started actual labor. With my first daughter, I barely made it to the nearby hospital in time for her birth, and that hospital had only been a few miles away, not a few hours.

I spent the last few weeks sleeping on the couch in the front room. During those long nights, I watched Orion's Belt shine through the front room windows. On and off throughout the previous months when I had moved back and forth from my bed to the couch so as not to disturb my husband's sleep and to give myself some extra back support, I watched that constellation change position in the night sky. To this day, it is like seeing an old friend to look up and spy Orion's Belt wherever in the night sky it may be.

Finally, one night, I found myself out on the couch wondering if those were real contractions or whether they would stop as they always did. But as the hours passed they seemed to get more regular and closer together. We had told the children if they ever woke up and found we were gone, they were to get themselves ready for school and go about their days as normal. We would have someone come by if we weren't there, but to not be alarmed. They knew we would be in contact with them if we needed to leave during the night to drive to Salt Lake and the hospital.

Most nights the Braxton-Hicks (false labor) would subside, and we would go about our daily routines.

Finally, as that long night continued, I woke my husband about 1 AM and told him the contractions were steady and getting increasingly stronger and that we better head for Salt Lake City.

I had called my sister Maxine in Pocatello, and asked her to come to be with our kids when they woke up. The plan was also that Paul's mother would come as soon as she could to stay with them. My own mother had broken her ankle recently and didn't feel that she was going to be very helpful as she was on crutches or in a wheelchair.

I lay in the back of the van with Paul's watch in my hand keeping track of the contractions as they continued to get closer and closer together. I knew I needed to sleep, but I was anxious, wondering if we would get to the hospital in time.

About the last image I remember seeing from my reclined back seat vantage were the Deseret Mill silos off the side of I-15 at Kaysville. When I woke up to the slowing of the van onto the highway exit, I was chagrined that my contractions had stopped altogether. But now we were in SLC, and we continued to the University of Utah medical center where we parked. I walked into the hospital. Since we were pre-registered there, they pulled up my file, and we waited and waited. I think they must have had a shift change, and we were lost in the exchange.

The account Ruth just shared took place the evening of October 19, 2006, and into the early morning of the next day, October 20, a Friday. I, too, had been nervous about the 240-mile drive and getting there before the baby decided to come. We had arrived at the hospital about 5 AM. When they finally checked Ruth, they said that Ruth was dilated enough that she should be admitted for delivery, and they would start labor that day if Ruth did not start again on her own soon.

It took a long time before we could finally get settled in a delivery room. Eventually, the doctor arrived and was able to further assess the situation. The baby seemed stable, and Ruth had not restarted labor. So, they finally started an IV and then began to induce labor. This was the first time labor was induced for any of our children. Here is more from my journal, bringing you closer to our real experience:

As I write this, I am feeling quite tired. Ruth has been induced and we are now waiting for it all to kick in. A moment ago, I gave Ruth a blessing. I said that the birth would go well. She is on oxygen right now because the baby doesn't do as well with contractions (the heart rate goes down). It makes us wonder what will happen when the contractions get really strong. Will they want to take the baby caesarean? I hope not, but that is something that has always been an option. Ruth just told me that she is not afraid of a stillborn situation. I still wonder if she hasn't had premonitions that I need to prepare myself for.

The labor proceeded somewhat uneventfully and routinely but seemed to take longer than normal. I guess a big part of that was due to Ruth always waiting as long as she felt it was safe before she indicated it was time to go to the hospital. She preferred to spend the majority of her labor in the comfort of our home. Deliveries came more quickly with each child that she bore. So, this time it was very different as we spent a long day in the hospital prior to delivery.

The nurses had a whiteboard on the wall with some basic information for others to see as shifts changed, etc. It contained Ruth's name, my name, and the nurses' names. They asked us the gender and the name of the baby. They were quite surprised when we said we did not know the gender. I guess most people want to know ahead of time so they can make plans. All we could offer was a potential set of names – male and female. So, they wrote on the board, "(Mystery Baby)" Josiah – Zion/Cherish. Ruth had picked out the name of Josiah for a boy only recently. The name Zion had been on her list for a long time. I had them add the name Cherish next to Zion because I felt strongly that that name needed to be included because of the experience Moriah had had years before.

Ruth was worn out because of the duration of the induced labor, plus the fact that she had been up virtually all night – over 36 hours of no sleep. For most of our children, she had given birth without any pain-relieving medication. But this time, when an epidural was offered, she accepted. Almost everything about this birth was different. I have been by Ruth's side for all six of our children, and each was a unique and amazing experience. To see a new life come into the world, one which you have co-created, is exciting and very humbling. There are many similarities to each birth. The pain, the pushing, the anticipation. This time was no different in that regard, but this time we knew there would be serious complications once this little one was out of the womb. In the womb, it was safe and doing well, as long as it was attached and contained within Ruth's body, but everything would change with birth. And it did.

I refer again to my journal entry from two days after the birth:

October 22, 2006

It is about 5AM and I find myself unable to sleep. I have had some thoughts that have kept me awake and thought perhaps I should write them down. I suppose that the first order of business ought to be to finish the entry I started the other day.

Ruth handled the contractions very well for a while, then they started to get pretty intense, so much so that she didn't refuse an epidural when it was offered to her. The anesthetist evaluated her situation, deliberated if it was too late, but had her curl up and gave her the epidural. He barely finished in time for the final efforts. It really did seem to help with the last few contractions. Ruth was on autopilot for the last couple. They laid her on her side and she told the nurse she felt like the head was right there. The nurse (Brenda) checked her and, very surprised, said, "You are right." There was a flurry of activity as they quickly found Dr. Draper. Coincidentally, our other doctor, an intern, was Jotham Manwaring. They delivered our baby at 4:02 PM on Oct. 20 at the University of Utah Hospital. The baby came out so easily at this point. I recall that Ruth was either asked to push or not push and she simply said – "I have no control, it is doing it on its own." The baby took its first breath and gave a sweet little cry. As we had the baby out, the question was asked, "Is it a boy or a girl?" I think Dr. Draper said that we ought to let the father announce that. I was barely able to speak when I saw that it was a girl. I was overcome with emotion. They quickly clamped off the umbilical cord and asked if I would like to cut the cord. As soon as the cord was cut, they whisked the baby into the ICU next door through the window that joined the two. Ruth never really was able to see the baby. They cleaned Ruth up after taking care of the placenta, sewing a small tear, etc. We got a phone call on the cell phone at about 4:15. It was Moriah – so she was the first to know she had a little sister. I wasn't the one who told her, however. When she asked, I had to hand the phone to Ruth because of the emotion that surfaced again. It hasn't fully stopped even now.

Newborn Intensive Care (NICU)

Zion had made her entrance into the world, and then everything we had anxiously anticipated began to unfold. The team in the Intensive Care Unit worked quickly to stabilize her little body and try and discern the true nature of her heart complications. For the time being, my attention was turned to Ruth. She was being cared for by the doctor and nurses to complete the process of birth and get her in a position where she could rest. We were happy, very happy. The long-promised girl had arrived, our second daughter. She weighed in at 5 pounds and 13 ounces. She was 17 ½ inches and beautiful.

I suggested that we officially name her Cherish Zion Manwaring because it flowed better than Zion Cherish Manwaring. It had meaning to it and was like a sentence, a statement, and seemed to fit perfectly. I also suggested that we would always call her Zion since that was the name Ruth had picked out some time ago. Later Ruth would say, "Now our family is truly complete. We have children from A to Z."

Indeed, our family was now complete. I had always wondered in the back of my mind, as each child arrived, if there was not yet another, even when Ruth had felt like she could do no more. But now, I too felt like our family was truly complete. Our eternal family was all here. The last little angel had arrived. After Ruth was cleaned up and resting well, I asked if I could see Zion. They led me to a door where I was gowned and masked. The NICU was a complicated-looking room full of different stations that had all kinds of medical machines and monitors. I honestly do not remember how many other babies were there. I only remember our baby, Zion. They had her little hands stretched out and attached to the sheet as they worked on inserting an IV and a catheter in her umbilical cord. She was hooked up to monitors to assess her condition and read her vital signs. The nurse had just put medication in her eyes, and Zion was trying to look around. She also had her eyes open after she was first born. I could easily see her Down syndrome features, but I could also see the typical Manwaring-Hanks features as well. She was a cutie! I was not able to touch her yet. Both Ruth and I would have to wait until later that evening to touch her and much longer before we could hold her for the first time. I took a couple of pictures and was allowed to stay for a few minutes. Immediately, a bond of love began to be forged as I saw our helpless little baby being cared for.

This was definitely a new experience to have a baby in the NICU, anticipating open-heart surgery and all of the potential challenges that might come with that. This could be a long and drawn-out process here at the hospital. It had only just begun, but at the same time,

what a wonderful thing to have
another child. The bonding
that began in the womb was
now being accelerated with
having her here where we could
see her and try to care for her
needs. One of the things that
amazes me is how deeply the
bonding can develop in such a short time. It is a connection that is so
profound, so emotional, and so spiritual. Perhaps that was all accentuated by the emotional investment that we had already made, and
yet would make, with Zion. In the weeks ahead, we would make large
deposits into that account.

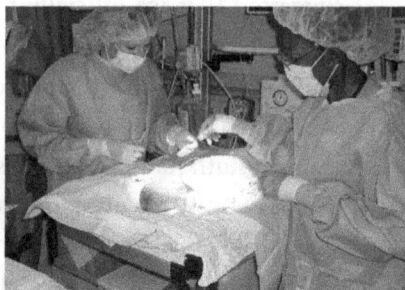

After Ruth had a chance to rest a bit, it was time to leave the
delivery room and go to the maternity ward of the hospital. The staff
transported Ruth via wheelchair and allowed her to see Zion in the
NICU. She was surprised at how well she felt for having just delivered a baby. She records:

> As I was cared for and moved to my post-delivery room, I felt
> really physically well. Hardly any pain or discomfort. I attributed
> that to the last-minute epidural. But as the days progressed, I
> couldn't get over how great I felt. I consider that blessing to be
> another tender mercy. Usually, postpartum, I have lain around
> and enjoyed taking the time to recover and wait as my body
> reassembled to normal. This delivery seemed to almost recuperate without hesitation or need of time. I was able to channel
> my focus and my energies and attention on my little girl. They
> brought Zion by in her Life Flight incubator to my room.

Life Flight
Zion was moved by a Life Flight transport team. The "incubator" Ruth
mentioned was a see-through container on a rolling gurney with all the

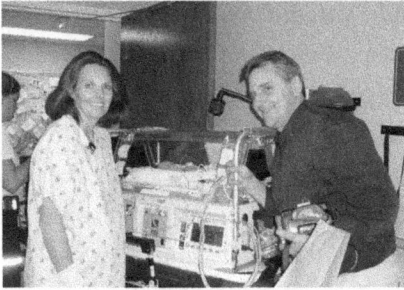

life support features she needed. They brought the baby by our room, and Ruth was able to see the baby and touch her now. After a few minutes, I accompanied the life-flight team to the Pediatric Intensive Care Unit (PICU) in Primary Children's hospital, where Zion continued to be monitored and cared for.

Despite the Life Flight name, there was no flight involved in the transportation of Zion from the U of U hospital to Primary Children's. The two hospitals are connected via an enclosed bridge/walkway. We now had a patient in each hospital.

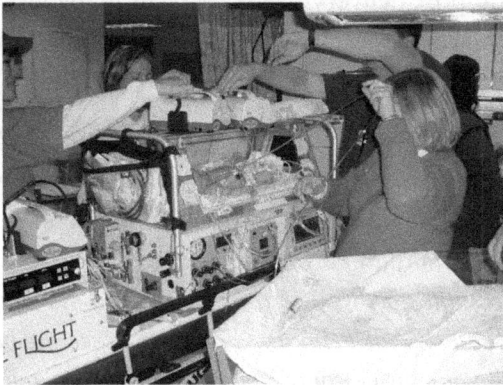

My journal entry for the rest of that evening:

One of the important things to mention is that they are keeping Zion alive with medication. They need to keep open a small artery between the pulmonary artery and the aorta called the PDA (Patent Ductus Arteriosis) because once it closes off right after birth, with the type of heart condition our baby has, the baby will die. I was able to spend a little time at the Primary Children's Hospital PICU before going back to Ruth's room. Mom and Dad and Ariane [my niece] showed up at Ruth's room. I took them to the PICU after we had visited a while. On the way there, we encountered Ruth's mom and Dell [Ruth's brother]. They also came with us to the PICU. Everyone took turns and had a chance to see the baby. I felt like Ruth needed to rest and encouraged everyone to move along. Both she and I went to sleep, and it was a much needed rest for both of us. I am sure I slept better than she did. I was vaguely aware of nurses coming in throughout the night to check on Ruth. It was a good night's rest. I had had only nine hours in the previous three days.

The next day was a busy day. The medical staff was overseeing Ruth's rest and post-delivery needs. We had many visitors, friends, and family who came to support us and to see Zion. I continue with my journal entry:

We had a lot of visitors yesterday. We have counted 41 visitors alone. We tried to accommodate them all. We also had a lot of phone calls. It was too much to make an account of right here. What is most important right now is to recount the visit we had with the doctors yesterday [Saturday] morning. I took Ruth to the PICU at Primary Children's to see the baby. She was finally able to not only see and touch Zion, but they let her hold the baby as well. Zion has all kinds of wires and tubes hooked up to her right now, so both of them needed to stay close to the monitors, but it was a tender event for both of us.

Ruth's own account of being with Zion is as follows:

Our little infant was hooked up to so many wires and tubes and such, it was difficult to hold her without alarms and machines beeping, and it was very intimidating and terrifying. She seemed so tiny and defenseless. They explained to us how her weak heart made crying a very difficult strain on her physical body. Things like sucking on a pacifier were tiring exercises for her. They had her hooked up with a feeding tube via her nose and I got outfitted with a breast pumping machine. They let us feed her sucrose water. I tried not to overdo myself physically, but I also wanted to be at the hospital as much as possible with Zion.

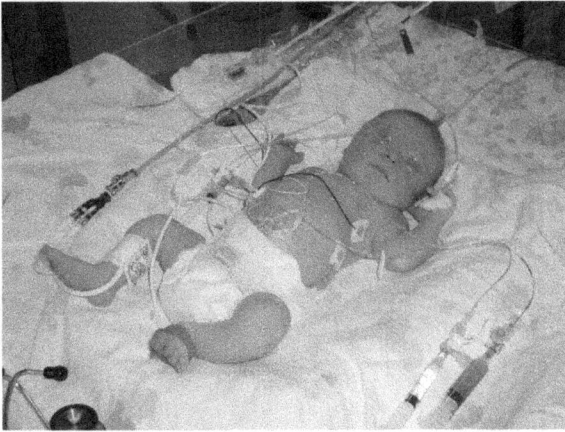

We were soon filled in by the doctors on the prognosis of Zion's condition. Now that she was no longer in utero, they had an accurate diagnosis of the situation. I share my journal writing of those consultations:

Dr. Etheridge, a pediatric cardiologist, spoke with us first. She told us that the diagnosis that Dr. Su had made was correct, this baby has AV Canal, single ventricle left heart syndrome and a hypo-plastic aorta. In addition to that, she also has a leaky tricuspid valve. She explained the complications to us, and it was very similar to what we have heard before, only with this leaky valve, and the Down syndrome, there are further complications that make this a very serious situation. Dr.

Hawkins came by and we were able to meet him. He seemed quite grave and serious as he explained the complications as they presently exist. Now, this is where I feel I need to try and put my thoughts to paper and sort them out to see if I really understand what is going on.

They told us that the tricuspid valve has leakage. This is not uncommon to have some leakage which may even correct itself within a few days after birth. We were told they rate leakage as none – mild – moderate – severe. Our baby has moderate leakage. If this does not improve over the next few days, then there is really no point in surgery because of the way the other problems all come together. They cannot correct the tricuspid valve. It becomes an issue of direction of flow that will ultimately prove fatal. Even without the valve problem, the success rate of surgery with the other problems is not the 90 percent they normally enjoy. Dr. Hawkins said the aorta is quite small, about the size of angel hair pasta (hypo-plastic aorta) and trying to sew that is very difficult to do without some leakage. I seem to recall he said the rate of success is less than 50 percent. When they do succeed, children with Down syndrome have other complications that normal/other children do not have that make survival even more difficult. One issue is pulmonary hypertension, which translates into too much resistance in the lungs, not allowing the blood to flow in the lungs like it should. Already the blood pressure is compromised with the single ventricle having to pump blood to the whole body, but when you add that resistance in the lungs, there is a concern about adequate oxygen to the body. There were so many things that were said, I think I would like to hear it all over again and take some notes to make sure I am getting it straight. I remember Dr. Etheridge saying it is very rare to see a child with all the defects this little girl has, and the survival rate is extremely low. They *have only had one child in her years here that has made it to the Fontan procedure, which is the last of the three stage surgeries. It sounds like the chances of having a very long life are very slim, and the life she would have could be fraught with difficulty. I am not really sure about this either. The combination of everything makes this an unusual case. As I said to the doctor, "I knew this baby was one in a million."*

That last quote from me is something I need to comment on further. This consultation with the doctors was a very serious one. Dr. Hawkins was quite candid about the complications we were facing. He has had vast experience with newborn heart problems. He was grave for a reason. I remember when I made the comment about Zion being one in a million, he did not crack even the slightest smile. It only lent to the gravity of what we were now facing.

I don't know if this is useful to anyone reading this book, but there was so much to digest, so much technical language. I had tried to read and inform myself about these issues we were facing so I could be true to my earlier commitment to prepare for this very moment in time. But with that education, I found I only had more questions because there was so much new information being thrown at us. I felt like I needed to talk to the doctors again, so I sat down and wrote out the questions that came to mind. I include those from my journal:

- *Why can't the tricuspid valve be repaired if it doesn't correct itself?*
- *Is this the only valve (considering the AV Canal), or is that part of the problem, that the two valves didn't separate, and the tricuspid valve is leaking because it just never separated enough from the mitral valve and cannot be separated as in AV Canal Surgery?*
- *Given the combination of problems, what can be done/ attempted, and what would the likely results be?*

- *Tell me about survival rates with the different procedures considering the combination of problems with this baby.*

- *When you said you had only one child make it to the Fontan procedure, what did that refer to (same set of problems? Heart, Downs, etc)?*

- *What happened/happens in the case of the others who didn't make it?*

- *The term Tetralogy of Fallot was used at one point? Does this apply to us? I read something which suggested a combination of defects that don't seem to fit our case.*

As was mentioned earlier, there were many visitors who came to the hospital. They came from many miles and hours away. We were astounded by how many family members (immediate and extended) and friends found their way to the hospital. Everyone had taken such a keen interest in our baby. It was humbling, and it still fills us with gratitude for their love and support. It seemed that everyone sensed there was something special happening here. As I write this, I tear up as those feelings resurface. In fact, this book is being written with many tears. Most tears are of gratitude, but there have also been some tears of pain and grief as we have relived these experiences. If those tears could be seen in some visible way on the pages of this book, you as a reader would understand better the hearts of the authors – there would be many tear-stained pages.

There was a constant stream of visitors on Saturday, with shifts of small groups going into the PICU every few minutes throughout the day. Maxine, Ruth's sister, brought our children down to Salt Lake City on Saturday. They came to be together as a family. This was such a special time for our family, to have us all together. We really did not know whether this would ever happen again. Would this be the only time our children could be physically present with their sister? They were allowed to come in, one or two at a time. Moriah was so anxious to be the first one in to see Zion, but she made a personal sacrifice and allowed Samuel and Nyal to go before her.

Moriah was next, and she just wanted to drink Zion up. Ruth confided in her that maybe there would not be the possibility of surgery. Moriah choked up because she knew what that meant. Each child was able to hold Zion for a long time. It was such a touching scene to see their love and devotion to their new little sister. They were curious (especially Jacob) about all the medical equipment, and they had to be very careful with Zion because of the wires and tubes she was hooked up to. But we were grateful the medical staff made it possible for them to hold their little sister and that Zion was allowed to feel their love for her.

We took pictures of each of them holding Zion, so they would always have this memory. It would have been nice if we could have had a family picture, but our family was too large to be in the PICU all at the same time. Moriah just begged to be able to go back again into the PICU, but there was no more time. It was 7 PM and visiting hours were over. Ruth said later, "I was haunted by Moriah's request, 'Please can I go back in? Can I stay longer?' Moriah absolutely loved her sister."

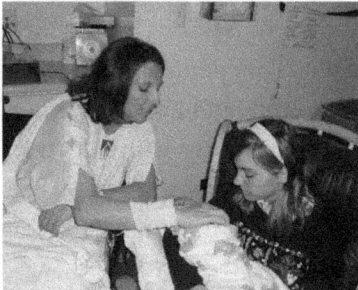

My mother went back to Twin Falls with the children to stay with them and take care of them. Eventually Ruth's mother would also come to help. One of the great blessings of my life is to have these two absolutely wonderful women as mentors and teachers, but also to have them as friends with one another. They get along well and have a mutual respect for each other. They are great examples. They are angel women.

I talked to Pres. Allen and Bishop Clark at some point on Saturday to update them on the birth and initial diagnosis. It was good to have this connection with such trusted and wise religious leaders. They had been such a source of help, support, and friendship in the past year.

Visions of Family

We eventually retired to Ruth's hospital room for the night. It was good to sleep. Ruth especially needed it. Sunday morning, I awoke early. There was much to ponder. As I lay there in Ruth's hospital room awake and pondering, an image came into my mind. It was an image I could not erase. In my mind's eye, I could see us bringing Zion home and having the family surround her in love as she took her rightful place in our eternal family. It was a vivid mental picture. I could see the children surrounding their sister and lovingly looking down at her. There was such a peace about this scene. I could see us giving her a baby's blessing (a name and a blessing). But the remarkable thing about the scene that played itself out in my mind is that it was set in the near future, and it was happening without any surgery being done. I felt uneasy because I did not have a confirmation of what was taking place with Zion's heart from the doctors, beside the fact that I had unanswered questions. But the impression this scene left on me was strong and caused me to wonder, "Is this the direction things are supposed to go?"

We spent just about every waking hour in the PICU with Zion. We wanted to be near our little girl and have her feel our love, know our touch, and hear our voices. Thinking back on our time with Zion in the hospital, Ruth shared the following about our daughter:

She was so kind – so undemanding, so gracious. Always ready when I was willing [to nurse]. What a great example of self-lessness. When her medication should have made her grumpy and grouchy, she didn't complain. I loved the nurse reports each time we showed up; the nurses loved taking care of her – she was so easy. I loved being able to sit in the rocker and hold

my baby despite the tangle of wires and tubes and beeping
alarms. It was awkward, but it was our reality.

Sunday morning, we were able to get some answers from Dr.
Etheridge about the seriousness of our daughter's heart. She said she
had never seen Dr. Hawkins so grave and serious as he was on the
occasion of delivering the news to us about Zion's condition. She
really laid some things on the line and basically told us that even
if the valve leak did fix itself, it would not be a very good idea to
proceed with surgery. The likelihood of survival was so slim that the
inevitable would take place even with a lot of surgery and difficulty.
"Sometimes it is better to spare everyone all of that and opt for no
intervention." She said there was still a chance the tricuspid valve
might not leak, and we might be able to better look at the other
option. It would be better to wait until Monday morning. We got
all this information just before we left to go to church in the hospital chapel.

Church at the Hospital

There were many others, like us, who were there at church because
of a child somewhere in the Primary Children's Hospital. Some of
them had their child with them in wheelchairs. We were able to slip
in just after the opening prayer. Ruth writes, "This was the first and
only time I attended a church meeting in a hospital gown and in a
wheelchair. It was short and sweet and such a source of the Balm of
Gilead." Indeed, it truly did feel good to be there in church and close
to God, to have the sacrament, and to feel His love. I remember
thinking how much we needed this. We needed peace and clarity. It
was a very emotional time for both of us. With Zion being born and
being able to hold her and love her, we wanted her to be able to live
and stay with us and grow up in our family. We wanted life.

I jotted down impressions that came to me during the meeting.
I was beginning to accept that maybe it was not the wisest thing to

seek medical intervention for Zion. I found myself gravitating more and more to the conclusion that we would be taking Zion home with us for the remainder of her time on earth. My grip on the hope of preserving her life through surgery was beginning to relax. Oddly, I found thoughts coming into my mind about what kind of a headstone she should have and sketched it out on this paper. Yet, we still hoped for the tricuspid valve to fix itself, but the medical advice and the impressions of the morning moved my thoughts in another direction.

"Ye Are My Hands"

Visitors continued to come on Sunday. My brother Jeff came from St. George, four hours away. We can't list here everyone who came; there were so many. One that needs mentioning is a woman from our ward in Twin Falls, Betty Jo Quigley. She left right after church and came all the way from Idaho to bring us notes that had been written to us from people in our ward earlier in the day. She wanted us to know right away of their love and support. There were scores of notes, each one congratulating us on our new addition and wishing us their best, expressing their love for us, offering their prayers for us and our new little girl. Once again, we were astounded, humbled, and grateful for the love and support from so many. I began to realize that it was something many people had invested themselves in. This was not just our baby any longer. This realization has only grown over time as we have realized that her life and story was meant to be shared and perhaps to strengthen many others.

Every time people have shown love and concern for us, it primes the pump of our wellspring of tears. I have said it before in these pages, but it bears repeating. It felt like the arms of God reaching out to us and wrapping around us.

Ruth had been serving as the president of the ward Primary. That Sunday was the annual children's program during the main worship service at church, a big deal, and one they had prepared for over the previous months. Naturally, Ruth was not there, so the following report was delivered in one of the notes by her counselor, Adria Sumsion:

My dear friend Ruth –

After we talked this morning, Jason and I prayed for your beautiful daughter Cherish Zion and feel such love for you, Paul, and your family. The prayers continued through church – everyone has you on their minds and hearts.

The Primary program was wonderful! Would it surprise you to know that Jacob sang loud enough for you to hear? ☺ *You would have loved it.*

The Lord has sent you such incredible gifts – you have an amazing effect on all of us. We love you, we are praying for you, and we have faith that we can accept the Lord's will and that you will feel His hand blessing you at this time.

Love and hugs, Faith and hope – always
Adria

The story is told of a statue in the town square of a small village in England that was damaged during the bombings of World War II. After the war, the townspeople were debating on whether to replace or try to repair the statue. It was a statue of Christ. Both of the hands had been broken off above the wrists. Finally, someone suggested to leave the statue as it was, but to place a sign at the base that read "Ye are my hands." And that is what they did.

I am convinced that we are indeed his hands as we act in love and support of our fellowmen. As it states in scripture, "When ye are in the service of your fellow beings, ye are only in the service of your God."[1] Thoughts of charity are thoughts inspired by God. It is one of the ways he shows His love for us. We are his hands to bless each other. It also gives us the opportunity to become more like Him – one of the great purposes of this life.

---

1. Mosiah 2:17.

The Ronald McDonald House

There was an opening at the Ronald McDonald House, and I was able to get a room there Sunday evening. I cannot say enough good about this charity. This was a large old house that had been converted into something like a bed and breakfast inn. It was close to the hospital and was there solely for people like us who had come from out of town and wanted to be close to someone in medical care. It was practically free of charge ($10/night), and they provided free meals for those who stayed there. In Salt Lake City, it was situated within easy travel distance of four major hospitals. Even though I could have stayed at my brother's place across town, it was good to be so close and be able to easily come and go without imposing too much on his family. Ruth was going to be discharged the next day, and then we did not know how long we would be staying in SLC with Zion. If we did do surgery, then we would arrange for a trailer as we had planned.

At the Ronald McDonald House, I remember there were local churches that traded off bringing in food each day, providing for those who were staying there. It was such a blessing to not have to worry about the basic necessities with so much else going on. It also provided a peaceful setting away from the hospital scene and the stress that often comes with the reasons why people are there. For me, perhaps more than anything, it became a place of peace and revelation.

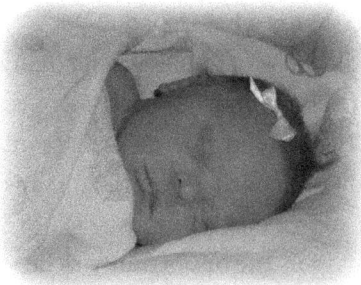

CHAPTER 8

Knowing the Will of God

Monday morning, I woke up early and felt like I wanted to do some reading and thinking. Today was the day we would find out whether Zion's tricuspid valve had stopped leaking. It was a big day. I had decided to fast also because it would be a day of decision. This was the contingency we had been preparing for. I was so grateful for Ruth's premonitions. They had prepared us for whatever might come next.

I sat in a small reading room at the Ronald McDonald House, just outside of the gabled room where I had slept. There was a desk and many books available, but I wanted to read my scriptures. I read in Mosiah, chapter 4, where it tells about parents teaching their children to love one another. As I read and pondered, I began to think about what needed to happen next, and I thought of Zion and giving her a baby blessing. I felt impressed to write down the things that should be said in Zion's baby blessing.

In our church, it is customary to give a newborn a name and a blessing. This is usually done in church as part of Sunday services, but it can be done anywhere, including the hospital. Many a baby has been given a name and blessing just after birth when there was a critical situation that might result in death soon thereafter. The father usually performs this ordinance. It is done under the authority of the priesthood, if the father has been ordained to the priesthood, which most men in the Church are. I knew this was my duty and responsibility. I began to contemplate what I should say in such a blessing, and when that blessing should happen.

Writing the Blessing – Knowing
I pulled out a paper and began to jot down my thoughts. What happened next, I want to record accurately and without exaggeration. Thoughts began to flow into my mind that I can only describe as pure inspiration. I wrote the words as they were given to me and continued to write until the words stopped. When I concluded with an "Amen" and a period, it was obvious this was a special blessing for a very special little girl. These were not my words. This was not a blessing from her earthly father, but one dictated from her Heavenly Father. This blessing was written under the inspiration of heaven. I have both given and received many blessings in my life, and I knew this one was more than just my own thoughts. From the content of the blessing, I also knew more specifically what God's will was concerning Zion. Everything was going according to His plan.

The day started with the Spirit, and it continued with the same divine guidance. I hurried to the hospital to be with Ruth and to find out Zion's condition.

Doctor's Diagnosis and Recommendation
I refer to my journal for the report of what happened next on Monday, October 23:

> *They did another echocardiogram. A doctor and a nurse came and talked to us, Dr. Cowley and RN Sherwood. They*

gave us the news we were truly anticipating – the valve was still leaking, and the prognosis was not good for a continuance of treatment. It was handled very professionally, and I think Ruth and I both handled it well also. We were able to ask questions about what was wrong with the heart, why it couldn't be fixed, if we tried – what could we expect; if we didn't – what could we expect. I feel like the answers were clear. Ruth interjected a specific question, "What would you do if you were in our shoes?" He replied that he would recommend for us to take our baby home and enjoy her for as long as we could.

I feel like Ruth has been right on with her impressions. We told them we would take a day to think things through. It was hard, but it was also filled with peace. They told us that they have never had a child here at Primary Children's Hospital with the combination of problems Zion has (and they have had a lot of children with a great variety of heart problems). This is even more serious than ones they have seen that have a very high mortality rate. All the doctors felt it would be better to not intervene.

Priesthood Recommendation

I received two phone calls that day, each independent of the other. One was from Bishop Clark. He said he had been thinking about our situation and wanted us to know his thoughts and impressions. I had not yet told him of the doctors' recommendation. He told me that he felt that this baby should not have surgery. That was his impression and feeling. I then told him what the doctors had told us earlier that day. It was all lining up. President Allen called also. He had not talked with Bishop Clark, but the conversation was a repeat of the one with Bishop Clark. He said that he had been thinking a lot about our situation since we had talked last Saturday. He felt that we should not do surgery. He said there was no need to feel guilty about anything – the Lord had chosen to take His daughter home after ful-filling His purposes for her. It was a very comforting conversation. From the mouth of two witnesses.

This was happening just as Dr. Smith had said. "It will be clear." Every item on my list to prepare for this moment of decision was being checked off. God's will had become very clear, without any room for doubt. In the blessing I had written that morning, it was clear to me that Zion would be coming home with us. Her purpose in life was to come to earth and receive this body, one that would allow her to live only a short time and then return to our Heavenly Father. She was to bring love and joy to our family and bless the lives of many for many years to come. Ruth had sensed all along there would be no surgery, perhaps with some feelings of guilt for even thinking in this direction, but it had been a critical part of our preparation.

Ruth was discharged from the hospital, and it was a beautiful short drive down the hill through the colors of fall, yellow leaves and green grass, to our accommodations. We were able to get comfort-able in our gabled room at the Ronald McDonald House. We had a lot to consider. The course of action was clear, but to actually com-mit to that path was a daunting and difficult prospect. We prayed together, we cried together, and we counseled with one another about what we needed to do.

The next morning, we arose early to go to the temple to seek strength and get a final confirmation from God about our decision. My journal contained the following thoughts:

October 24, 2006

I am fasting, and we are going to the temple this morning. I think Ruth and I are ready. She has been so sweet and tender. This will be a very hard thing for both of us. I will need to be strong for her.

We spent the early morning at the temple. As we sat pondering quietly in this peaceful atmosphere, we were approached and asked if we would like to help with doing sealings, which we agreed to. "Sealings" are religious ordinances performed by proxy (living people) for ancestors and loved ones who have passed on from this life, binding together – "sealing" – families both on earth and in heaven, that they can be together, with God, for eternity. When we entered the sealing room where these sacred ordinances are performed, to our delight, Bruce Lake, a friend and former colleague of mine, was the officiator performing the ordinances. This ordinance can seal married couples to each other, and also seal children to their parents so they are maintained as a family beyond the portals of death. Families can be eternal. This particular morning, the ordinance being performed was for children being sealed to their parents. It could not have been more perfect timing. We felt like it was a wonderful and comforting reminder that we will have Zion as a part of our family in the eternities. This was just another of the many tender mercies we would experience over the next few days. I once heard it said, "When it comes to spiritual things, there are no coincidences." We felt like we had the strength to move forward in the direction we knew we needed to go. Truly, it is one thing to know what is right, and an entirely different challenge to find the strength to actually do the right thing.

Ruth had found her peace, a peace that had taken months to fully realize. All of her dark premonitions and uneasiness made more sense now. She could see a purpose in all the feelings she had grappled with. She later recorded:

I began to understand the preparation I had been receiving all along this journey. My hesitation in stepping on this road, my struggles, had all been not a foreboding of ill to come, but preparation to go through the dark, unlit channel and walk through to the light. I knew what to do and felt calm and at ease with the direction we were travelling. I was at peace finally knowing the path we needed to continue down. I feel like it was a tougher conclusion for Paul than for me.

When we got to the hospital, we counseled with the doctors and informed them of our decision. We would forego surgery and take Zion home with us. We had a number of questions, very important questions. How long would she live after she was taken off the life support system and medication she was now on? What could we expect? What could we do to make her most comfortable? What kind of care would she need from us? How would we recognize when she was failing? What signs should we be aware of? They answered our questions, but some of the answers were very worrisome. Those had to do with the longevity of her life.

We were told that once she was disconnected from the monitors, the IVs, etc., they could give no guarantees as to how long she would live. It just depended on how long it took for the PDA (Patent Ductus Arteriosis) to close off and shut down. "We cannot tell you. We do not know. It could be a couple of hours or it could be days. Sometimes it can be weeks, and at the *very* longest, a month or two." We did not even know if we would be able to make it back to Twin Falls! This was getting very real and very scary, very fast. We discussed options and it was finally decided to bring our little girl home the next day, Wednesday.

A Blessing to Make It Home
We spent Tuesday with Zion and enjoyed holding her and being with her. She was able to nurse, and Ruth took care of her needs. We really needed God's help. We did not want to leave the hospital and not be able to make it home without Zion still alive. It was a terrifying thought. I called my brother Brent and asked if he could help me give her a blessing so that she would make it home all right and that we would be able to enjoy her for a while. Later that evening,

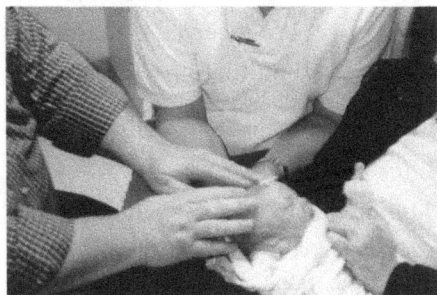

we gave Zion that blessing. Paula (Brent's wife) and my dad were there at the hospital as well. My brother anointed Zion with oil (James 5:14-15), and I sealed the anointing and was voice for the blessing. It was a very emotional and heartfelt prayer and blessing. I blessed her by the power of the priesthood, which we hold, and in the name of Jesus Christ. I felt impressed to call upon all the faith and prayers that had been exercised by so many family and friends to bear down on this moment. I blessed Zion that she would live to make it home and be with her siblings, and to enjoy their love and the love of her family. I felt prompted to say those words, and they came with power and authority. I felt God would honor this blessing. It was a source of peace and something I could put my faith in. We spent the rest of the evening getting everything finished up so we could leave the next day.

As we lay in bed that Wednesday morning before we got up to bring Zion home, I gave Ruth a blessing. About this, I wrote in my journal:

> She has had such a tender heart. She asked, "How can we bring her home? I am terrified of bringing her home. How can we do this?" I blessed her that she would be able to handle everything. She has been so wonderful – I cannot even express my gratitude adequately.

The next part of the morning was spent packing up everything we had brought for a long stay in case of surgery. We bid farewell to the wonderful staff at the Ronald McDonald House. This had been our own peaceful place where we could think and talk and ponder and pray together. We have never forgotten those feelings and have continued to make donations, so others can continue to enjoy the benefits of this great charity and service. We received a thank-you card from the Ronald McDonald House Foundation with a poem that expresses our sentiments:

This is the house
Where families meet
To continue their lives,
To eat and sleep,
To find strengths
And dry their tears,
To look forward with hope
To better years.
This is the house
That becomes their home.
This is the house
That love built

When we left to go to the hospital one last time, it was a cold, rainy, and blustery morning. I remember the cold rain blowing in my face and the wind trying to whip up the wet autumn leaves plastered on the ground as we loaded the Suburban. The weather had been so wonderful the preceding days, an "Indian Summer", warm and sunny with gorgeous colorful autumn trees. I wished it would not be so gloomy. Of all days, it would have been nice to have physical rays of light and hope to lift our spirits.

We arrived at the hospital, and things were set in motion for Zion's release. Ruth describes the scene:

We watched as the medical staff made preparations for Zion to be released to our care and send her home to be with her family. Social workers joined the stream of people coming and going with forms and instructions. The difference was the social workers were doing funner things. One lady came and asked us questions, and she used the answers to make a beautiful, big, colorful poster of all of Zion's "favorite" things. Another brought a baby book and files filled with helpful tips for going home and through hospice care. Another not so fun conversation was to get information to set up hospice care once we did get back to Twin.

The preparations to leave included receiving instructions and signing necessary paperwork. The precariousness of our present situation was heightened by a letter handed us from the hospital on official letterhead and signed by our critical care nurse and physician, in the event Zion did not make it home alive. It was dated October 25, 2006, and read:

To Whom It May Concern,

Zion Manwaring is a 5-day-old female with Trisomy 21 and Hypoplastic Left Heart Syndrome. She is being discharged from Primary Children's Medical Center in Salt Lake City to home for hospice care.

They began to disconnect Zion from all the monitors and life-preserving devices that she had been tethered to for all five days of her life. It was as if she was being born a second time, released from a second womb that had been sustaining her life. But now she was truly, completely, on her own. Her little imperfect heart would have to fully carry the load of life from this point on. She had been on the timetable of doctors and science, but now she was on God's timetable. And we were all at His mercy. It was about 11 o'clock in the morning when they finished unhooking her from her IVs and monitors. Ruth describes her memories of those moments:

Slowly as the tubes came out, signatures were written, instructions given, items packed up, wires removed, and as Zion was dressed in a little traveling outfit and snapped into a car seat, I took a deep breath and almost sighed in relief. Seeing her untangled and wrapped in blankets, I realized that she was a little baby and that I knew what to do for babies; I could take care of her. Whereas when she had been hooked up to monitors and machines, I felt unequal to the task of caring for her, but minus the tubes, I saw the little babe that she was.

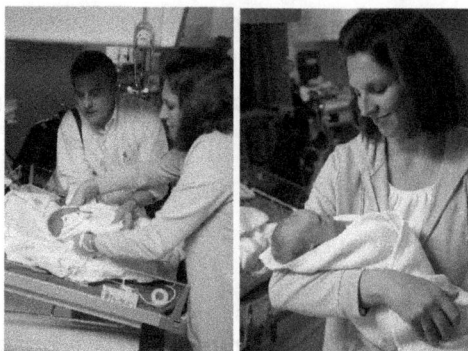

We had received so much love and care from the staff at Primary Children's Medical Center, the doctors, the nurses, the social workers. Our hearts were full of gratitude for them. We had also made friends with some of the other patients' families, and we bid them all goodbye and God's blessings for their own specific challenges.

My older brother Craig came to the hospital that morning. He is a photographer and took a bunch of pictures. As I have looked back through the pictures my brother took, there were a few he took with us and another mother and her baby in the bay next to ours. Ruth and this mother held our babies next to each other for a picture together. The contrast is very apparent. Her baby appeared quite blue next to Zion. Apparently, it was oxygen deprived because of its heart condition. Zion's color was so normal and healthy. It always was.

My father was there and helped carry things to the car. Once we were loaded and ready to pull away, I felt like we were not too much different from Zion. We were now on our own too, stepping outside of the safety and security of the hospital. It was reminiscent of our experience with leaving the hospital with Adam, our firstborn. The feelings of stepping into the unknown were similar, but so much heightened by this new situation. We were embarking on a trip that was more than just a three-and-a-half-hour drive home. We were heading into territory we had never experienced before. We knew there was heartache and pain at some points ahead, but those landmarks were not with mileage markers. There were so many unknowns. I felt better as we looked around us and saw that the sun had broken through the clouds and was shining down on us. This was just another tender mercy. God was with us and would accompany us on the journey ahead.

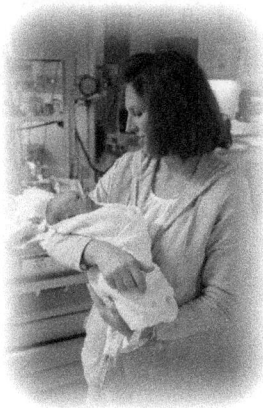

CHAPTER 9

Home, and Eternal Family

A s we got on the road, I felt anxious about getting home. Little things were stressing me. I didn't want to stop for gas although I knew we had to. I was anxious about making it home with Zion alive. Everything felt so tenuous. It seemed like we were teetering on the edge of a cliff with the ground crumbling under our feet. My fears were starting to work on me. I had to take a little time to regroup when Ruth asked if I was all right. I realized I was not exercising my faith, and yet I truly believed we would make it home and have at least a few days with Zion. We had a very heartfelt conversation, somewhere just past the Utah-Idaho border. I will never forget the raw emotion of the moment. I had been trying to be strong for Ruth and put on a good face, but it belied what I was feeling at my core, the absolute reality and difficulty of what we were doing. We looked at each other and cried openly, asking the question, "How can we bring our baby home to die? How can we do this?" I sat there in the driver's seat just sobbing, my chest heaving as I finally let all my emotions out. Now it was Ruth's turn to comfort me. Indeed, we comforted each other.

We knew this was the right thing to do. We just needed the strength to carry through with God's plan. I have found that the exercise of faith is a true workout indeed. We have moments in life when our circumstances overwhelm us. Our thoughts are focused only on the realities before us, and our emotions give way to fear. All we can see are the obstacles in our path. Our negative thoughts and fears breed discouragement, and it feels like a huge weight pushing us down. It takes great effort to push back against that weight, to shove aside those doubtful thoughts and fears. It takes mental work to look for those thoughts of faith, to look again to God, believing that "He's got this. Hang in there. It will be okay." It is a struggle, but a struggle that with persistence eventually pays off. Our efforts are rewarded with peace and with hope that with His help and strength we *have* got this. And like any exercise, you grow stronger the more you do it.

I stated earlier that we can expect tender mercies. I have a testimony of this. We experienced many. It was as if God was saying, "I know this is something very difficult that I am asking of you, so I am going to smooth out some of the rough spots along the way. You are not alone in this. I am with you."

Ruth and I talked about what needed to happen when we got home. We decided that there were a few things we needed to do, certain goals and desires we had for the time ahead. As I wrote in my journal:

We do not know how long we might have with Zion. It could be literally hours, or perhaps days – even weeks. This will be very interesting and challenging, living with the knowledge that we can lose her at almost any time. Each moment will be precious.

Interestingly, just a week prior to Zion's birth, a friend of Ruth's shared a forwarded email written by Jack Rushton, a former colleague of mine in Southern California. Jack had suffered a broken neck from a body surfing accident at the beach. He instantly became a quadriplegic reliant on life support. In this email, he spoke of the Sword of Damocles from classical Greek mythology. The sword was precariously suspended over the head of Damocles by a single horse-hair, and therefore, could fall at any moment (or not). Jack Rushton goes on to express his thoughts about how this relates to all of us:

> In a sense, we all have the Sword of Damocles dangling over our heads. My expression for the Sword of Damocles – "an ever-present peril" – is "living on the edge." I have been especially sensitive to the "Sword of Damocles" philosophy while living on life support for 17 years. I have had numerous brushes with death, all of them convincing me that I indeed am living in "an ever-present peril." You may think this is a very negative way of looking at life, but I don't think so. Realizing that I am "living on the edge" and under the dangling "Sword of Damocles" helps me to appreciate and value each good day I am given. It motivates me to make the best of every day of life I am granted.
>
> You may not want to believe it, but we are all "living on the edge" and directly under the dangling "Sword of Damocles." I personally believe it is a healthy thing to realize how fragile life is, but I don't think the Lord wants us to face the present or the future with fear and trembling. To feel at peace and secure each day of our lives is what living the Gospel should do for us, isn't it?[1]

His email observations expressed very well the situation we found ourselves in at this time. Literally, we were living with an "ever-present peril," not knowing how long we could enjoy our daughter, but we didn't want to live this period of time in fear and trembling. We wanted to live it with love, peace, and happiness.

1. Email written by Jack Rushton, October 12, 2006, 11:49 AM - received by Ruth on October 14, 2006.

The Goal and the Miracles

Our desires were few and simple: We wanted to enjoy Zion and make those precious moments count for as long as we had her. We wanted to have a family picture done to preserve our memory of Zion's time with our family. And finally, we wanted her to have her baby blessing.

We hit only a couple of short snowstorms on our way home, and as we pulled into Twin Falls, the clouds gave way to a blue sky. The next few days the weather cleared, and we enjoyed some wonderfully warm autumn days. I recorded the following in my journal about our arrival home:

We brought Zion into our home about 3:30 in the afternoon. Moriah stood vigil at the door and was there to greet us. My mother had been with the kids and prepared them for our arrival. There were some challenges to be met. Samuel was struggling emotionally, Nyal was upset because he knew what this meant, that we were "bringing her home to die," and, "How could we do that?" … and "She should have the surgery."

We gathered the family together around the kitchen table and talked. When our children left the hospital the previous Saturday, surgery was still the main option in our minds. The children were expecting this would be the case. They knew that without surgery Zion could not live. To have us come home with her was something we had not been able to prepare them adequately for in advance. We realized that they needed to hear our thoughts and experiences and to know what we had gone through, so they might be able to accept the course we were taking. I recorded the following in my journal:

We had a wonderful talk around the dining table and helped the kids to understand all that had happened in the past few days, and to bear testimony that this was the will of our Heavenly Father. We also brought out something that I think changed the whole mood. It was a plaster cast of Zion's hand.

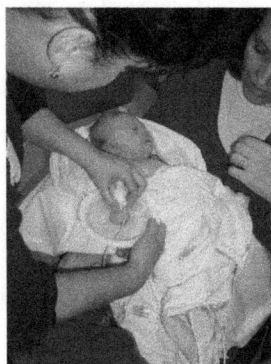

A couple of days before we left the hospital, a social worker, Joy, came to us and asked if we would like to have a memento of our daughter, plaster casts of her hand and her foot. We were delighted at the offer, something we would have never thought of. She placed Zion's foot in the latex goop until it congealed and could be removed, leaving an impression of her foot. She did the same with Zion's hand. She then took the impressions and made plaster casts of her hand and her foot and brought them to us. She said the foot came out just fine, but she was disappointed with the hand. Zion had closed her fingers and made a fist, probably because of the goop being cold. She asked, "Would it be alright if I tried it again?" Of course! We were more than happy for a second attempt. Another impression was made, and Joy brought back the second plaster cast of Zion's hand. A second time, Zion had clenched her little fist. Joy apologized, but wondered, "Would you like to try one more time?" Yes! We did want to try again. This time, I offered to help her to get Zion's fingers outstretched and get a better mold of her hand. We wanted this physical remembrance of our daughter. I flattened out her hand and pressed it in the goop, holding it down in the goop by pressing on the back of her hand with the shortened index finger of my right hand. We were pretty sure we got it right this time.

When Joy came back, she did not return alone. She had with her an entourage of seven or eight nurses. We could see that something special was going on. Joy had the cast of Zion's hand in a small box, so we could not see it. She seemed close to tears, and the faces of the nurses were also full of anticipation. Joy said, "I have the cast of your daughter's hand in here. In all the years I have been making these plaster casts, I have never seen anything like it, and I would keep it for myself if I did not know this was meant especially for you." She then opened the box, and there on white tissue paper rested the tiny cast of our daughter's hand. What we saw was indeed unique and marvelous. And now, with our children huddled around us at our kitchen table, we opened the box again and shared with them what we had seen:

She [Zion] had somehow pulled her middle two fingers in and her little hand had formed the symbol in (ASL) American Sign Language for "I love you." When the kids saw the hand cast, they burst into tears as we told them we felt like God had allowed her to give us a message. I truly do believe this with all my heart.

It was a message that was clear to Joy and the nursing staff, and it was immediately clear to us. Ruth adds that when we first saw the cast, "It literally took our breath away. Her little message of love was broadcast so loud and clear to our hearts that she was aware, that she loved us, and that a loving Heavenly Father had provided a way for her to communicate in the only manner that she could, an everlasting message of love and thanks." We could almost hear the words she could not speak: "I love you for all you are going through, and will yet go through for me, so I can come to earth, albeit for a short time, and fulfill God's purposes for me. I love you for bringing me into this family – _my_ family. I Love You!"

This was a wonderful blessing for us personally, but I believe her message also speaks for all children who never had the opportunity to express themselves to their loved ones before passing away, no matter what age and stage of life they were. If they could speak and you could hear, I think you would hear a message very similar to this. If the world could only understand what a precious gift life is in the grand scheme of eternity, we would know how grateful the Zions of our lives are to us for bringing them into this mortal existence, no matter how brief the time may be.

I hope this message finds a place in many hearts. It has an eternal place in ours. The hand cast of our daughter is a priceless memento for us, but it is also a symbol of something much greater than Zion and our experience. It is a symbol of love, of hope, of families, and of God's tender mercies. I know He cares about all our pains and our heartaches. I think this was also *God's* message to us as well. *He* is saying, "I love you – for all you are going through to fulfill my purposes in your life. For your struggles and stress. For the grief and pain still ahead. For your willingness to submit to my will – for trusting me. I Love You!"

Ruth's testimony:

That cast touched us, and it touches ALL who hear her story. I testify there is a God, and He loves each one of us. He doesn't shield us from difficulties, but He does carry us through difficult times. He provides help along the way. If we will trust Him and submit our wills to Him, He can do great miracles. He is real, and He is powerful, and He is all-knowing. He led me through this experience in the way that I needed to go. He guided my husband in the way he needed to travel. He watched over each one of our children through this journey in the way that each needed.

The children accepted our decision when they understood the process we had gone through and especially when they saw Zion's hand cast, but there was one little boy who was still struggling with one aspect of the whole thing. Samuel, our eight-year-old, stuck close to me and followed me into the bedroom, where I started to unpack and put things away. I sensed he wanted to talk and I asked him if he did. He poured out the pain of his young heart with a simple question, "Dad, can't Heavenly Father cure her heart?" He began to cry. I did, too. I sat down on the edge of the bed with him, took him in my arms, and we had a good cry together. I was so touched by his tenderness and sensitivity. I realized he was still hoping and praying that Zion could live on and on and stay with our family, that he still had this hope and his tender little heart was breaking. Mine was, too. He believed God could heal her. I wasn't sure what to say to him at that moment, so I said a little prayer asking for help to know how to respond to his question.

A thought came into my mind that fit everything I had already come to know. I told him, "Samuel, Heavenly Father has a special mission for each one of us. Your special mission is to help prepare the earth for the coming of the Savior. Zion's mission is to get a body, bring love to our family, and then return to Heavenly Father and help prepare the earth for the Savior's second coming from the spirit world. Each plan is important." I told him it was all right to cry and that his mother and I had also been doing a lot of crying. We held each other for a long time. I know I was trying to comfort him, but it was also a comfort to me. I was very grateful for a boy who was so caring and loving of his sister. Our hearts were knit together in grief and solace and faith. As I reflect back on this tender moment, I can't help but remember that I too had once been that little boy, outside the French doors of my brother Mike's hospital room, hoping and praying for the healing of my baby brother.

This Is Not about Me
Ruth was grateful for the recovery she had experienced after the birth of Zion. She was amazed at how much she was able to do

and how comfortable she was physically. Ruth also felt like she was blessed emotionally. She records the following:

"This is not about me." My new theme. This was to become my focus as I came home and found myself frustrated with the same challenges here ... kids not doing chores, not getting ready, not watching the time. The thought hit me, "This is not about me," and it became easier to let go – my job is to love – to do more for my family – to teach by righteous example.

What a great mantra – something we would all do well to live with as a guiding thought.

Our Home – A Temple
We really enjoyed having Zion at home. The children understood that we didn't know how long she would be with us, and they took all the time they wanted in holding her and loving her. Their prayers changed to "Please bless Zion that she can enjoy her time with us." I have absolutely no doubt that those prayers were answered. She was rarely alone. She was constantly enveloped in the love of her family.

We set up her bassinet in the front living room of the house, not back in our bedroom which would have been normal for us with a newborn. We wanted her to be accessible to everyone who wanted to spend time with her and love her. Her little bed was right next to the couch. This is where one of us slept each night, right next to her. Because of her condition, she slept a lot, but she always had such a peaceful look about her. Ruth wrote of these vigilant night watches, "I didn't begrudge being up with her. I didn't want to sleep. I felt it a privilege to serve her. I knew I could sleep later – there would be lots of time for sleeping, resting recuperating – I just wanted to be with her."

We did not mind visitors. We found out later that many would have liked to come by but wanted to respect this private and sacred time our family had with each other. I use the word sacred, and indeed, that is what it was. Those who came often commented on the feeling they had when they entered our home. They said it felt like a church or a temple. A sacred feeling truly was present. A spirit and feeling of reverence surrounded Zion, accentuated by her closeness to the boundary between mortality and immortality.

One note we received exemplifies this point and the effect it had on those who did stop by. It was from a retired couple we had grown close to:

Dear Brother and Sister Manwaring,

Your little Cherish Zion has blessed our lives, as have you two, during these last months of your adjustment, acceptance, and anticipation, and we wanted to share with you our private thoughts.

First of all, the two of you are personal witnesses to us of refined, dedicated followers of Christ. Your love, devotion, concern, and support of each other in this situation lend a sacredness to little Cherish's visit here on earth. We felt that same sacredness in your home today as we stopped to meet her. Pure, precious, porcelain, with an aura of eternity, she touched our hearts. While she may have a "broken heart," yours are the willing and accepting hearts, the loving hearts that are blessing her short journey. How blessed she is to feel so much love! How blessed you are to feel her love!! For your family, Zion has come in a very real way. Cherish is a link in your family's circle, perhaps a welding link in ways yet to be seen. Thank you for sharing her with us this morning.

Know that we are grateful for our association with your family.

Brother and Sister Stowell

The following are some of Ruth's memories of the next couple of days:

*During the days Zion was home with us, Paul and I took turns
sleeping on the couch with her. He'd either take the early or late
shift. Paul liked to be up with the kids in the early mornings –
they'd share some private moments bright and early. I always
felt bad because it seemed I could hardly get her fresh milk. By
the time I'd pump, they'd already fed her the old, and it was a
vicious cycle – poor child. She never complained. It was a great
blessing/lesson to me. She was so undemanding – but she
needed to eat to keep her strength. I'd never been able to sleep as
long as I wanted after having a baby. Seems they always wanted
to eat. That was a new experience also to be the milk cow and
let others feed Zion. It allowed them to bond. I was grateful
because it took that stress off me. I could rest. Moriah was the
one who got her to eat the best. I thought she looked like she was
gaining weight. I thought her face was beginning to fill out. She
didn't like her first and only shower with dad – didn't like the
spray on her face – but she did enjoy the bath tub with dad. She
looked like a little frog with a big round belly/torso and little
tiny arms and legs. All her clothes were too big. But I didn't
have anything small enough to fit her.*

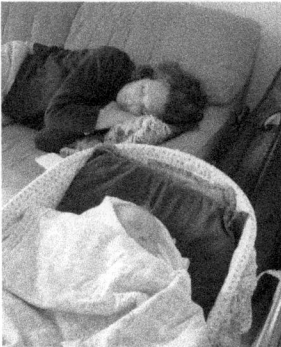

Hospice

Shortly after we arrived home, a hospice nurse came to the house to give us some instruction and to ascertain our situation. Ruth says: "I hated hospice because the phone calls they would make to check up on us were a reminder of what was coming. But they are angels because they took care of so many little things, paper work, getting things lined up for the inevitable, preparations that we really did not know how or want to deal with at this stage. It was a love-hate relationship." Ruth goes on to say that the hospice nurse was so good and knowledgeable and was able to answer any concern or question. She was both a blessing and a harbinger of ill tidings because of her purpose in our lives.

A Priceless Gift

Friday morning, we had breakfast together as a family. The kids had been up early and had completed their paper routes and their chores of feeding the cows and chickens. Today was a day of no school, probably due to teacher conferences, so we had everyone around the table. We began to discuss what we wanted to do to meet our next goals and talked about having a family picture done. We thought of taking everyone to a portrait studio, but Ruth and I were nervous about taking Zion away from home. Everything felt so safe and secure here, and we did not want to upset that balance. Who did we know that was a professional photographer who could come to our house? I know I was also concerned about the cost (I always am), but that should not have even been a concern given the circumstances. A family portrait was the most important thing. It would be treasured for the rest of our lives. We thought of someone we could call and were hoping to arrange for a sitting, perhaps the next day if possible.

Only a couple of minutes after we had concluded our discussion, as we were still sitting around the table, the phone rang. My journal entry describes what happened next:

It was truly an answer to prayers. We received a phone call from Amy Haake, a woman in our ward. She apologized for intruding in our family's special time together, but she was wondering if we had considered having a photographer come to do a family picture. She said that her sister was a photographer and would like to come and take pictures of our family – pro bono. The kids were out of school, and the timing could not have been more perfect. It seems like all of the timing of this episode of our lives has been perfect. We have felt like the Lord has been walking this path with us and even directing the events as they have needed to happen. Ruth says that she feels like there have been stepping stones placed in front of her and that the options have been made clear – one step at a time.

This was a blessing from heaven. Amy said, "My sister can come by anytime that is convenient for your family – including today." Ruth's reaction to the offer of this personal photo shoot:

My jaw was on the floor. Could she? Of course! How kind an offer. I had just been wondering how I was going to dare schedule an appointment, groom everyone, and get to a studio to accomplish this goal. I hadn't wanted to take my tiny, susceptible baby out into such a cold, germ-filled world. And here was someone offering to come into our home to do for us exactly what we wanted?!!? And the fact that the kids had the day off from school ... How perfect, you say? No kidding! So, my mother-in-law and I went through the kids' drawers and closets to see if we could pull together some semi-matching outfits. It was determined that we could get everyone in white tops and khaki bottoms. Truly another tender mercy for our family.

I have often said about these events and the way they unfolded that if I'd had a year to prepare, I could not have planned everything to turn out as perfectly as they did for us. We marveled at the miraculous confluence of blessing after timely blessing flowing into our lives. The timing of this phone call was beyond coincidental. It was a gift from heaven. We are sure that Amy and her sister were inspired by God to call when she did.

Amy had written one of the many notes that were delivered to us in the hospital by Betty Jo Quigley on that first Sunday after Zion was born. It said, "You have been on my mind and in my prayers. I'd love to help in any way." Boy, did she!

The Photo Shoot
We arranged for Amy's sister, Jessica Randall, to come about mid-day to our home. There was a feeling of love and harmony present as Jessica placed us in various positions and combinations. We had our entire family together for this special moment in time, and the precious pictures preserved it for posterity. Also, everyone in the family had his or her picture taken individually with Zion, including my (Paul's) mother who was helping with crowd control. Jessica was so good with everyone, so patient and happy and knowledgeable about what to do. We comfortably followed her lead. It was a wonderful time. Ruth wore a white dress, and so did Zion. Zion's dress was also the same beautiful little dress that Moriah had been blessed in as a baby. Some of my favorite memories are of mother and daughter. They were both so beautiful and pure.

A very special moment of this sitting for me was when Jessica had the children gather around their little sister as she lay in her bassinet. I immediately recognized the scene from that early morning in the hospital room when I saw Zion at home with her family, her siblings gathered around her. This was the exact scene I had pictured! I realized now that that had been a prophetic moment, something Heavenly Father had allowed me to see beforehand, with the eye of faith. What was happening now in front of my physical eyes was its fulfillment. It was a humbling moment and a confirmation that we were on the right path, and God was walking it with us.

It brings to mind this scripture: "And there were many whose faith was so exceedingly strong, [who] truly saw with their eyes the things which they had beheld with an eye of faith, *and they were glad.*"[2] (Italics added). And *I was* glad. This picture is a reminder to me of the ability of God to foresee and sometimes give us a glimpse of the future. He knows the path that can lead to our greatest joys and richest experiences.[3]

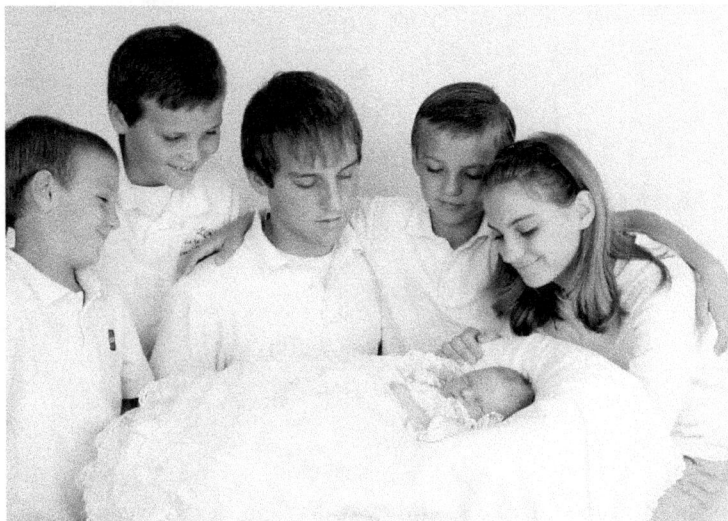

We were excited to see how these pictures would turn out. We knew they would be invaluable to us, and this has proven to be true. The photo sitting was a major milestone, and we were relieved it had now been accomplished. Not knowing what we could count on for a timeline was difficult. Zion was doing so well. She did not seem to

---

2. Ether 12:19.

3. I found the piece of paper that I had written on in the hospital that morning in church. Here is the text: "This morning I could not sleep. I was thinking of the possibilities that face us in the days ahead. I wondered if it won't come to taking this baby down a path that will result in no treatment and ultimately death. I wondered how that should happen. I could picture that instead of having a death take place in the hospital, we bring the baby home to Twin Falls and surround this little one with family. I see Zion surrounded by her brothers and sister - her eternal family. I see us enjoying her for a short time, a tender time, a holy time."

be struggling, her color was good, and she seemed so peaceful and content. It seemed like maybe she could be with us for a long time. And yet, everything seemed like such a gamble. We were truly going on faith and prayer.

Ruth & Zion

My thoughts turned to the next item on our very short list: the baby blessing. In my journal, when I had recorded my thoughts about the writing of Zion's blessing that early morning at the Ronald McDonald house, I also wrote the following as to the circumstances under which I felt it should be done:

...the time was not yet for giving the blessing. I sensed it needed to happen at home, maybe even in church.

As I have stated before, we had seen such a deep interest from people at church. We realized that many had invested themselves in our situation, and we needed to do this at church if at all possible. The normal time for giving a baby blessing in church would be on the first Sunday of the month, which was still over a week away. It would be nice for her to be blessed on the normal Sunday for that kind of event, like any other child. Dare we try and wait that long? Maybe if we scheduled it for that day, Zion would be allowed to stay with us at least that long. We loved having her with us. We truly did not want her to ever leave. We hoped against hope that her life would be extended. Was I trying to cheat fate? Maybe.

I shared with Ruth my thoughts about waiting until the first Sunday of the month, which is called a Fast Sunday because the members of the church fast for two meals on that day and give the money they would have spent on their meals to a fund to be used for helping the poor and the needy. Initially Ruth had been okay with my suggestion.

> *[But on] Friday, she began to feel very uneasy about having the baby blessed on Fast Sunday and said that she felt like we should do this right away, on the upcoming Sabbath. I have learned to listen to her feelings. I asked her again on Saturday morning how she felt after a good night's rest, and she still felt the same. There was no debating in my mind – we needed to set things in motion for that to happen. We called family, and those who were able to come made arrangements to be here.*

I called Bishop Clark and asked if it would be all right for us to bless Zion in church the next day. He said, "Of course, that would be no problem." So, it was all arranged for October 29, 2006. Baby blessings are significant events for our families. We did not expect many to be there on such short notice, but we knew some would be able to come.

Sunday – Zion's Blessing
Our sister-in-law, Teriann Hanks, had been busy making a beautiful little dress for Zion for the baby blessing. She brought the dress with her. Ruth's parents and many of her family came from eastern Idaho (over three hours away) for the blessing. My father and many

of my brothers came from an even longer distance to be with us. Our house was beginning to fill up with visitors and relatives.

I wanted to prepare personally to give this blessing, sensing the sacred nature of what I was about to do. I took some time in the privacy of my study to go over the words and to ponder their meaning. I knew the words and sensed the power they could have in the lives of those who would hear it. In the midst of my preparation, something interesting happened that I want to mention here because of its significance to me. A thought entered my mind that I am embarrassed to admit even came into consideration. I had a momentary glimpse of the impact the blessing could, no, *would* have on the hearers. I could almost hear and see them in my mind's eye, praising me for the words that were spoken for their eloquence and meaning. I began to anticipate the compliments that would come and the admiration along with it.

Immediately, I felt a sense of anger for even thinking such a thing. This was so unworthy. I felt so ashamed that I could even consider using my daughter's life and special circumstances to aggrandize myself or my status. This was not worthy of her, of me, of God, or any part of what was happening! I considered where this thought had come from because it was not at all in keeping with my normal thinking, and I realized it was a temptation that originated from the source of all unrighteousness. Satan tempted even Christ himself. Once while He was standing on the pinnacle of the temple in Jerusalem, Satan taunted Him to cast Himself off from that great height and let the angels catch Him in full view of the crowds below. He was being tempted to do something for the glory of the world, to be admired of men.

I did not think of this event from Christ's life at that moment, but as I look back on it, the similarities describe my situation. It angered me that the Adversary would try to use the purity of this situation as a temptation. I remember the strong and intense commitment I made there in my study as I swore, "I will not give this blessing if it is done with such unworthy motivation!" I meant that statement as much as I had ever meant anything in my life. I remember very clearly my clenched jaw and resolute mind and the hot tears that accompanied this commitment. This has been my continued resolve since then. In the years that have elapsed since that moment, I continue to keep that promise in my mind and heart.

Zion's life will not be used for self-gain of any kind. Not then, not now, not in the future. The purpose in writing this book is singular: If there is anything in the telling of her story that might help others, then it is worth the effort and time and expense.

The time came for us to go to church:

Zion looked like a perfect little angel. Ruth wore the same white dress she had worn when we had the family pictures done. She looked like an angel mother. There were so many others who were there for the blessing. Bishop [Dr.] Smith, Pres. Allen, Bishop Clark, and from our family – all of the grandparents, many siblings, and their families.

The members of our ward who had been so interested in our daughter and had offered so much love and support to our family were finally able to see our precious little girl, alive and well. Everyone knew Zion would only be with us for a short time. It had to be touching, even heart-wrenching for those with tender sympathies.

The blessing was given near the beginning of the meeting. I held Zion alongside others who held the priesthood, both family members and our priesthood leaders. We placed our hands under her little body and held her in the middle of the circle we had formed around her. After addressing our Heavenly Father in prayer and referencing the priesthood authority by which we were performing this ordinance, I gave her the following blessing:

Heavenly Father, we take this child in our arms to give her a name and a blessing.

The name by which you will be known upon the records of the land and the church is:

Cherish Zion Manwaring

*The name by which you shall be known in our family in mortality is **Zion**.*

I bless you that your spirit may be aware and understand the words spoken to you this day. You are an exalted spirit of high and holy station whose main purpose in mortality is to gain a body and bring love and blessings to others through your presence. As in your premortal life, you are fulfilling your mission here with exactness. You are true and faithful to our Father's will. Your spirit was anxious to come to this family, and we are grateful and honored by your presence. Your birth was foretold to your mother by a faithful stake patriarch years ago.

Your name has been carefully chosen. Zion was chosen by your mother many years ago. It reflects the teachings in the scriptures. Mt. Zion in Jerusalem is a Holy and Sacred place and is associated with the future coming of the Lord and the concept of the atonement. Zion means pure in heart. This could not be more perfect of a name for you.

Even though your physical heart is not perfect, your heart is indeed pure. As Jesus said, "Blessed are the pure in heart, for they shall see God." The concept of Zion is what all faithful Saints strive for: as we read in the scripture, "and the Lord called his people Zion because they were of one heart and one mind and dwelt in righteousness...." Your heart has brought our hearts to a oneness. Your life gives us more purpose and desire to live in righteousness. You are exalted in our eyes for we understand the doctrine of infant children and their place in eternity. We know that those spirits who come into a body that is mentally impaired also have an assurance of eternal life with God our Father.

You sought a body such as you have been blessed with in order to fulfill God's plan for you. We are so blessed to have you as a part of our eternal family, born in the covenant, sealed for time and all eternity.

Your name – Cherish – has a special meaning in our family, especially to your sister, Moriah, and reflects your eternal nature – that you lived before you came to earth as one of God's choicest spirit daughters. It also reflects how we will honor you throughout our mortal lives. You have watched over this home with love and tenderness, with understanding and patience as you have waited for the timing to be just right. We bless you that you will become our family's guardian angel to watch over us, to bless us to come and join you in our Father's presence. You will be blessed to greet your grandparents as well. It is your purpose and mission to help us to cherish one another even as we cherish you now in our hearts and our home. We look forward to knowing you in your full spirit stature. Zion, we cherish you, we love you with all our imperfect hearts and pray that our hearts may become as pure as yours, that we too may have a broken heart and contrite spirit in the pure figurative sense.

We bless you that your short life will accomplish great good in this world for a long time to come, and that there will be a rippling effect which will influence many and be the means to build faith, testimony, and a deep and abiding trust in a loving Heavenly Father and His Son Jesus Christ. We bless your good mother that she will be honored, blessed, and comforted for her great sacrifice in submitting to our Father's will.

We promise you all the blessings and ordinances requisite for exaltation. We bless you with a continuance of your natural gifts and talents to be used in the service of God in preparing for the second coming of the Savior of this world.

And now Zion, we seal these blessings upon you, and seal you up to our Father in Heaven and his timetable, for you are now, always were, and will forever be in His Hands.

These things we say in the name of Jesus Christ. Amen.[4]

I do not have much memory of how the rest of the meeting went that day. I will always remember the blessing though. It has continued to have significance for our family in the years since then, which I will touch upon later. Ruth remembers the following about this occasion:

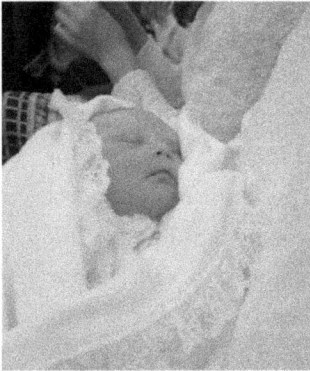

She was beautiful. I couldn't believe Paul snapped a picture of her in sacrament meeting – but I treasure that picture because I remember that moment and the joy of holding her in church. The kids (Moriah, Nyal) all wanted a turn after the blessing. Carter (our nephew) came over and sat between Paul and I. He just looked. I asked if he wanted to touch her. I showed him the still visible and healing IV/needle hole on the top of her hand. Carter asked why his dad (a doctor) couldn't fix her. What a loaded question. "Even the doctors in Salt Lake City couldn't fix her. Heavenly Father wants her to come back home soon."

As it was stated in the blessing, Zion was sealed up to our Heavenly Father and was on his timetable. Our simple desires for her were all being realized. We had our family pictures and the baby blessing in church. We had been loving her every minute since she arrived home. Our main objectives were all being met. We were very grateful.

4. Zion's Name & Blessing, October 29, 2006.

Loving Zion – Cherishing Every Moment

Ruth and I began to wonder if she would be with us for a long time to come. She was doing so well, had such good color, was so content. Maybe she wasn't going to pass away soon after all.

That Sunday was a wonderful day. We enjoyed beautiful warm fall weather. We enjoyed one another's company. Everyone took turns with Zion. Three of my six brothers had come great distances. Most of Ruth's family had been able to come, including some of her cousins, nieces, and nephews. Everyone helped with the food and other necessities. Children played outside. Adults visited with each other. It was wonderful to have so much family present and so much family support. I recently reviewed the pictures taken on this and other occasions, marveling at how many of them show people – dozens of them – holding Zion. I think everyone sensed the window of opportunity was small. They did not want to miss the opportunity to connect with this precious, beautiful gift from God.

When we gathered to offer a prayer and blessing on the food, I tried to express my gratitude to everyone for being there, but I choked on the words and had to pause to collect my emotions. I quipped, "I think we need to put a sign on the front door that reads, 'Warning! Anyone who enters here and shows the least bit of love and concern may be met with tears of gratitude.'"

Family. I believe that families are the basic building block, not just of society but of eternity. Families are what God began with – Adam and Eve, and then their children, and the next generation of families, and so on down to our present time. He intended them to form strong relationships and to teach and learn from one another, to care for and support each other. We have been blessed to have such families. God does not intend for families to be formed here and to discontinue those relationships in the next life. Families can truly be together forever. We are all God's family.

Eventually the crowd began to dwindle as people departed for their hometowns. Once again, a journal entry captures another important moment of that day and my daughter Moriah:

> *Moriah has been so very attentive to Zion. She has a very personal interest from many angles. She is a sister, first off, but she has a tender heart about this whole thing – also because of the natural love she has for others, her family in particular. I believe she was also the first contact that Cherish Zion had with our family. It all is clear now. Every moment that she was able to hold her, feed her, be with her, you would find Moriah there. I think the Lord was also preparing her heart for what was to come.*

I took Moriah upstairs to her bedroom at one point in the day, when things had quieted down, and I had her bring Zion with her. I asked her to stand on the spot in her bedroom where, on that night, years before, she heard the "lady's voice" say over and over again, "Cherish, Cherish, Cherish!" We talked about that experience and reflected on that significant event. Could it be that Zion was now here in her sister's arms on the very spot where her premortal spirit once had been? We think so. I took a picture of Moriah as she stood there with her baby sister – Cherish Zion Manwaring.

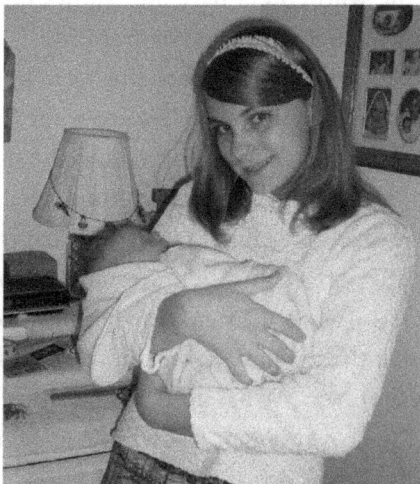

I need to say something about Ruth as well. These were days and moments not to be forgotten as we enjoyed the coming together of family and loved ones that the intense interest in Zion had brought about. Here Ruth was truly in her element. More journal thoughts:

I cannot express how impressed I have been with Ruth and her deep sensitivity to everything that has transpired with this baby. She has often given vent to tears as she has anticipated what would eventually happen. She has been strong, but she has been so tender. She loves our little girl like only a mother who has carried, sacrificed, prayed, and fretted over a baby can. I love her with all my heart for all she has done. She felt like her mother should be here, and when the blessing was over, her mother stayed. It has been so wonderful to have both of our mothers here. I can't say enough about what a blessing they have been as they have quietly taken care of various small tasks, so we could enjoy Zion and each other.

Sunday had been a beautiful sunny day, but late Sunday evening, the 29th, the weather turned cold. Monday became chilly as a cold front moved in. Looking back on it, the timing of the weather was once again significant in how it seemed to match or portend upcoming events. The warm days of fall were now turning to winter. Monday was the 30th of October. Zion had been with us for ten wonderful and unforgettable days. I recorded the following in my journal:

I decided to go back to work Monday. It was to be a scaled-down version of work. Zion has done so well, it seemed probable that she would be around for weeks. We knew we were in the "icing on the cake" period of time.

About that Monday, Ruth says:

We settled into as normal a routine as possible. With the kids in school and Paul at work, I was able to spend more alone-time with Zion. I could relax knowing that all of the tasks we had planned were taken care of. Loving Zion was never a task, but such a natural exercise of the heart, such a privilege. When the kids came home from school they washed their hands and held their sister. Adam was especially tender in feeding her with a tiny bottle. She didn't eat much and each day she seemed to eat less and less. The hospice nurse kept coming to check and offer any needed help. She really was an angel, but I hated being reminded of the eventual outcome of this story.

Nyal turned 11 that day, and it was a special birthday for him and for all of us. (The October birthdays are easy to remember in our family. Ruth was born on October 10, so we now had birthdays on 10/10, 10/20, and 10/30.) This was also the day that Zion was supposed to be born, the day that was originally scheduled for Ruth to be induced. It was the first family celebration Zion got to enjoy with her family. I say "enjoy" because I believe there is a consciousness of the spirit even with an infant. Some may think their newborn state does not allow them to know or experience anything around them, but anyone who has nurtured a newborn child can tell you they respond to their surroundings. This is even true while they are still in the womb. We know she felt our love.

I once had an interesting experience with Moriah when she was a newborn, perhaps only a couple of weeks old. It was night, and I was up with her for some reason. Perhaps she had been fussy because she needed to burp or had some gas. I was letting her mother sleep. After a while, Moriah calmed down and was peaceful. I had her on my lap, looking down at her and talking to her. I gazed at her, wondering at this precious gift of a baby girl. It was a very peaceful moment. And then she looked back at me with a recognition in her eyes that was unique and filled with intelligence. It felt like I was with a person full of understanding of her situation and that her veil of forgetfulness had not fully closed upon her mind. She understood who I was and where she had come from, from the presence of God, who is the Father of our spirits. If she could have spoken, I felt like she could have told me things about the spirit world from which she had just arrived, things about God that she still remembered but the rest of us have forgotten, and which she too would soon forget. It was such a vivid and clear moment. I sat there in awe and there was a feeling of truth about what I was thinking and experiencing. I wish I could adequately explain what happened. It was not like looking in the eyes of a baby, but the eyes of a fully conscious adult, a fully mature spirit. There was a connection between us. This moment lasted for only a few minutes. Then it seemed as if her little mortal body made its presence known through a small pain caused by some natural discomfort and then that intelligence in her eyes began to fade.

There is a poem by William Wordsworth which expresses this concept of our having lived in the presence of God before we came to this earth. It is a lengthy poem, but there is just one stanza I quote here:

Ode
Intimations of Immortality from Recollections of Early Childhood

Our birth is but a sleep and a forgetting:
The Soul that rises with us, our life's Star,
Hath had elsewhere its setting,
And cometh from afar:
Not in entire forgetfulness,
And not in utter nakedness,
But trailing clouds of glory do we come
From God, who is our home:
Heaven lies about us in our infancy![5]

---

5. William Wordsworth, *Ode: Intimations of Immortality from Recollections of Early Childhood,* Literary Licensing, LLC, 2014, 48 pages.

We cannot underestimate our presence and influence upon these little ones, nor should we discount their potential influence upon us. Our children are not entirely our own. They have been lent to us by God for our care, and we have a responsibility to Him to raise them and nurture them in love and righteousness.

Zion was never alone. Adam had a pose that was iconic of his relationship with Zion. He too formed a special bond with his sister. He would sit on the couch with his feet on the floor and his legs together and lay Zion on his lap, in the crease of his legs, face up. He would hold her hands with her little fingers wrapped around one of his own fingers on each hand. He would lean forward looking down in his sister's face and talk to her, or just stare at her, loving her. He was the big brother, the protector. He was fifteen, almost sixteen, and had grown out of his childhood, now the tallest in the family by far. There was something very grown-up about the way he approached his time with Zion. Ruth gives a wonderful description of Adam and Zion:

> *Adam. The word gentleness describes his relationship with Zion. He liked to lift her arms up and put his thumbs in her grasp. He liked to unwrap her and look her all over. She was*

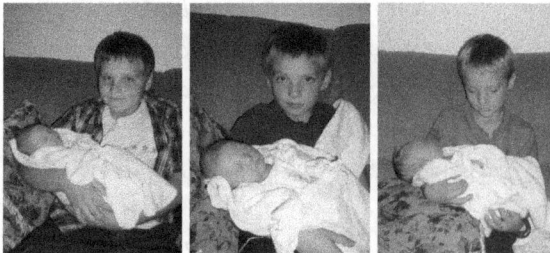

so tiny next to his bigness. He opened his heart to her – looked past her handicaps, her weaknesses, and loved her whole-heartedly without holding back.

Adam found his own way of bonding with her and cherishing her. Each of the children did.

Zion just seemed so healthy and was doing so well. It was hard to imagine that she had a fatal condition. Ruth recalls, "Paul asked me Monday night, did I ever just think she'd get better, that she was fine, that the doctors were all wrong? I agreed – she was so perfect."

CHAPTER 10

A Hallowed, Sacred Evening

Tuesday was Halloween. The kids were looking forward to fun parties at school with everyone dressed up in costumes. It was nice to have our mothers there to help with everything. After the normal morning beginnings, the kids were off to school. Ruth now had time to devote her attention to Zion with no distractions. As she cared for Zion, Ruth began to notice a change. Zion seemed to have discomfort not evident before. Ruth shares the following about the day:

> *I grew concerned as Zion didn't seem to have many messy diapers, and I was able to communicate these types of worries with the nurse. Zion seemed to be a bit out of sorts. Whereas she normally was quiet and subdued, she had been crying out in short bursts randomly. The nurse didn't really have any suggestions for me, but I felt a bit tense that day. I called Paul home early from work to see what he thought.*

Ruth wanted the hospice nurse to come over, but apparently, she was occupied with another client. Ruth sent my mother to the pharmacy for a medication the nurse had recommended. She recorded the following about that afternoon:

How do I write/record what transpired this day? When she cried in pain, it terrified me. I didn't know what it meant. Was it a tummy ache? Where was she hurting? What was I to do? I am so overcome with guilt that I might have choked her giving her the medicine. She would stop crying if you stood and gently bounced her. I would turn her on her right side and rub her back. She would calm. I tried to feed her with her bottle. She wasn't interested. I wanted her to be comfortable, to be well, to not hurt, to be happy, to not be in pain. Did I try too hard? I was distracted, hopeful, then afraid.

Ruth knew that expending energy by crying and fussing weakened Zion. Zion needed to eat to keep her strength up. It was a very difficult day for Ruth.

When I came home from the office, Ruth asked me if I would give Zion a blessing. She was anxious about her condition. I took Zion into our bedroom where I could have privacy for a few minutes. I took one of the pillows from the bed and laid Zion in the middle of it with my arms underneath her as I knelt beside the bed. I prayed to Heavenly Father that He would bless our precious daughter and that the discomfort she was experiencing would go away and be replaced with comfort and peace. Was her discomfort the kind that is normal for babies? Or was this discomfort particular to her situation? Her color was still good, and she looked healthy. Maybe this was just normal? Once again, I was watching Ruth, listening to her anxiety, and it made me wonder. I knew I could not discount it.

As we prepared for trick or treating that evening, everyone was getting dressed in the front room. My mother was helping Samuel get wrapped up as a mummy with torn strips of bedsheets and safety pins. I was the one who went out with the kids around the neighborhoods. Where we lived, the houses were not close together. Each property was at least an acre, so I drove the van and the kids would enter and exit if the distance was too far to walk efficiently. It was a cold night. I had a cell phone with us in case Ruth needed us to come home. We ended up in a neighborhood a couple of miles away. The home of the Caspersons had a spook alley set up in the barn, and the kids were enjoying going through it.

Meanwhile, back at home, Ruth recalls the following:

Our stake president and his counselor (Presidents Allen and Browning) and their wives stopped by to visit. I handed Zion over to our dear stake president and watched Zion's little body. Her face was sallow and a bit chalky. She was so unnatural. I tried to visit, and I appreciated being surrounded by friends. But I was so anxious for the family to return, and yet not wanting to infringe on the kid's fun. I finally called Paul and encouraged him to come home quickly.

When Ruth called, the kids were still in the spook alley. There was an urgency in Ruth's voice, "Please come home – now!" It was an anxious moment as I tried to round up everyone so we could get home right away. Ruth says, "When I heard the garage door open and then the back door and the clatter of many feet, I was somewhat relieved." Adam, who had been with his friends, was also called. "Come home now. Hurry!"

When we came in, Ruth was with our mothers and our visitors in the front room. Sister Allen was now holding Zion. We could see that Zion was fading. It was time. We all sensed it, but she was so peaceful and quiet. She showed no pain or discomfort. The Allens and Brownings recognized it was time for them to let our family have these last moments alone with Zion, and they excused themselves.

The children had gone upstairs and were taking off their Halloween costumes. My mother remembers sitting by Ruth while

Ruth was holding Zion, and she recalls that Zion was alive. But then Ruth made a comment to my mother and said, "Mom?" My mother quickly went upstairs and gathered the children.

We were all together in the front room. Ruth's intuition was once again manifesting itself as we watched our bright little light fade. Zion became very still and unresponsive. I don't remember right now who was holding her, but I think it was Ruth. She had prayed that Zion would pass away peacefully and without any pain. As Ruth later wrote, "She was so peaceful – then too peaceful – then I wondered."

We tried to feel a pulse or see if we could detect breath, but it was difficult to be sure. Ann Babble, a friend who was a nurse, lived close by. We called her and asked if she could come and bring a stethoscope. We did not know what to believe for sure. At this point, Moriah was holding Zion. When Ann arrived, she listened to Zion's heart, and listened, and listened. She finally said. "I don't hear anything. I cannot detect a heartbeat."

We have never really known the exact moment she passed away. As Ruth says, "I am not sure at what point she left us. So quietly, so sweetly, so serenely she left us. Our little angel was gone."

Her death was like her life – very peaceful. But now that we knew for certain, the grief we had been holding in check was released. Our hearts broke, and our tears flowed. We had come to love Zion with all our hearts and wanted to have her and cherish her forever. Everyone cried as sadness and loss overcame us. We had known this moment would come, and though we were as prepared for it as much as anyone can be, we were not prepared for this kind of pain and heartache.

I somehow had the sense to take a picture of the scene, having felt all along that I needed to chronicle this experience for our family. The scene of anguish is plainly etched on the faces of each child. Adam held his little sister on his lap with a solemn sadness, his grandmother Manwaring standing beside him with a hand of consolation placed on his shoulder. My mother had been an oncology social worker. Her job had been to prepare cancer patients and their families for these kinds of experiences. Death was not foreign to her, and you can see in her face both the concern and sadness, and also the peace that comes from her personal testimony of life after life, and knowing this is not the end. Zion is not gone for good. Next to Adam is Moriah, kneeling near Zion and embraced by her grandmother Hanks. The pain and grief in both of their faces is accented by the tears streaming down their cheeks as they hold each other and openly sob, their emotions unchecked as they give vent to every feeling of love and grief inside of them. These are emotions that any who have lost a dear loved one can understand. I am experiencing all of this again with this writing. We all missed her so much already. We did not really want consolation in these first moments as much as we just wanted – needed – to cry and cry. Ruth, Jacob, Nyal, and Samuel were on the couch in that order next to Adam. Jacob is nestled up against Ruth, being comforted by his grieving mother; Nyal is next to him, red-eyed with tissue in hand. Samuel is crying with his hand covering his eyes, wiping them with a Kleenex. These are the images preserved in the picture and in my mind. I can't help but think of Ruth's mother and the intense sorrow she was feeling and how it must have taken her back to the time when she lost her own child, her little Nyal. She is tender-hearted and full of empathy.

Ann Babble had quietly excused herself at some point. I don't remember when, but we are so grateful to her for coming at a moment's notice, and at such a moment as this. Her service was important for us because we did not know where we were at or what to think until she provided a reliable diagnosis.

As I reflect now on what was happening, I think of a scripture that expresses so well what was transpiring here:

"Thou shalt live together in love, insomuch that thou shalt weep for the loss of them that die."[1]

---

1. Doctrine & Covenants 42:45.

We had been doing exactly that – living together in love. Love always leaves us vulnerable. And with that love, any love, comes a great liability of sorrow and grief when we lose a loved one. But the greater tragedy would be to never have loved at all. We should never shield ourselves from potential grief by withholding our love. It is fully appropriate to cry, even if you have a strong belief and personal testimony that death is not the end. And so, we cried for a while. It was a deep soul-felt cry. But eventually we cried ourselves out, at least for the moment. Ruth recollects, "We cried so hard we laughed at each other."

I wondered what we should do next. It seemed like the right thing to do was to call the funeral home and have them come and pick up our little girl. I hadn't thought this through ahead of time; I had not anticipated what to do in this circumstance. I guess I thought the hospice people would be present and tell us what to do, but it was late in the evening and everything had happened so quickly and naturally that they had not been notified to come. As Ruth put it, "There are no manuals to be read about what to do when you welcome a baby into the world, or what is the right protocol upon their exit from the world."

I will be forever grateful for what happened next. Ruth was in no hurry to make that final parting. She asked if we couldn't delay the call to the funeral home for a while. She said, "We need to give each of the children any time with their sister they want to have, to be able to cherish her here in our home one last time and to say goodbye." I knew immediately that what she was saying was the right thing to do, but under the circumstances, I don't think I would have ever thought of it myself, nor would I have thought of the next thing she suggested: to give each of the children a blessing of peace and comfort on this occasion with their little sister.

Blessing Each Child

And so, I took the children one at a time and laid my hands on their heads and expressed the thoughts that came into my mind. In going through notes in Ruth's file box, I came across her notepad where she recorded some of the words expressed in the blessings given that night. Adam was first, and he made a request which was unusual. He asked, "Can I hold her?" He wanted to hold his sister while he received his blessing. I probably would have thought this request to border on the morbid prior to our experience, but there was nothing of that here. It was absolutely the right thing for the moment. It was inspired. Some of the other children followed suit as they received their blessings.

Each child received a blessing from their Heavenly Father according to their need and circumstance. Adam was blessed with comfort and peace, and that through this experience he would gain a deeper testimony of truths of the gospel. He was told to conduct his life so that he can have assurance to be with Zion eternally. Moriah was told, "…you are pure of heart, like your little sister." She was blessed to feel Zion near at various times in her life. Samuel asked "Can I go next? Is it okay?" Samuel was blessed to know in his heart that Heavenly Father has a special plan for Zion, a special mission, and she is happy to fulfill it. He was reminded that he too has a special mission. Samuel was blessed that there will be times when he will feel Zion is close, and he will feel her kiss on his cheek. Nyal was blessed to know that everything would be okay with Zion. He was blessed to feel Heavenly Father and His spirit close to him, and as he grows, he will have a special bond with his sister. He was told, "I bless you, to be able to feel your sister near, who is now beyond a thin veil, and to remember things about her that will help you in times of difficulty." We have no account of Jacob's blessing. It is possible that Jacob was so tired that he went to bed. Somewhere in our writings, I recall Adam took Jacob up to bed that night.

The holy feeling and reverence which we had felt since Zion had come home was accentuated on this occasion. It began to turn our great sorrow into peace and comfort as we felt God's love surround us in our home at this critical time.

It is significant to me that this evening was Halloween. Some might think it is a cruel joke for Zion to have passed away on such a date, but considering the historical origins, it really fits quite well. Halloween comes from the term "All Hallowed Eve." The actual holiday, All Hallows' Day, started the next day. Later this became All Saints Day, a Catholic holiday in which saints and dear family members who have passed away are remembered and honored. It celebrates all those who enter heaven. Celebrating the evening before a holiday, such as Christmas Eve and New Year's Eve, carried over to this eve as well. In some traditions it was also considered the end of fall (October 31) and the beginning of winter (November 1), a straddling of the line between "fall and winter, plenty and paucity, life and death."

So, the word 'Halloween' means hallowed evening or holy evening, even sacred evening. This evening certainly became that for us.

Ruth shares the following about each child saying their goodbyes to Zion:

They were each tender in their own ways. One son held her for so long, turning her over and rubbing her little body, almost as if trying to touch every bit of her and exercise her little features, stirring life back into her appendages. One sibling didn't want to hold her and was uncomfortable with her deceased condition, which was totally fine. Everyone had their own reactions and spent whatever time they wanted or needed. I wanted there to be no rush and for everyone to understand there was no right or wrong way to spend their last moments with their littlest sister. It was a very tender evening.

We had a family prayer together, and Grandma helped get the other younger children to bed, but Adam and Moriah stayed up a while longer. When Moriah finally retired to her room, she did not go to sleep. She wrote a long poignant letter to her little sister that truly encapsulates her thoughts and feelings. I include only a few excerpts here:

Dear Zion,

Thank you so much for coming into my life ... Even though I know that you, your spirit, is alive and happy and healthy and well, I still miss you ever so terribly. How can I ever express my feelings to you? All the love and gratitude and peace? But I know that you understand, and [I] realize fully that it is quite probable that you feel the same way.

Oh – my wonderful, dear, sweet sister! How I love you! ...I held you dear in my heart before you were born, and also in life and in death. I have held you in my arms, cuddled and loved, watched and touched, soothed and fed you, and more. Even when you died I held your small little form close. Dear Zion, I know that you must understand why I couldn't stay near your dear lifeless body too long after you had departed it. I couldn't bear to see the changes coming over it, and I need to remember the you that was full of your bright and sweet life.

Dear Zion, how happy I felt when our father told me in the blessing he gave me that I had a heart as pure as yours! I do know that I will see you again, my sweet sister, and I am so, so thankful to know that.

...Do you remember how I would cuddle you and croon to you and just love to be with you and hold you? I never, ever wanted to let you go, just keep you and love you to myself forever and ever. But I shared you, and I'm glad that I did, and now I have no regrets...

Zion, you remember how I'd come to you and talk to you while you were sleeping, just before I went upstairs to go to bed? And the promises I made you? ... I firmly believe that you too will help me and each and every member of our wonderful family because there is a great bond of love between us all. I feel sure that you want each and every one of us to have eternal life and joy. We all love you, Zion! We all love you so, so, so much!

155

Oh, sweet Zion ... your spirit still lives with our family, and no one is ever "truly dead" because we will all live again. Oh Zion, thank you eternally for your message to us all that you love us. It is an amazing miracle to us. Maybe every time a message of love is communicated or shared, it too is a miracle. My dearest sister, please guide and help our family and me, and comfort us and let us feel your presence whenever you can. We love you and miss you so much!

From your eternal sister, and with eternal, joyful, undying love that only I could give you. Oh Zion, I just can't possibly tell you in all eternity how much, how badly, how intensely I love you!

Moriah Manwaring[2]

As I now reread this, my heart is full. How can a father read such things from his daughter without being filled with emotion? She expresses herself so well, writing from the depths of her soul. How can anyone who reads her words not be touched? This is the pain and the joy of love.

I will never forget Adam as he took that iconic pose one last time with his sister. She lay on his lap, still, silent. He held her hands and looked at her and held her and loved her. Ruth wrote, "Once again, he opened his heart to her – looked past her stillness and loved her wholeheartedly without holding back." He stayed up late with her, taking all the time he wanted to say goodbye to his sweet little sister.

Finally, it was Ruth's turn to be alone with Zion. She wrote:

I'd hoped to hold her all night long. I undid her sleeper and rubbed Zion all over, rubbed her legs, her feet, her back, her arms, her hands. I uncovered her limbs one by one and rubbed

---

2. Moriah's footnote at the end of her letter: "I wrote this the night she died, October 31, 2006 and wrote past midnight into the next day (November 1, 2006)".

them. I just wanted to feel her, to love her, have her come back. I tried to memorize everything about her. Not wanting to let her go – wanting to rub the life back in. This was too soon.

We could not bear to have Zion picked up and taken away from our home. We decided we would take her to White Mortuary ourselves. I drove while Ruth held Zion in her arms. Ruth writes of the painful trek to the funeral home:

It was very late/early into the morning before I felt like I could even approach the subject of making the long drive to the mortuary. At some point, Paul called the mortician to inform him that our daughter had passed away. Because of her status and all the help and guidance we had been provided, all the needed preparations had been made. It was up to us to determine the particulars. I will never forget the kindness he proffered in telling us to take whatever time we needed and to let him know when we were ready, and he would meet us at the funeral home. "Anytime you are ready. Don't worry about the time or the hour." He was so kind and considerate.

I felt like I could never walk out our door. I didn't want to leave our home. I didn't want to take that final, inevitable step. The dreaded time had come, but for right now, she was still ours. She was still in her home and still bodily a part of our family. I didn't want to make it final. She was my tiny baby. She was our little miracle. She was the love that filled our home in her quiet way. She hardly made any sounds, she rarely had her eyes open, but her sweetness pervaded and filled our home to the brim. You could feel the love that exuded from her. She had filled our hearts and our arms. She was such a part of us.

But at some point, the inevitable reality was that I had to let go and escort her to her next stage. It was so heartbreaking.

I held her close and just kept smelling her tiny head and holding her little body and rubbing her hands and feet wanting so much for her to open her eyes and smile and cry and be normal and healthy and alive, but knowing that she was gone and her little journey was over and now we had to take care of what remained of her.

The drive to downtown Twin Falls passed too quickly. It was dark and lonely on our drive. The world was asleep, and so was she. I really didn't want to hand over my little girl to the mortician, but he was so gracious, kind, and patient. He talked kindly with us. He held her tenderly as I transferred her body to his arms. The finality almost killed me. I sobbed all the way home and felt like my heart would break as we drove back through the lonely, dark streets of our little town. I was angry that the world had not stopped just because her heart had. People were asleep snug in their beds and homes and in a few hours they would wake and go about their lives and no one would notice that a tiny life had been snuffed out and it wouldn't matter to anyone but me and my family. I couldn't help but feel a bit angry that we had just had our hearts broken and it would be business as usual for humanity and the rest of the world. Our little girl was gone. Her body would be prepared for interment and we would feel the loss, but the world marched on. On the one hand, I was glad for the routine that my children would step back into. They would get up and go to school if they chose. We would let them choose how to deal with their grief and luckily, they continued on brave and strong.

Oddly, it was comforting to know that my baby was just the other side of town. She wasn't really gone, just somewhere else for a short time.

And so, we returned home, empty-handed, and with aching hearts. It is hard to describe how our hearts hurt. It was a real, actual pain. Our feelings seemed to vacillate between heartache and comfort. There were constant reassurances because of our faith, but there was also the constant longing for our little girl and the tremendous heartache of our loss. I was amazed at how deep my feelings were, how intense my love for Zion was considering how short a time we had her with us. I have commented numerous times to others on this fact. And yet, it is a fact. I cannot imagine my grief being any greater had one of our other children passed away. I wrote the next day:

November 1, 2006

I cannot tell you how my heart aches and how I miss this little spirit already. Ruth's heart is nearly broken in two. It makes us cry every time we see something that reminds us of our little girl's presence in our home: the diapers by the couch where we changed her, her empty bassinet, her little clothes that were always too big for her anyway. When we got home from the funeral home, I went into the bedroom and saw the pillow still in the same position I had lifted her from earlier in the afternoon. It still had a crease in the pillow where I laid her.

Ruth describes in her own words what she was going through:

I cried myself to sleep that early morning and my mothers (mine and Paul's) got the kids off to school and took care of the house and meals and everything. I just remember the following weeks feeling like I had a giant hole in my chest. Like a cannonball had been shot through my trunk. There was a definite pain and hurt – almost tangible. I kept pressing my hand to my chest trying to push away the pain. I kept sighing, trying to get enough breath to fill the giant abyss that was my lung cavity. I felt limp and useless and empty and doleful. I had no appetite, no desire to move. No mental capacity to function as a mom, or wife, or person. I just grieved.

I am so grateful to my mothers who just stepped up and in and ran the household that I couldn't even find to care about. My heart just was aching. I wanted to love my children and to be there for them, but I just hurt inside. I wanted to help them as they dealt with their emotions and their grief. I like to think that we all grieved in a healthy manner, but I was surprised at how real the pain was. It was a long time before the hollow feeling in my chest left.

Of that next morning, I remember coming into the bedroom and finding Ruth sitting on the end of the bed, clutching her heart and rocking back and forth in tears. She looked at me and said, "My heart hurts! It feels like it has been broken, shattered, into a thousand pieces." And she just rocked back and forth and cried. I sat next to her and held her, and we cried together. How we missed our little girl!

Ruth had been nursing Zion and also pumping milk, so the family could alternately feed her. And here she was, her heart breaking because of the loss of Zion, her body ready to feed her baby, but no Zion to feed. Her own body was a constant reminder of her loss, of Zion's absence.

Somewhere Over the Rainbow
Sometime during the day, we received notice from Jessica Randall that the pictures from the family photo shoot had been made ready for us to see online. What she had done was both amazing and perfect. The pictures were beautiful, intimate, personal, and heartwarming. She had put them in a slideshow format with music. The song was a heartfelt rendition of *Somewhere Over of the Rainbow* performed by Israel Kamakawiwoʻole, known simply as Iz, a large

Hawaiian singer with his ukulele. The song, the lyrics, and the mood it created were perfect. Our emotions were already on the surface. The tears came as a flood again, welling up from the heartache of missing Zion, mixed with an intense gratitude that we had been blessed with her presence in our family.

That evening, I gathered the family and took them to my office to share with them the slide show of Zion and our family. We needed something right then to fill the void that had been created by Zion's departure. We gathered around the monitor, and I started the slideshow. It was a beautiful moment for our family. It brought back all the good and wonderful memories of when Zion was alive and with us and the happy days we had just experienced with her. We cried again as a family, all for the same reasons I had cried earlier in the day. Pain and gratitude. Those pictures are a priceless gift. You can hardly know how they have blessed our lives in the years since. They are a reminder and memory of our wonderful time with Zion. Thank you, Amy, for calling that morning. Thank you, Jessica, for the absolutely priceless gift of these pictures and memories. The sweet, moving song by Iz has become our Zion/family song. We love it. Every time we hear it, the memory of Zion and the evening we watched the slideshow comes flooding back. More specifically, whenever we hear it, we remember Zion and our hearts are filled with love. Somewhere over the rainbow, we know we will see Zion again.

I think of what we would have missed if she had been in the hospital the whole time and passed away there, instead of coming home with us. It is scary to realize we would have missed this profound, life-shaping experience. It has changed us eternally. I am so grateful that things did not go as I was determined they should go. The miracle God had in mind for us was and is much greater than the miracle I had desired. Oh, how we ought to trust Him.

You are probably tired of all the crying at this point, but maybe I am wrong. Maybe you have shed some tears too as you have been reading Zion's story. Tears are a way of cleansing the soul. We all need cathartic moments in our lives. It is crucial to our growth and development to feel things deeply, to be moved in ways that also move us in the right directions, to make appropriate commitments to change, to do better, to be true to what is right and good. It is often in our feelings and emotions that God can find us and speak to us. He can take these heartaches and turn them to joy, as I hope you will see as this story continues. In the Book of Revelation, we read: "And God shall wipe away all tears from their eyes; and there shall be no more death, neither sorrow, nor crying, neither shall there be any more pain: for the former things are passed away."[3]

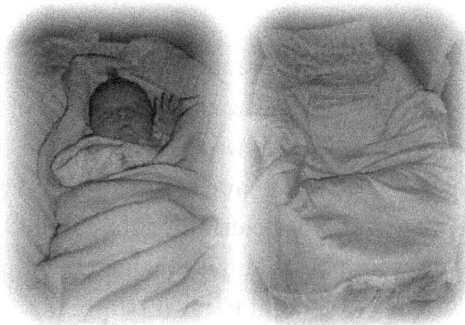

3. Revelation 21:4.

CHAPTER 11

Sunday Will Come

W e thought it would be a good idea to have the children write a message to Zion. We thought it might be helpful to them to express their feelings and thoughts about her. So, we had them sit down and write whatever they felt like writing. Those messages to Zion have become precious expressions that we will treasure.

We began to make funeral plans for Zion, and thought it would be best to have a funeral/memorial service that upcoming Friday evening and then take her to the family cemetery in Parker, Idaho, for interment on Saturday. Many helping hands and thoughtful hearts assisted with preparations. Ruth recalls:

I had two wonderful women from church who showed up after Zion's death and asked how they could help, and in their sincerity refused to be assured that we were all right. I remarked that the plants lining the house entry were a bit overgrown as I had not been able to trim them in the weeks prior to Zion's birth and I knew we would have a lot of visitors coming in and out through that entrance for the next while. They left and quietly and quickly trimmed out the dead foliage and cut back overgrowth without fanfare or thanks. It looked fresh and clean and welcoming. I can see God's love and guidance manifest through His children here on earth through little and big things. We were inundated with meals and flowers and cards. I really wished I had had an appetite to eat all the delicious foods that were delivered. Unfortunately, everything tasted like sawdust to me. I ate because I knew I needed to keep up my strength, that I needed to stay healthy, but I had no desire for food. Because of the circumstances so many things were well on their way to being done, but we needed to finalize and make determinations about the details. Halloween was on a Tuesday, which had morphed into a Wednesday, and we had her funeral service on a Friday.

We notified family again. We didn't expect them all to come for a third successive weekend to be with our family, but we knew they would want to know and come if they could. The funeral service was to be held in the same chapel where we had blessed Zion only a few days before.

It was a challenge to write an obituary. Ruth took on that important task. As Friday neared, there were a couple of things that needed to happen before the funeral service. Actually, we called it a memorial service, perhaps because funeral sounded too strong, too stark, too final a word for the brief life of a little girl.

Truly, it was not just a time to mourn Zion, but a time to remember her and share her life with others. We wanted to allow others to know her. So many people had not had anything more of a connection to her than to know she was born to us and lived a short life. Some had seen her in church when she was blessed. Close family and friends had held her. We wanted to do something special for those who would be at the service. I had begun putting together a

PowerPoint (an audio-visual) presentation on Thursday and spent most of the night and a good part of Friday working on it. I wanted it to be just right for the memorial service. It included Zion's story in brief, with pictures and text so everyone who attended could experience her life through our eyes, our thoughts, and our feelings.

Dressing Zion

We had been given a choice of either letting the staff at the funeral home dress Zion, or we could do it. This was a hard choice, but in the end, we decided this was a service we wanted to do for her. I have had the experience of helping dress others for funerals. I helped Ruth's father do this for his own father. There were a couple of other times when I had been asked to perform this service, but Ruth had not had this experience. I was concerned about her, but she showed a great strength in her resolve to try. Ruth recorded her thoughts about this occasion:

> *I had always heard that it was a sacred experience to dress the body of deceased family members, so I encouraged Moriah to come with Paul and me when we took Zion's dress to the mortuary. I did not have a sacred experience. It was very difficult for me to want to handle this shell that had once been my Zion girl and was not anymore. Death does have an effect on the mortal body – duh! – I know, but even the best cannot remove the change that is wrought on the body when the spirit leaves. Though her body will be preserved for many decades, it is still and lifeless and is only the shell that housed her great spirit. I don't know what to expect when I meet her in her resurrected and perfect body, but I will know her and I will love her when we meet at some future day.*

We brought with us the clothes she would be buried in – the same dress that she had worn only five days before. Her blessing dress would become her funeral dress as well. As Ruth expressed it: "Our sister-in-law Teriann did a beautiful job with her blessing/ burial dress. She told Paul it was a pleasure to make. "No big deal", she kept telling me. But she did say she felt the spirit so strong while she was sewing it. We knew what it would be for – we just didn't want it to be so close together."

The details of this experience are not necessary, but it is sufficient to say that it was a tearful experience. It was tender to the greatest degree. As Ruth said, "It was hard to see Zion again in this cold and lifeless state." The thing that always impresses itself upon my mind in the presence of death is that the body is now an empty shell without the spirit. The spirit of the individual is what gives the body life. It is best to focus on the fact that the spirit of Zion, or any loved one, still exists and is very much alive. This body is just a part of her, and yet a very important part. I was reminded that this was one of the significant purposes of her life and mission, namely, to obtain this body so one day she will be able to take it up again, incorruptible and perfect, in a glorious resurrection. Her mission in mortality was now complete, but her immortal life as a resurrected being is yet to be.

Everything was finally ready for the memorial service.

The Viewing – A Little Casket, Eternal Gifts
So many people came. Maybe we should not have been surprised, but we were grateful. For those who wanted to see Zion for the first time or for one last time, a room was provided at the church for a viewing. Many chose to stop in and to give our family their condolences. One of the things that I remember was Ruth comforting others as much as they were comforting her. Her thoughts: "We welcomed and received well wishes during her viewing. I was so overcome with gratitude for the many people who came to celebrate her life with us. That meant a lot to us. I dreaded her little life being forgotten or never remembered – thinking that she would not have mattered to anyone but us."

There were many family members who showed up despite another long drive. Neighbors and acquaintances came to show their support to our family. Some of our children's friends from school were brought by their parents.

As they entered the room, they received a hug from Ruth who stood near Zion's beautiful little casket. My father had let us know that he wanted to take care of the casket. Ruth observes, "We had been learning some things about infant burials. The standard casket looks like a sewing machine case. I was grateful to Paul's dad for offering to provide a more normal-looking casket for our baby girl."

He picked it out, and he paid for it. It was so thoughtful. It was also so fitting. It was a beautiful little white casket. Both beautiful and heartbreaking at the same time. But it was perfect for her. I had never seen a casket this size. It is not very often someone dies so young.

Once everyone had come through the line, the door was closed with only close family left in the room. Each of the children had been told they could give a final gift to Zion and put it in her casket before it was closed for its final time. What gifts did each leave in the casket? Moriah left a copy of the letter she wrote late into the night on the evening Zion passed away. Samuel had made a mold of his hand in class at school, and that is what he left as his personal gift for Zion. Nyal picked out a toy unicorn that had been given to us by the staff at the Ronald McDonald House. It had been donated by a King family from Ohio. Adam's gift was the pink blanket from Adria Sumsion, "because of the story..." He was referring to the dream Adria had shared with Ruth, and afterward, she gave Ruth the blanket with the statement, "Think Pink."

Ruth had embroidered a green apron over a period of many months, and she had spent many hours on it. This was the gift she wanted to give Zion. She wondered if it would be appropriate to include in the casket. My response to her was, "Green is the color that is symbolic of eternal life. I think it is more than appropriate." It was a message of hope and of faith. So, Zion was tucked in one last time by her mother with this beautiful handmade apron. Some final thoughts were offered by Bishop Clark, and a prayer was offered by my brother Steve Manwaring. Before the casket lid was closed, I gave Zion one last kiss on the forehead. That was my parting gift to her. There is something about the closing of the casket that seems so final. It is the last time you see the loved one in mortality. In fact, every event from here on seemed like another final step. The memorial service was the next one. We all filed behind and accompanied her little casket into the chapel for the service.

The Memorial Service
The chapel was filled. Ruth's observation: "I was shocked at the number of people who came to her funeral. She was an infant, barely over a week and a half old, and she completely filled our church with family and friends and on short notice." Our family sat on the front row. Ruth continues, "Jacob came and sat on my lap. I said, 'We have our whole family here.' I asked him, 'Do you think Zion is here?' Jacob: 'Yes.' He joked that Zion (Zion's spirit) was on the bench with us, that she took his place when he sat on my lap."

Bishop Todd Clark conducted the service. Pres. Allen was on the stand with his counselors. The service was simple in many respects. It began with singing an opening hymn: "Dearest Children, God is Near You." Many family members participated in the program. Our brothers (Dell Hanks and Richard Manwaring) offered opening and closing prayers. A musical number "Be Still, My Soul" was provided by my sister-in-law Paula as she accompanied (on the piano) our daughter Moriah who played the violin.

Normally, in a funeral service, someone gives a life sketch. But with such a short life, we determined that it would be best to present Zion's life through the PowerPoint presentation. That responsibility fell to me. As mentioned, I had been working on the presentation practically nonstop for the previous two days. Ruth recalls that I hardly slept. I wanted it to be a perfect representation of her life. She says this was my "gift of love to Zion" that night. It began with text narrating our story of finding out that Ruth was expecting and then finding out there would be complications with this birth. Music accompanied the text as each slide continued to tell the story in both word and images. Everyone in the congregation was able to relive our experience in the hospital and see the scenes we had seen as they were preserved in pictures. I also shared what each of the children had written to, or about, their sister.

Messages to Zion From Her Family

With each of the following messages, pictures of each family member holding Zion in the hospital were displayed.

Jacob (6 years old) wrote:

"Zion you are great, I love you. Zion, I hope you have a great time here. To Zion from Jacob."

Samuel (8 years old):

"Zion – You are the best, most lovable baby ever to be born, and we all love you. I remember whenever I held you I felt warm inside. I love you more than anyone I've ever met and will meet. I LOVE YOU! Samuel"

Nyal (11 years old):

"I love you and I always will. When I meet you in the spirit I will have open arms to you. Every time I was around you my heart melted with love for you. Love Nyal" [He wrote all around his note many times – "I love you."]

Adam (15 years old):

"Zion,

We will miss you, but I know we'll see you again. I wish I could see you now, though. We love you – and Mom probably misses you the most. Your name is so fitting because I will always Cherish Zion. You were the greatest blessing our family could have gotten. I love you.

Eternally loving you,
Adam (Your biggest bro)"

I only included in the slide presentation a couple of excerpts from the letter Moriah wrote the night Zion passed away (shared earlier, in the last chapter).

Moriah (14 years old):

"Dear Zion,

Thank you so much for coming into my life. In just eleven days you made a wonderful difference for me. I love you with all my heart, just as I did when you were alive. Even though I know that you, your spirit, is alive and happy and healthy and well, I still miss you ever so terribly. I do know that I will see you again, my sweet sister, and I am so thankful to know that."

"...Zion, you remember the promises I made you? ...I promised I would be the best person that I could be, that I would say "I love you" to my family and each member in it more, that I would not just try to be worthy to live with you and Heavenly Father again, but that I actually would do so, and that I would come to you. I was afraid to make a promise, fearing that I wouldn't be able to keep it, but I know that I'm

capable of doing all these things because that is what my Lord wants me to do and he will help me all through my life."

"We all love you Zion. ...I love you. Oh, how intensely I love you.

Your Eternal Sister, Moriah"

Ruth's and my messages were intended as expressions of our faith to those attending.

Paul's message:

"This has been an incredible journey. We would not trade our experience with Zion for anything in the world. We have been blessed more than we can express. Heavenly Father has been so gracious and kind. We will again hold her in our arms. This I know."

Ruth's message (which came from the obituary she wrote):

"We're grateful for the love and peace our littlest angel brought to our hearts and home in the short time she was with us. We are grateful for the many prayers and much support that have been offered in her and our behalf by dear friends and family. Those prayers allowed her to come home and enjoy being loved and surrounded by her family and friends until she slipped back into the arms of her Heavenly Father and others on the other side of the veil.

"She endured her challenges with patience and peace and left us with aching hearts and empty arms, yet she was allowed to leave us with a tangible message of love. We look forward with hope and faith in a resurrection, restoration, and future reunion knowing she is ours eternally. We will forever Cherish Zion."

We shared the story of Zion's hand cast, of the initial failed attempts, and we showed the picture of the final result. This was a part of our story no one was aware of until that moment. The presentation covered the entire span of her 11 days on earth. It was a touching remembrance for all of us. The children cried as they watched this review of her sweet life. The scripture from Job 1:21 was included in the slide presentation. It highlighted our deepest faith and belief: "…The Lord gave, and the Lord hath taken away; blessed be the name of the Lord."

Pres. Paul Morgan spoke next and provided us with a copy of his talk. I include only a few excerpts of it here, hoping that the words are useful to some who may read it, as it was for us on the occasion of our daughter's memorial service.

Brothers and Sisters and Friends, I express to you the gratitude of my heart for this treasured opportunity to speak a few words. We have come together in circumstances that are surrounded by the deepest of sorrows and the most glorious of Gospel doctrine and hope. And we do so because of the love we, as a community, have come to experience through the Manwaring family. And so, we wish in some way to share, or even lift, some of the burden of sorrow that they are experiencing.

…The greatest of sorrows brings forth the brightest hope. We recall the sweet words of Elder Joseph Wirthlin. The darkest and most terrible Friday this earth has ever experienced occurred when "the Savior of mankind was humiliated and bruised, abused and reviled." His crucifixion caused the earth to groan and tremble and be shaken to its very depths. And this great sorrow brought forth the brightest of all Sundays in His resurrection, portending the resurrection of us all; and in His atonement, bringing to each the potential of the gift of eternal life. And as Elder Wirthlin so eloquently declared,

"Each of us will have our own Fridays – those days when the universe itself seems shattered and the shards of our world lie littered about us in pieces. We all will experience those broken times when it seems we can never be put together again. We will all have our Fridays. But I testify to you in the name of the One who conquered death – Sunday will come. In the darkness of our sorrow, Sunday will come."[1]

The Sunday of this occasion is the sweet, sublime, inspiring, and uplifting doctrine of the exaltation of little children, who – having fulfilled the requirement of their eternal progression of receiving a physical body – transcend these mortal experiences and return directly to our Father in Heaven. As we observed this little baby, so frail and dependent, it is somewhat overwhelming to consider that she is now beyond us in knowledge, in eternal progress; she is now the example of that which we wish to attain, life with our Father in Heaven.

…Brother and Sister Manwaring, and each of your children, we rejoice with you in this great victory over death and sorrow. And we wish to bear with you the burden that is coincident. Your Friday has reminded us of our Sundays.

We arrive, with you, as we gain understanding of the wisdom of the Proverbs:

Trust in the LORD with all thine heart; and lean not unto thine own understanding. In all thy ways acknowledge him, and he shall direct thy paths.[2]

It was a wonderful talk, full of hope and wisdom and comfort. "Sunday will come." We are grateful for that teaching and fact. We believe it and rely on it.

I personally wanted this service to be a very positive experience

---

1. Joseph B. Wirthlin, "Sunday Will Come," *Ensign*, Nov. 2006.
2. Prov. 3:5-6.

for all and decided that another slide presentation was important to share. The slide presentation was listed on the program as "Zion at Home." This consisted of the pictures Jessica Randall took of us enjoying Zion at home, accompanied by music. These pictures became a centerpiece and a representation of the time that Zion spent with our family. These were scenes of life and joy. These are the images we wanted to leave with everyone. I believe every heart was touched, some powerfully.

It was a beautiful service, but not without many tears. As we relived Zion's life through these pictures, we were spectators with everyone else, and it brought back all the feelings of love and grief, of heartache and hope. Ruth remembers, "Sam sobbed so hard at the memorial service it twisted everyone's heartstrings. I finally had Jacob move off my lap and motioned for Sam to come over and take his place."

On the back of the printed program we included the following scripture:

"The Lord gave and the Lord hath taken away; blessed be the name of the Lord."[3]

And then the following statement:

The Manwaring Family wishes to extend the most heartfelt thanks to so many people. We cannot express how your prayers have sustained us. It has felt like Heavenly Father has reached down and embraced us with each prayer, gift, card, meal, or kind word you have offered. We are truly overwhelmed. Please accept our love and appreciation in return. Paul, Ruth, Adam, Moriah, Nyal, Samuel, Jacob & Zion.

Pennies from Heaven
"Find a penny, pick it up. All day long, you'll have good luck." This couplet has been around a long time. So has a song called "Pennies

---

3. Job 1:21.

from Heaven." Somehow these two concepts were put together and the result was, "When you find a penny, it means your loved one in heaven is thinking of you and is nearby." Ruth shares the following about this happy idea:

> *When we drove to the Kimberly Stake Center for Zion's funeral, I was surprised to see a penny lying in the parking lot, so I leaned over and picked it up. I think I noticed it because I walked around with a bent head those days. It kind of went with the hole in my chest feeling.*
>
> *Then as I walked into the foyer of the church there was more change lying on the floor which I picked up. That was very unusual, I had never noticed money laying around the church before. When we attended church the day after her burial, I found another penny in the parking lot.*
>
> *I was reminded of something my mom had always said about pennies from heaven, and I smiled to think that Zion was sending her mom a smile and a hug from heaven. She always seems to get us little messages that brighten our day in thinking that she is aware of us and wanting us to smile.*

Of course, we don't know absolutely that this is true, but it did become for us a means of sweet "communication" and remembrance from then on. Whenever we find a penny, not only do we think of Zion watching over us, but inversely, we think of her and remember her.

Ruth found a penny as we left the church at the end of the memorial service. It was in the foyer, just outside the chapel. Ruth taped it in the journal she had begun at the time that we returned from the hospital. This journal I call "Zion's Journal." Interspersed among its pages are pennies that have been taped, with little notes as to when and where they were found, and by whom they were found. Ruth shared with the family about her pennies from heaven. The kids were keen to spot pennies and to retrieve them and give them to their mother. This is something that has continued over the years.

Of course, at some point, there
were too many pennies to put in
a journal, so a jar or receptacle
became the depository for our
"Pennies from Heaven/Zion." We
have collected many hundreds of
precious pennies over the years.
It is amazing how many show

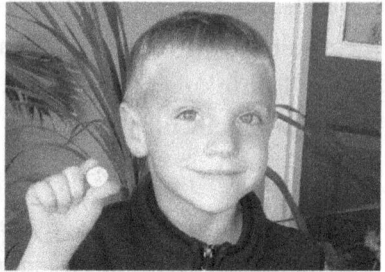

Jacob found a penny from heaven

up on special family occasions. Each one represents a moment of
fond memory, a reaching beyond the veil of death into heaven, and
from heaven back to us on earth. To quote Ruth, "The pennies from
heaven help as gentle reminders that always bring a smile ... an
encouraging lift/pat on the back/hug."

The next morning, November 4, 2006, we took another one of
those final steps. While Ruth and my mother got the kids ready, I went
to the funeral home to receive the casket for transportation to the
family cemetery three hours away. It was a solemn occasion to put
Zion's little casket in the back of the Suburban, the same vehicle she
came home in only a few days before. This would be her final journey
back home to that God who gave her life. Ruth also observed, "I do
remember thinking and remarking that this would be the only time
we would have our entire family together in the same vehicle. We had
purchased the Suburban recently, watching our boys grow bigger and
needing a vehicle that could fit all of us, including a new arrival. It was
comforting to know that we were all together at least once in this
world for a road trip, even if it was for a sad occasion."

CHAPTER 12

The Crown without the Conflict

Ruth grew up in a small farming community in eastern Idaho. Her parents and a few of her brothers still live and farm there. In Parker, Idaho, there is a cemetery where many of Ruth's relatives are buried. Early in our marriage, years before Zion's death, Ruth's brother, Doug, was appointed as the sextant of the cemetery for a term. He was in charge of interment and the selling of grave plots. When Ruth found out he had been given this assignment, she approached me and asked how I would feel if she bought a couple of funeral plots for us in the Parker Cemetery? That was a new thought for me. I had no plans to die anytime soon and thought that death was many years away for both of us. It seemed not only premature, but ... Parker, Idaho?

My people are mostly buried in Utah. I had often visited the grave sites of my ancestors there, and supposed it is where I would find a final resting spot, although I had not really pondered the thought. As I contemplated further this new option, I realized that it didn't really matter – so long as I was next to Ruth. I consented, and she made the purchase. I later found out she had purchased three burial plots. That seemed strange to me, and I had asked, "Why three?" She simply responded, "I don't know. It just seemed right, so I got three." At the time, I chalked it up to the fact that Ruth is a planner and likes to cover all contingencies, but in retrospect, it is obvious there was inspiration involved. Zion would be buried next to us in the Parker Cemetery – only she would precede us by many years. Even in her death and burial the little miracles continued to flow.

The graveside service was to be fairly simple. Ruth's brother, Doug, who was now a bishop in Parker, Idaho, was to conduct the service. Typically, a couple of people would say a few words to those who had gathered and then someone would dedicate the grave at the end of the brief graveside service. As we discussed who should do this, I thought perhaps one of our brothers could do the grave dedication, but Ruth said she would really like me to do it. In fact, she said, "*You* have to do it." I knew with those words that she was right. She drove much of the way to Parker while I worked on putting together a few thoughts about what I should say. In retrospect, I am so glad that Ruth insisted on me doing this last act of service for Zion. Once again, inspiration flowed, and it created a memory that continues to be significant for me. I wrote down the words of the dedicatory prayer so I could remember them.

When we arrived at the cemetery, the weather was cold, almost freezing. A frigid light drizzle persisted throughout the day. It was a stereotypical funeral/burial scene. Many family members were present. Bishop Clark and his wife had also come the distance to be there with us.

The pall bearers were Zion's brothers. Moriah brought the flowers. It was a heartrending, yet at the same time a heartwarming, sight to see them carry her casket from the vehicle to the gravesite and place it on the ground next to the open grave. Children carrying a child.

Ruth's brother gathered everyone around and welcomed them. Most of us stood under umbrellas, many with shoulders hunched together against the cold. My brother Jeff offered a prayer. Ruth's sister was asked to share her thoughts and reflections. She talked about Zion's short life and how much everyone had been touched by her. Bishop Clark also spoke briefly about the blessing of resurrection. After Ruth's brother, Doug, said some appropriate words, it was my turn to offer the dedicatory prayer and to dedicate the grave. Here are the words I spoke in prayer:

The Dedicatory Prayer

Heavenly Father,

We meet in thy presence and in the presence of thy holy angels and those interested ancestors who have gone before, including our littlest angel. We meet this day to dedicate this grave for our sweet baby Zion.

And so, Heavenly Father, by the power of the priesthood of Thy Son, even the Holy Melchizedek Priesthood that you have graciously given to us, I dedicate this grave that it may be the final resting place for Cherish Zion Manwaring. We are grateful to you Heavenly Father for sending her to us for this short time. She has changed our hearts and the lives of her siblings forever. Thank you.

I bless this casket that has so lovingly been provided by my parents, that it may house the contents therein, protected from the elements and corroding nature thereof. I bless Zion's little body that was created by a loving mother over many months of sacrifice and challenge – that it may be well preserved until the day of resurrection. I bless the dress that, sewn with threads of love and inspiration, clothes her body.

I bless the other contents, symbols of the love and devotion of Zion's family, especially the temple apron, lovingly sewn by her mother for a different occasion, but now a wonderful and appropriate symbol of the eternal life and exaltation that is

Cherishing Zion

promised to this special daughter of God. Her calling and election is sure.

I bless this grave, that it may be left undisturbed until the time of the morning of the first resurrection, Cherish Zion Manwaring's time for taking up again her little body, whole and complete, with a perfect heart and void of any other defects. A time when this cemetery, in this peaceful community will be a place of great activity and great glory, a time when the cemeteries and tombs and forgotten graves throughout the earth will yield up all their righteous dead at the day of our Savior's second coming.

I dedicate this grave and all its contents to come forth on the Morning of the First Resurrection, when you will be brought forth by the power of the Son over death and placed again in your mother's waiting arms. This will be a time of greater joy than any of us will have ever known. You will be like Him for you are pure even as He is pure. And now Cherish Zion, this completes your journey in mortality. Thank you for letting us provide the means and letting us accompany you. We love you.

Heavenly Father, I say and do these things in the blessed and holy name of our Savior, who makes all this possible, even Thy Son, Jesus Christ. Amen.

I had an unusual experience when I wrote out this dedicatory prayer. At one point, I could see clearly in my mind's eye this little cemetery on Resurrection morning. It would be full of light and joy beyond description, even as I stated in the prayer. I could imagine all the cemeteries throughout the world, and even the many millions of unmarked graves yielding up their righteous dead on that bright and beautiful day.

The contrast between that dreary November day in 2006 and what is yet to come will be amazing. It left me with a sure conviction

of what lies ahead. I know without any doubt that we will see Zion again, alive in the flesh. It is a reunion I look forward to with great anticipation. On that glorious day, everything will be made right. I give my own witness to the words of Joseph B. Wirthlin who said, "The Lord compensates the faithful for every loss. That which is taken away from those who love the Lord will be added unto them in His own way. While it may not come at the time we desire, the faithful will know that every tear today will eventually be returned a hundredfold with tears of rejoicing and gratitude."[1] I have even found that I do not have to wait until that day to shed many tears of gratitude.

As we left that scene to go to the church for a lunch that had been prepared for everyone who had traveled so far to be at the service, Ruth remembers the visual impact of seeing our daughter's casket for the last time, and the feeling that came with walking away from the gravesite:

"I think Paul and I were the last to leave the hillside as those in attendance went to the local church for a meal my sisters-in-law had provided. It wrenched my heart as I took one last look at her little white casket left on that lonely cold hillside outlined

1. Come What May and Love It, *Ensign Magazine*, Nov. 2008.

against a dark gray sky, awaiting her uncle and cousins to come and place her body in the cold earth and cover her with the dark soil. I don't think I will ever be able to erase that sight from my mind and I don't think I would want to. My heart was in my throat, and I was so grateful to know that my brother, Zion's uncle, and my nephews, her cousins, would take care of her little remains and her tiny casket. Whereas I left it there alone on a cemetery hill, they would lovingly watch over her tiny grave with love and respect, always a short distance away."

The Crown without the Conflict

My father came across the phrase "The Crown without the Conflict." The origin of this phrase has to do with the idea that a crown is given to the righteous who are allowed to sit down in the kingdom of God. In James 1:12 we read, "Blessed is the man that endureth temptation: for when he is tried, he shall receive the crown of life, which the Lord hath promised to them that love him." The crown is a symbol of righteousness and victory. We also read: "...and they shall come forth – yea, even the dead which died unto me, to receive a crown of righteousness, and to be clothed upon, even as I am, to be with me, that we may be one."[2]

2. Doctrine & Covenants 29:13.

For most of us, we have a lifetime to work through the challenges, the trials, the adversities, the temptations – the conflicts. We receive the crown only after overcoming much conflict. But Zion and the many little children who pass away early in their mortal journey receive this crown without having to endure the conflicts of life as we know them. As stated in scripture: "Little children are alive in Christ, even from the foundation of the world. ...all children are alike unto me; wherefore, I love little children with a perfect love and they are all alike and are partakers of salvation."[3] The words of another scripture confirm this promise: "...the infant perisheth not that dieth in his infancy."[4]

We have a firm conviction that Zion is okay, that she is well and happy with her Heavenly Father and with family members who have gone on before. When people ask us how many children we have, we say "Six." When they ask about each one, we respond on the status of each, but when we get to Zion, we explain that she has passed away. Then we will often say, "She is saving a place for us in line to get into heaven."

I came across a note from my father in which he recounted a conversation he had with my brother Jeff. My father concluded his note, stating simply, "Zion – she wears a crown without the conflict of mortal life." In all my father's communications, in his letters to us from this point forward, he placed a sticker of a golden crown.

---

3. Moroni 8:12, 17.
4. Mosiah 3:18.

CHAPTER 13

The Reality of Grief

We returned to our home in Twin Falls. There was a sense that something was missing. There was an emptiness and a void that was physically and emotionally felt. We were very grateful for the comfort we received from friends and from God, but even these did not completely fill the expanded space Zion had created in our hearts. We tried to resume a normal life, the life we had known prior to Zion, but it just was not the same. It was impossible to ignore the fact that a significant part of our lives was missing.

Our children continued with their daily chores and went back to school. We did not try to make any special accommodations for them at school. Their teachers were aware of our loss, and we trusted them to be sensitive to and aware of our children's needs in that setting. Ruth did what she could to attend to her daily routines; but my mother was there, and it allowed Ruth to spend time privately with her thoughts and her grief. We had been given brochures and booklets from hospice and family members with valuable information about how to deal with death and loss.[1]

We continued to have family prayer and read together in the scriptures every night. We knelt with our younger children for their personal prayers. Without fail, they expressed how much they missed their sister and how grateful they were that she had been allowed to come to our family. Our faith gave us great comfort and perspective to help us deal with our loss. However, it did not completely take away the need for grieving. In one of the brochures we received we read: "It is important to give yourself permission to grieve. Grieving the death of a baby may last far longer than you and others expect. ...Be patient with yourself, and do not expect too much too soon." One bit of counsel said it may be helpful to "create a baby book or a special box containing hospital records, certificates, sympathy cards, pictures, and blankets." Ruth spent some of her time doing exactly that. Ruth's grief was deep and left her little motivation to do the things that needed to be done in a household. It was with great effort that she was able to make any progress.

As for me, even though I saw myself as a person who was full of faith and knew without question that there were beautiful, timely, and tender mercies giving us assurances along the way, I was privately dealing with a loss I felt deeply, more deeply than my optimism allowed me to see at the time. I tried to present a face of faith and strength – which were honestly and truthfully there, but I concealed at least some of my secret hurt in an effort to be strong for others.

I always had an open-door policy at my workplace. A few years into my career, a wise superior gave me this advice: "Always leave your door open so others know you are available and approachable." But in the weeks following Zion's death, my door was often closed, the first time in the 16 years since receiving that counsel. I spent time privately doing my lesson preparations and other necessary

---

1. There is a variety of helpful literature covering a broad range of topics like: Helping grandparents deal with the loss of a grandchild, symptoms of grief, the impact of grief on marriage, surviving siblings, questions about religious faith, etc.

work. But everything I did was subjected to the constant memory of Zion. Whenever I could, I immersed myself in writing and creating an audio-visual presentation (PowerPoint), that expressed the things of my heart, the lessons I had learned, wanting to keep Zion near and my memories alive. There were times during this process when I would miss Zion so terribly that I gave vent to my tears, and I needed the privacy of a closed door.

At some point, someone said something that caused me to realize that those who were closest to me, those who knew my normal daily patterns from before and then after Zion's life, were concerned about me. Ruth said of me that I was "unfocused." My Area Director mentioned his concern for me and referred to an observation my secretary shared with him. The process of grief was something I, too, needed to go through. We can have peace and comfort because of our faith in God and, yet at the same time, miss – deeply miss – the presence of a loved one.

In trying to be strong for my family, I believe I did much good for them, but my one regret is that I wish I had been more attentive to Ruth. I assumed she was at about the same point I was in terms of the balance between comfort and grief. Perhaps I was blinded by my own needs. Only recently, as I have reviewed her personal writings, have I discovered elements of her private grieving I was not aware of at the time.

A Mother's Grief

Just as the experience of giving birth to a child is unique to a woman, so is the death of her child. There are things a man just does not experience in the same way. His experience does not and cannot cross into her realm. He lacks the physical, mental and emotional constitution, and the exclusive experience of motherhood to fully comprehend her distinctive form of grief.

Ruth experienced tremendous pain and inner turmoil immediately after and in the weeks following Zion's death. These are some of her thoughts and feelings of the grief she endured after Zion died:

> *I want to say this as strongly as I can. Grief is real, and it needs to be gone through. There are no right ways or wrong way to grieve. It would be tragic to try and ignore grief. Grief is as real an emotion as love and anger, peace, hate, joy, sorrow, pain, etc.*
>
> *My crying was unusual. It was guttural, almost animal like. A primal groan to match the heartache. The ache makes its hurt vocal ... as a sigh ... during sobbing. There is a physical pain/ache – it literally feels like the heart is broken in pieces. I kept pressing my hand to my chest trying to push away the pain. I kept sighing to get enough breath ... I had no appetite, no desire to move. I just grieved ... I was surprised at how real the pain was.*

Ruth was experiencing that which is described in one of the publications given to us: "Reality comes and sits on your chest. You will never see this person again. The pain hits and you can't breathe. You can't go around the pain or the grief – you must go through it."[2] Ruth's words about the role of grief in healing are also confirmed by others. "Grief is necessary – in fact it is critical. Without grief, healing cannot take place. Simply stated, grief is your method of sorting out your emotions about your loss; it is your way of gathering yourself up and eventually moving on."[3]

Ruth's mother left soon after Zion's passing. She didn't feel like she could offer much help in the present situation as she was recovering from a broken ankle and had such limited mobility. The death of our little girl was also heartbreaking for her. We witnessed that grandparents are not immune to grief from the death of a grandchild. They hurt on multiple levels. They hurt for their own loss of a grandchild, but also for the pain and grief of their child who is in pain.

2. Doug Manning, *Understanding Grief* (Special Care Series) (In-Sight Books, 1993).
3. Brent Q. Hafen and Kathryn J. Frandsen, *Faces of Death* (Morton Publishing Co., 1983), p. 12.

On November 2, Ruth wrote: "Mom called after she left and said she'd had a dream. She had seen her mom, Grandma Quayle. Grandma looked great—wavy black hair, dress, and holding a blonde baby girl, 1 ½–2 years old, happy and smiling. Mom said she started to run to her mother and then she was gone. 'I have never dreamed of her since she died,' Mom said between sobs."

As I ponder this dream, its symbolism enlightens and comforts me. Ruth's grandmother had lost a child, and so had Ruth's mother. In the dream, Zion is alive and well in the loving arms of Grandma Quayle. This presents a wonderful scene of comfort, understanding, and healing for multiple generations. Zion is in the devoted care of loved ones on the other side of the veil. Perhaps Zion's life and death were already having a healing effect on others.

Each day was filled with all kinds of thoughts of Zion. She was a part of our beings, our souls. She was in our thoughts and in our dreams. The following from Ruth's journal is representative of this period:

November 9th - Thursday night. Paul kind of woke me up and in that neverland between waking and sleep, I had such a brief glimpse – a flash, but I felt it was Zion – I wanted to have a clearer image, to focus, to see, but it was gone. I forgot until lying down again tonight. I wanted more.

I have her beanie, blanket & last sleeper worn by my bed and I love to press my nose in and smell her every night, and every morning and sometimes in between. It is a mixture of sour milk and lotion and it just smells like Zion. The smells of the hand antiseptic remind me of her.

In "Zion's Journal," Ruth explains:

I was given a journal that became my way of recording my journeys to Zion. It is my way of remembering and expressing my emotions and thoughts and remembering the details and the impressions and experiences. But some things are so indelibly imprinted on our hearts that I will never forget certain moments and feelings and experiences.

Some entries she writes directly to Zion; others are more general expressions about what she is feeling or experiencing at the time. Ruth continues to record her thoughts and feelings, even to the present day. The healing process takes time. It is counted in days, weeks, months, and years. There is a gradual lessening of grief and a growth of gratitude. Only a couple of weeks after Zion was gone, she wrote the following:

November 16 - One of the big [initial] moments of healing for me came in the parking lot of the Twin Falls public library. I had dropped off the "Strings Alive" crowd, returned library books, and looked over at White Mortuary. I had my yellow pad of paper I had been writing in, and I turned over the backside of a paper and started writing down snippets to help me remember all the things I wanted to remember and record. I just sobbed and sobbed. But I was able to relax and know I wouldn't forget all these moments and experiences. Now I need to just record all these vignettes. They may not flow, but they will be written.

My mother stayed for more than a month and a half after Zion died. She was such a blessing to our family. Sometimes kids need a grandma, and sometimes grown adults need their moms. Ruth took time for herself during those weeks to process everything; she was fairly private most of the time my mother was there. When my mother's bags were in the car and she was about to leave, she and Ruth began to say their goodbyes. It was at this time that Ruth opened up to her like she had not done in the previous weeks. For two hours, nonstop, Ruth shared her feelings. My mother delayed her departure for as long as Ruth wanted to talk, and she just listened as Ruth poured out her heart. It was cathartic, an unburdening of the soul, something very needful in her healing process. Ruth personally discovered a truth shared in one of the pamphlets she had received: "We work through our grief by talking it to death."[4]

My mother made an observation to me regarding postpartum blues that is worth mentioning. Postpartum means "after the parting." This is a type of depression many women experience after the birth of a child, the separation of the baby from the mother's womb. It can be very confusing because this should be a time of joy and gladness, so to feel unexplained sadness and melancholy is not congruent with what one "should be feeling." It can range from being mild (blues) to severe or very severe (clinical depression). For postpartum blues, there are many symptoms, including mood swings, crying, sadness, insomnia, and irritability. Postpartum depression symptoms are more severe and are longer lasting. They can include an inability to care for one's newborn and, at the extreme, even thoughts of suicide.

My mother had been present for the births of two of our children and stayed at our home for a period afterwards. She had observed that postpartum blues was something Ruth had dealt with in the past. I remember Ruth saying something after our son Samuel was born that gave me a special insight into what she might be experiencing: "I miss feeling life inside of me." I have never forgotten what she said. This is something I can only try to imagine. It is a phenomenon a man cannot fully comprehend. Once again, he does not have the biological capacity to understand something so unique to women who carry a life within them for months.

If one can imagine having postpartum depression compounded by the loss of a child, then one may begin to grasp the depth of grief and the difficulty of the challenge. For some women and their families, it can be catastrophic. I am aware that some never fully overcome the trauma. It can be recognized and dealt with, often with

4. Doug Manning, *Understanding Grief* (Special Care Series) (In-Sight Books, 1993).

professional assistance. Ruth feels she was spared the most extreme after-effects of postpartum depression because of all the preparation and the many tender mercies we had experienced. However, it still had its repercussions.

"My Best Christmas Present Ever"
That first Christmas was rough, but it was also beautiful. There was so much to be grateful for. Many of the gifts centered around Zion and came from the heart. For example, we found a *Willow Tree* sculpture of a male figure with a baby on his lap in the same pose that Adam had always cradled Zion. We knew this needed to be one of his gifts, and there was no need to explain why it was chosen. When Adam saw it, he just sat there and cried.

Ruth and I received a very simple gift from Samuel: Johnson's Baby Lotion. As we held it to our noses and breathed in its fragrance, it was the scent of Zion. The smell of this baby lotion will always be associated with Zion. What a powerful and overwhelming reminder smell can be, and how strongly it can attach itself to our emotions. This gift brought more tears, especially from me. We cried and then laughed at how we cried about such simple gifts. It was both a grief-filled and a gratitude-filled Christmas.

But flowing beneath all of this was a difficult countercurrent. In the weeks since Zion's death and leading up to Christmas, Ruth had been struggling and often had a hard time being around family. This was stressful to her, especially when the kids got out of school for Christmas break and were at home all day long. She found herself easily annoyed and angered by little things the children were doing, which made her feel even worse. To keep this from happening, there were times when she simply avoided us. She expressed it as follows:

My heart feels physically broken again. I cried more in the last two days than the last month. I have struggled for a long time with feeling happy. I have blamed it on my family – my kids – my husband. I have been so impatient, so demanding, so frustrated, so angry. Zion brought me the message of love, hope, patience (wait and watch), peace, inspiration, promptings, etc. I knew God was aware of me and my fears, my selfishness, my anger, and He sent His Comforter, His Spirit to guide and prepare me/us. I knew He knew – I had to trust Him – even though I didn't want to. Zion also showed me how wonderful, good, and kind my family was. To see Adam so tender with Zion, so involved and caring – so non-judgmental; Moriah, so doting, careful, constant, giving; Nyal surprised me with his detachment – his seeming to want to hold back. He is my cuddly bear. So intelligent. Sam just sobbed it seemed every time he held his little sister. He sobbed so hard at the memorial service it twisted everyone's heartstrings. Jacob just flitted – bouncing here and there, in and out – everywhere and nowhere.

But now, my kids are driving me nuts and I have been so nasty. I was back where I had started from. I don't know what I need. I treat them badly, yet I long not to. As determined as I am to not lose it – I always do. Get the kids off to school, calm down during the day – then lose it when they come home. I am fine at home – determined to act right, until they come home and barge through the door. The disarray will commence – bickering, teasing, yelling again. Asked to "pick up," ignored; asked to "stop teasing or torturing for pleasure," ignored; asked to help, ignored. I try to keep my tongue civil – but I can't. I try to give clues about what kids should do – disobedience. It's as if whatever mom asks is just the opposite of what is done. Paul tries to give a hug – so not wanted. I've so forgotten anything Zion gave me.

It seemed to Ruth that her senses were in hyper-mode, especially her hearing. Everything was so loud and amplified. Our kids could never be accused of being quiet, and certainly they could be unruly and disobedient at times. But for Ruth, it had become a constant and more than she could bear. She felt like she had lost control of her children and of her own emotions. It was overwhelming. It was a silent suffering I was unaware of.

We had planned to take the family to St. George, Utah, stay at Ruth's parents' condo, and spend time with my brothers and their families, to give the children some cousin-time. It was something we all looked forward to. The plan was to leave the latter part of Christmas day, after presents were opened and things had settled down. But then Ruth dropped a bombshell. She told us she did not plan to go with us, and she just needed some time alone. Initially, I was very worried and concerned that she did not want to join the family on this trip. This was out of character for her. We were to be gone for a week. I was worried about her, leaving her alone. I was also hurt. I felt personally rejected, like I was being abandoned. I took some time alone to think, ponder, and pray about what she had said, and to understand what she needed. I truly struggled to set aside my own needs and hurt. In the end, I was finally able to come to a feeling of relative peace about what Ruth needed. I wrote her a short letter before we left. Here is a part of what I said:

I don't know how much personal space you need – but you have it. I would love to talk with you every day, but I will be content with whatever you need. I know I will miss you, but I also know that this is the right thing for you and for our family.

Ruth had not shared with us all her struggles and feelings, but she knew she needed a break. She needed peace and quiet time for introspection. I wish I had better understood how much of it was associated with the grief and loss she was still experiencing. She wrote the following about our departure:

I can't believe Paul supported me. What am I supposed to do? I can't believe they're going without me. I want to go. I want to go to the temple, shopping, visit. I want to be with my family – but I'll criticize, nag, belittle. They don't need me to be critical. They don't need to be criticized.

Ruth stayed behind, alone at home, in Twin Falls. She spent time doing the chores that needed to be done, but at her own pace and schedule. She relaxed and began to "breathe" again. She ate, or didn't, according to when she felt hungry. She took the dog for long walks. She shoveled a neighbor's driveway. She played in the snow and made a snow family. She cleaned and organized, and as she put it:

I enjoyed wandering around creating order; it dulls, it doesn't require thought, just movement/action. Establishing order allowed me to relax. The quiet soothes my soul. I loved the stillness. Everything was so quiet. I am surprised by the peace that envelops me when everyone is gone. Like I told the kids, maybe my ears are too good, my eyes all-seeing, my brain too active, because I sense and feel so much it overwhelms me – overstimulates me. I didn't think I would do so well so quickly, as brokenhearted as I felt for the past two days.

As the week progressed, she continued to do productive things. She also dealt with her grief and inner turmoil:

I know I am blessed. I love my home, my family. I write as if they are horrible – but they are not. They're incredible ... they just drive me insane.

...Yearning to hold my dear baby again, to feel her small, soft head, to feed her and watch her grow and be healthy. Yearning to feel her inside me again, to provide nourishment for one so helpless ...Yet the time was so short and sweet. Infant stages always are. They grow so quickly. I'm grateful to be able to have control of my life. I can sleep, eat, go, come whenever I want. Freedom again – but I want to hold my baby. Where's my baby? How can I learn to treat my other angel children better? They need care and nourishment also. Aching arms – definitely. I'm tempted to go buy a baby doll. I like to smell Zion's sleeper, blanket, and beanie every day when I make my bed and when I climb into bed. A broken heart – definitely! A physical ache as if my heart was broken in pieces. A feeling of heaviness, pressure. The Quigleys asked if I had heartburn because I kept pushing my chest – but it helped alleviate the pain and hurt. I felt like someone hit me in the stomach when I received a baby shower invitation the week after we buried Zion – that hurt. I have had that baby gift sitting around for 2 months now and can't seem to get it to that person. I know it's not their fault and they need the baby gifts – but I just don't do it – I do just want to be left alone.

Ruth's journals from that week contain quotes from things she read that impressed her, for example: "Grief is like peeling an onion – it comes off one layer at a time ... and you cry a lot."[5] She shared random thoughts as they came to her. I am very grateful she wrote so much. It has been a blessing to read them and to share some of

5. Doug Manning, *Understanding Grief* (Special Care Series) (In-Sight Books, 1993).

the things that impressed her most.

In an earlier chapter (when I wrote about losing my fingers), I talked about the stages one goes through with loss. It may sound like everyone goes through these stages in a step order process, but this is not necessarily so. Grief is very individual. Doug Manning wrote some great advice in a booklet, *Reconstructing Our Lives*. Ruth copied and kept some of his insights:

> *Grief is not an orderly process. We do not walk through grief in a straight line. The problem I have had with describing grief in stages is that the explanation suggests clear cut lines of demarcation with orderly progress being made. We flip-flop through grief. We can be well advanced one day and retreat all the way back to ground zero the next. We can be in two stages at the same time. There is no step-by-step orderly progress. Gradually, we do not retreat quite so often and not quite as far back. But there may be times when we will think we have not made any progress at all. The first anniversary is one of those times. Preparing for the day can stir up all the feelings once again and drive us back to the first layer of the onion. We will not stay there as long nor hurt as deeply as we did back when the death first happened, but we will certainly hurt and wonder how long this surge of pain will last.*
>
> *This is a time when some people begin to have some questions about their progress. They begin to ask such questions as: Should I be further along than I am? For some reason, we have decided that grief should not last very long. A man-on-the-street survey revealed that people thought grief should last from forty-eight hours to six months. From my experience, I think people will allow three months and then begin to think the person is not trying to get over their pain. Since you are living in the pain, you know the fallacy of getting over it in three months. But it is easy to decide that after a*

whole year you should have made more progress than you did.

...You have a broken heart. It will never completely heal, but you will learn to live again. It is not well yet because it takes longer than a year to heal. That does not mean you are weak or slow, nor lacking in will power or in faith. Grief seems to grip us very tightly and then relax its grip for a time. About the time we think we are past a lot of the pain, it will hit again with a vengeance.

...One of the keys to grieving properly is to give yourself permission to grieve. Remember that there is no schedule for grief. Everyone goes through it at their own pace.

...Grief is as unique as a fingerprint. No two people grieve alike. No two grieving experiences (even in the same person) are alike. We grieve each loss in a manner unique to that loss. [6]

There is great wisdom and experience in these statements. I find truth in them from our own experience. I also feel to temper the comments above with this thought: Although each person's grieving is indeed very different, it is always made easier when God is invited to be part of the process. I know that if we reach out to God and accept His loving help in those unexpected times when grief revisits us, when it descends upon us and takes us in its grip, we will find the challenge more manageable and the path smoother than if we attempt to handle it on our own. I cite the account and experience of one man whose nine-year-old son passed away:

"The pain I felt was a combination of everything, and it had gotten to a point, where I could not take it anymore. ...It felt like I was going to burst inside, or I was going to be crushed. I could not bear any more of that pain, and I dropped to my knees and I prayed to our Heavenly Father. I said, 'Would you

6. Doug Manning, *Reconstructing Our Lives* (Special Care Series) (In-Sight Books, 1993), pp. 12-15.

please take this pain from me, I can't take it anymore.' And at that moment, I felt Him speak to me, not to my ears, but like He spoke to my spirit, and He said, 'I can take away the pain, but I'd have to take away the nine years you had with your son. Or you can keep the nine years you had with your son and endure the pain that comes with losing him.' And at that moment, it completely changed my perspective, because I would not give up anything for those nine years I had with my son. I knew that the road ahead was going to be long and hard, but I knew that it was going to be okay."[7]

Grief is a time to find God. As He gives us comfort and peace, and as we feel His love for us, our hearts are knitted to His. I can even see God's wisdom in not giving us immediate and lasting relief at times, because in doing so, He is shaping us and molding us into the kind of person that is more useful to others and to ourselves.

As Ruth's writings continued during that week, she often referred to a small book we had received, *Gone Too Soon,* and wrote down quite a few quotes from it that were helpful to her.

I used to find myself consumed with grief ... Before I knew it, hours turned into days, and I knew I was learning to deal with my loss. Now I can concentrate on the simple beauty of [her] life and the good that has come out of the experience.[8]

The evidence of her processing is in the notes she kept, the scores of scriptures and articles she read, referenced, or quoted. Other quotes that were helpful to Ruth included the following:

It's OK to never 'get over it.' You certainly never can or want to be 'over' your child's life and death. Get on with your life.

7. Transcript from video, available at: https://www.facebook.com/lds.jeffrey.r.holland/videos/324519501747213/.
8. Sherri Devashrayee Wittwer, *Gone Too Soon: The Life and Loss of Infants and Unborn Children* (American Fork Utah: Covenant Communications Inc., 1994), p. 10.

Grief is a part of a parent's life. The parent is experiencing some of the most poignant and significant emotions in the human experience. These emotions are an essential and normal part of life and parents need to experience the full spectrum of emotions involved with grief until they can enjoy happier times.[9]

To survive and emerge even stronger from the tender loss of a baby, we must believe in the goodness of God, believe in his love, justice, mercy, and wisdom and trust that all things will be resolved in a manner pleasing to Him, as well as to ourselves.[10]

The Lord takes many away, even in infancy, that they may escape the envy of man and the sorrows and evils of this present world; they were too pure, too lovely, to live on earth; therefore, if rightly considered, instead of mourning we have reason to rejoice as they are delivered from evil, and we shall soon have them again.[11]

Another thing Ruth read that was helpful for her was from the booklet, *Gift of Understanding*:

Grief overloads every part of our lives. You can expect a loss of memory as your mind seeks to protect itself from the stress. Your mind will occasionally stop working properly. 'Brown outs.' Don't panic, your mind will return.[12]

At one point, Ruth began to question herself as she sorted things out in her mind. She wondered if she had been more willing to have a baby a few years earlier, would Zion have been able to be born in a healthy body, and would she have been with us still? This was a guessing game that could not have any clear answers. It is also typical

---

9. Source unknown.
10. *Gone Too Soon*, p. 89.
11. Joseph Smith, *History of the Church* (Salt Lake City Utah: Deseret News, 1908), p. 4:553.
12. Doug Manning, *Gift of Understanding* (Special Care Series) (In-Sight Books, 1993), p. 22.

for people to blame themselves, to second guess their choices. The advice of Dr. Rettmier to me the night I lost my fingers is so applicable here. "Don't worry about the would've, could've, or should've(s)." With hindsight, all of us would make different decisions than we do. The value and lesson here, however, is for the future – to take from our experience and employ those insights in future decisions. Nothing can be done to change the past. There is no need to torture ourselves with the past. Nothing good comes from it. It is my conviction that our experience with Zion has happened according to a higher divine plan. God works with our weaknesses, shortcomings, and choices in the best possible way. If our shortcomings or weaknesses contribute to the course of events, I believe God incorporates them into his design. He is both all-loving and all-knowing. For God, there are no surprises. Everything we experience gives us opportunities to learn, to grow, and to become more like Him.

As you can see, Ruth really needed this time to be alone. She needed time to grieve and to process everything in her own way. During the week she was alone, she began to write in Zion's Journal about her memories of the past year. She sought insight and perspective. She took time to organize things and carefully store some of the physical reminders she wanted to keep from Zion's life. She wrote, "Doing something good is never a waste of time. This has been the best Christmas present ever. I can process. I can shop, do errands. Progress. This is all great – I know my family is happy and I'm happy – I'm vacationing at my own home. If I get Zion's piles organized, will it mean closure? I don't want closure … but how do I have a change of heart?"

In the hymn *I Know That My Redeemer Lives*, there is a stanza that deeply touched Ruth. She wrote, "I was comforted by the words, 'He lives to hear my soul's complaint.' I had never thought anyone would live to hear another's complaint."

Ruth's journals contain other quotes and scriptural references meaningful enough for her to record them. All are evidence of the intense studying and pondering she did during that week she had to herself. As she found answers, insights, and further healing for her own soul, she began to better understand that she wasn't the only one whose life was disrupted by this loss. She was impressed by the following quote which she recorded (source unknown): "Death intrudes on a child's typically quiet and peaceful life – taking away innocence." And then these:

> *Count your blessings, at least you have other children. People who grieve are grateful for what they have. But nothing, including other children, can make the pain go away. Support and love can be a positive factor at a time when everything seems hopeless.*[13]
>
> *There is no way you can go through the loss of a baby without coming out of that loss a better person. You become more loving, caring, compassionate, and generally kinder because you have learned the hard way what a miracle life is.*[14]

Along these lines, there was also another quote that seemed to offer instruction and encouragement in dealing with difficult and energetic children:

> *Nothing is so much calculated to lead people to forsake sin as to take them by the hand and watch over them with tenderness. When persons manifest the least kindness and love to me, O what power it has over my mind, while the opposite course has a tendency to harrow up all the harsh feelings and depress the human mind.*[15]

Ruth resolved,

> *I've loved this vacation/me-time in my own home by myself. How can I keep this peace, when insanity walks back in the*

13. *Gone Too Soon*, p. 76.
14. *Gone Too Soon*, p. 35.
15. Joseph Smith, *History of the Church*, (Deseret Book Co., 1991), 5:23–24.

door? Gratitude! Be thankful I have a healthy, noisy family. Maybe this solitude would get old – but I'm enjoying it now. Reorganization – stepping back into life.

...I should see each of my children as a miracle and love them all the more. Spend time each day with the children. Reassure of your love. They may need more touching/holding than usual.

And finally – "Thanks, gang, for the breather."

Ruth's entry in Zion's Journal from the New Year's Eve at the end of that week was addressed specifically to Zion:

Dec. 31st - 11:30 PM - "Happy New Year, Baby Girl. Everything is packed away or tucked in an organizer. All the 'thank yous' have been handed out. The photos [of you] that the kids picked out have been framed and hung ... I love you. Please help me love your family better. They're angels, too."

On the envelope of the letter I wrote to Ruth before the children and I left Twin Falls, she wrote: "The best Christmas present ever." I understand now. I can see this was a critical step in her healing process.

As the year progressed, Ruth's journal entries continued as she periodically recorded some of the things that touched her or the struggles she had. She records finding her pennies from heaven at random times, many of them when she needed a boost. She was asked to speak to the women of our congregation at the end of February 2007 about her experiences with Zion and what she had learned. She was grateful for the opportunity, but the preparation was an emotional challenge. She entitled the talk "Small and Simple Things." The day she gave her presentation, she recalls, "I sobbed in the shower and cried on my walk, but somehow was able to present to the sisters the things they and you [Zion] did for us. Thanks."

Ruth received many expressions of gratitude for her sharing

these things of her heart. One woman said she was finally able to gain some insights about her own loss of a baby. One written compliment included the hope that giving her "Small and Simple Things" presentation provided closure for Ruth. Of this, Ruth says, "I don't ever want closure. I don't ever want to forget. I love my little angel." There is a balance that can gradually be achieved between not forgetting and replacing the pain with gratitude.

I could not help but think of the lessons I had learned from the loss of my fingers a year before which were appropriate at this point. The lessons from my accident and subsequent healing are so applicable to what Ruth and the rest of us go through with any significant loss:

- There is real pain and discomfort associated with loss, but that pain lessens with time and experience.

- Seeing my hand for the first time after the surgery and facing what was there (not there) was reality. When we lose someone, it is the same. They are not there anymore for us to see, to touch, and to talk to.

- Like the seeping, stitched-up wounds that looked like they would never heal, we too wonder if this heartache will ever go away, if we will ever be able to function fully again. In time, the wounds begin to heal, the pain subsides, and the stitches come out, having served their purpose.

- There is a new stage of healing. The old dead skin sloughs away and there is new skin, and the hand of our life begins to look and feel more normal, though very different.

- Adjustments must be made because with this loss, some things can't be done the way they used to be done. You adjust, and it works. You learn new skills, new ways of doing things. You find you even need help from others on occasion. It's okay. It gives others an opportunity to serve.

- There is nothing you can do about the fact that the member, the loved one is gone. As the doctor said, "Just move forward and realize that everything will be all right. Those who do well are the ones who accept their circumstances and face them head on with a determination to be happy and enjoy life."

The year 2007 became a year of remembering and reliving the previous year. Some of the phrases that were often repeated were "Last year at this time…" or "A year ago we were…."

The grieving and healing process has distinctive mile markers. Anniversaries are a very real thing. Anyone who has lost a loved one knows that holidays and birthdays and the annual anniversaries of death are tender times. Those who understood this were cognizant of our situation, and it was amazing to us how many people sent cards or a thoughtful note on such dates.

In Zion's Journal, Ruth wrote about how other people continued to remember Zion long after she left us, and the effect it had upon her:

Amazingly, at the time I think everyone's forgotten or gone on with life, more cards show up, a letter is given, etc. It is just right. It is appreciated. It heals. It is so gradual, I don't realize when the peace replaces the pain. The heartache is bearable, then patched. The trouble now is to remember. To not let her life/example/love be in vain.

Ruth wrote in July,

Very emotional – mental, to be going through the "last year at this time, I was…"

Last 4th of July we were in St. George for a family reunion. That was our first announcement to the family about our pregnancy. Last year people were starting to get suspicious or openly asking, and the ensuing "congratulations" followed. It was so hard. I wish I knew then what I know now – I would have cherished every moment – but I fought the good news instead. How I miss my littlest angel. I miss feeling life inside. I am so grateful for the peace I feel. I shared my testimony with others last month (June) about how I was sitting, looking at our blooming peace lily [we received at Zion's funeral], and recognizing I did feel peace. It slowly filled my aching heart. I didn't think my broken heart would ever mend … but the pain is gone. I have joyous memories. I am so grateful.

With Ruth, the gratitude did not stop with the reception of such notes and remembrances. I have watched how she has become very sensitive to others on their own anniversaries. Just recently a friend of ours who lost her husband a few years ago called to thank Ruth for sending a birthday card (again) for her husband who had passed away! She said, "Ruth, thank you for remembering Bob's birthday. I can't tell you how much that means to me." And I ask, "Who sends such cards anyway?" The answer, "...Someone who understands and knows these are tender times and cares enough to reach out and let a friend know that her feelings and his life matters."

Looking back on these months (and years), Ruth recently reflected: "I am so grateful and was so blessed to go through that time of pain and grief. I think allowing myself time to grieve helped me heal and process the loss of our baby girl. I don't think I could have healed without going through the grieving process."

CHAPTER 14

Lessons from Zion

Zion's presence in our lives had left a high-water mark. After a flood passes, and the waters recede, the affected buildings and structures, and even nature, retain a visible line of how high the water had reached during the flood. So it was with our experience. Our family had a high-water mark left upon it by this experience that had fully flooded our lives. It was a mark of growth, an expansion of our souls. We had learned to love more, and to love more deeply as a family. Zion had unified us in ways we had not previously been unified. We had come to better know the presence of God in our lives as a family and as individuals. The mark that was set also became a goal for our future, to try to reach that level again by taking the higher path and being true to the lessons and principles we had learned.

I heard recently that the relationship that begins after a loved one dies is one no one tells you about. It is very personal; therefore, each person needs to work through it in his or her own way. Certainly, this was the case with us. I came across a quote that caused me to ponder this concept. It provides some understanding for why some people do not let go of grief and pain after the loss of a loved one: "The pain I feel ... I love it. I am afraid to let it go. It is the last piece of him I have left."

This puts an interesting twist on the idea of pain. We do not like pain, and we do everything possible to make it stop and go away. Yet, on one level, this quote makes sense. We do not want to forget the people we have loved, lost, and continue to love. The pain we feel is a constant reminder of them and what they meant to us. But the pain need not stay with us. It can eventually motivate us to find better, more productive ways to remember our loved ones. It can evolve into good works and gratitude. Our pain and grief can be a catalyst for future joy and happiness.

Life did not stop, thank goodness, and there were many things that needed to be done. Life with its abundant demands marches on. Work is cathartic. Productivity is positive and satisfying.

I needed to process everything that had happened. I spent time thinking and writing and trying to learn the lessons I felt I was supposed to learn from this experience. I did not want to let this opportunity for growth and learning pass without gaining from it everything God had to offer me. I did not want to waste one second of Zion's life, or death. I did not want to squander her life by wallowing in self-pity and depression, or in just moving on and forgetting. There was something higher to strive for – to let this experience change us forever, to become better people, to love and serve others more, to give back to God in gratitude for all He had given us.

This was an important time to figure out such things, while the memories were fresh and the pain and grief were still present. One must find good and productive ways to deal with the loss and the void that is created. The best way to do that, I have found, is to serve others. Take some time for introspection, but don't be consumed by it. Take the lessons you learn and turn them outward. Do some good in the world around you. I believe that every trial God gives us or allows to come into our lives is intended to be turned around and made into a blessing for someone else.

I understand more deeply now the motivations of people who create charities in the name of a loved one or who create laws to prevent and protect others from the same kind of hurt they or their loved ones may have suffered. For example, the Amber Alert is the result of an effort to protect abducted children from harm or possible death. According to the U.S. Department of Justice, of the children abducted and murdered by strangers in the USA, 75 percent are killed within the first three hours. Amber Alerts are designed to inform the general public quickly when a child has been kidnapped and is in danger so "the public [would be] additional eyes and ears of law enforcement."[1] As of February 2017, the U.S. Department of Justice estimated that 868 children had been successfully recovered as a result of the existence of the Amber Alert program. This program has now grown internationally. From the tragedy of a young girl by the name of Amber Hagerman from Arlington, Texas, who was abducted and murdered, we now have hundreds of children who have been spared a similar fate. This all started through the efforts of her parents, who suffered the unimaginable grief and pain of Amber's abduction and murder and wanted to spare others what they had to endure. They had not been able to protect their child, but they found a way to protect other children and prevent them from suffering in a similar manner. Great good can come out of great trials and difficulties.

Cast Your Bread Upon the Waters

We often wondered why so many people took a deep personal interest in our family's experience with Zion. The answer came to a degree from Carol Morgan, the wife of President Paul Morgan, when she wrote the following note to Ruth and the family:

---

1. Steve Irsay, "Cold War technology helped save lives of abducted teens", *CNN.com*, (August 5, 2002, retrieved March 7, 2014), http://edition.cnn.com/2002/LAW/08/05/ctv.alert/index.html.

Dear Paul, Ruth & family,

When I asked if there was anything I could do to help, you asked for a letter as to why we were so involved with your family and Zion.

As I have thought about this, it goes back to when I heard you were pregnant. Your concerns and feelings about the pregnancy. As a mother of seven I could relate in a small way as to those feelings. I had a few pregnancies which were not planned, and my emotions were on the surface.

It was not until a couple of weeks ago during our visit that I learned of your thoughts and feelings that this baby would have medical problems. No wonder you were concerned.

I think the reason so many felt such love and concern was because as a family you shared your thoughts and feelings with us. But you also shared Zion with us. Her blessing was beautiful, it touched so many hearts that day. What a powerful message concerning the plan of salvation. She needed a body and you provided that for her.

The memorial service gave us another opportunity to share your precious moments with the rest of us.

Your family has been so involved in our ward. How many times you have opened your home to the new members, trying to help them feel welcome. Your leadership skills and positions have touched many lives.

I think because you have cared for us, we wanted to be there and help you if possible. I know there is still grief and sadness, but what you have done for us by letting us experience some of your special and heartfelt emotions will always be cherished.

Zion is a little Angel who brought a special love and spirit into the lives of so many. As to why, I don't completely understand, but she did.

Love, Carol Morgan
Nov. 19, 2006

As a footnote to Carol's letter, the following should be known. Ruth had started the practice years before of arranging occasional potluck dinners at our home. She invited large groups of people for the sole purpose of helping them get to know each other. She invited people who were new to the area along with those who were more established. She often invited a broad mix of people. If a new family had small children, other families with small children would be invited so they had someone to get to know and to play with. These dinners also gave us an opportunity to become better acquainted with others and to let them know they were welcomed and cared about. Our home was always the happiest when it was shared with others. Ironically, this all started because we had once lived in a place where we were the newcomers and, even after many months, we hardly knew anyone. The solution was not to condemn others for not reaching out to us, but for us to reach out to them and to create an opportunity for people to get acquainted and build friendships. These dinners continue to be an important part of our family practice.

There is a phrase that perhaps many of us have heard: "Cast your bread upon the waters, and it will come back to you." It comes from the Bible in the Old Testament (*"Cast thy bread upon the waters: for thou shalt find it after many days."*)[2] The scripture calls on people to believe that their good deeds will ultimately return to their benefit. I think this is a lesson we learned unintentionally. We were not doing good things for others with the intent that they would return the favor, but we found that good, caring people do respond well to kindness and generosity, and desire to do the same.

In Ruth's file box are many cards and notes from people who expressed their love and sympathy at every stage of our journey. It is gratifying to read their words of love and encouragement. It still touches me to consider the caring of these good people. Ruth expresses her own unique thought about this subject.

---

2. Ecclesiastes 11:1.

My big question – (I have gotten some replies): Why are others touched? She was our baby, we should cry. Why are others so kind, tender, emotional? Margie Coats (a neighbor) said, "because we imagine our own feelings if we lost a child." I was overwhelmed at the kindnesses shown to us by so many. It really helped to know others cared. They were human in their godliness and godly in their humanness. Sister Morgan answered that some understand the pain from similar experiences, but it just seemed more than regular. I think it was her little spirit and her mission that drew others to us through her.

I have thought of how fortunate and blessed we have been to be in a community where, as Ruth stated, people were so "human in their godliness and godly in their humanness." They exemplify people who naturally fulfilled their promise to be "willing to mourn with those that mourn; yea, and comfort those that stand in the need of comfort."[3] Of all the good reasons people had for their intense interest in our situation, Ruth's reason feels especially right: "It was her little spirit and her mission that drew others to us through her."

Zion's Tree

After the first Thanksgiving of Zion's passing, I went to my office, and there was a four-foot artificial Christmas tree that was beautifully decorated with lights and ornaments. At the top of the tree was a picture of Zion in a little frame. Accompanying the tree was a note from the Institute Women's Association (IWA)[4], a sorority, a service club of college-age girls. Placed on the tree, along with the silver and red ball ornaments, were five angels of silver. The note read:

Manwaring Family...

This tree is in memory of your daughter Cherish Zion Manwaring.

3. Mosiah 18:9.
4. "Institute" refers to the private education program for college-age students which I supervised and where I taught classes.

The five other angels are your five other children, Jacob, Nyal, Samuel, Adam, and Moriah. We put Cherish Zion on the top of the tree because we know she will be watching over your family this Christmas season.

In this time of year, it is so important to remember the angels watching over us, and the IWA Pearl Chapter wants your family to know we remember your daughter as one of the most special Angels!

It was signed by all the girls in the chapter and their advisors. What a wonderful and thoughtful gift. We could not thank them enough for their kindness. It once again evoked tender feelings and tears.

The tree came home for the holiday season and occupied a prominent spot in the living room where the family spent most of our time together. This tree has become very special to us, or as Ruth says, "A treasure." In fact, when the Christmas season ended, and all the other decorations came down, we did not have the heart to take Zion's tree down. Ruth explains, "It was too depressing to consider taking it down, so that first year we left Zion's tree up until Easter. That seemed more fitting to celebrate her life, and I was more able to bear taking her tree down then."

The reason for this was the significance of Easter, the celebration of the resurrection of Jesus Christ who broke the bands of death for all of us, so we will all be resurrected in perfection and live again eternally. It was in the celebration of this hope that we felt we could take down her tree. This would become our tradition for years to come.

That Easter, the IWA girls came a couple of days before the holiday to see the tree before we took it down. On Easter Sunday, we had a special meeting with just our family. We talked about the significance of Easter for all of us and about the Atonement of Christ. We talked about the words of the sacrament prayer and why we partake of the sacrament every week. Why so often? So, as it states, we can always remember Him. When we remember Him, we can have His Spirit to be with us. We then talked about the life of Zion and the spirit she brought to all of us, which was really the Spirit of the Lord. We spoke of her and remembered her and spoke of how she also brought us something in our family that we must not ever forget and must ever strive to maintain. I then showed the family the PowerPoint presentations we had played at her funeral. Ruth shares the result:

> *The spirit was strong. We were all emotional. Lots of tears. Moriah and Sam cried during the shows. Adam didn't melt until I asked him for a hug. We miss our baby sister. "We're so grateful for the joy she brought our family," as Samuel always says in his prayers.*

We took the tree down last, after talking about Jesus Christ's resurrection and that because of Him Zion would be resurrected too, and we would see Zion again. The spirit was indeed strong, and we all felt it. Ruth recalls "Adam was very tender that Easter night as he led the family prayer, and Nyal suggested we hold hands as we knelt together."

While I was packing up the tree and Adam was putting away the silverware, he came over to me and asked if we could talk. He told me he had been feeling guilty about something he had done. He confessed he had not told me the truth about something. I was truly astounded and pleased with what I was seeing, something uncharacteristic of him at that stage of his teenage years. This was a rare and wonderful moment. I just wanted to rejoice. I wrote in my journal of that incident:

> *I learned a great lesson. When we feel the spirit, it changes us, prompts us to do what is right and good. I was so surprised and pleased by his actions. The best thing we can do for our children is to have the spirit of God in our homes, so they*

feel it and can respond to its promptings. His feeling the spirit did more for him than all the lectures combined that I have ever given him. Maybe the lectures have actually done a little good, but the Spirit had such a wonderful effect.

It was during this Easter season that Ruth recorded some other poignant, comforting thoughts:

I was rolling out pie dough in a quiet kitchen. (Moriah was doing homework – Paul and the boys were clearing out the Olive Tree area behind the Parrots, our neighbors). I found myself in tears as I thought of how nice it would be to be with Zion in heaven. I want to return to heaven and rest my weary soul, to see my little grown girl. As excited as I was with that thought, I don't think I could ever bear to be away from Paul. He is the love of my life. Again, I find myself teary-eyed thinking about that situation. I know I don't have to choose between the two because we are an eternal family.

We are grateful for the thoughtful gift of Zion's tree and the tradition that emerged from it. It is also gratifying to know that Zion's life touched the hearts of the girls in the IWA club. Incidentally, Ruth wrote in her journal a number of months later, "Pauline Meyerhoffer, the IWA advisor, informed me that they combined the Pearl and Ruby chapters of IWA and spent an evening trying to decide on a new name. When she got home, she said the name came to her, and everyone agreed. 'Zion' is right."

Ruth's Letter
Ruth wrote a letter to extended family and friends and shared the monumental events of the past year. In her letter, Ruth tells the story you have been reading. The details that you, the reader, are already familiar with have been edited out. At the end of the letter, Ruth shares important lessons she learned along the way.

We have spent some tender moments together as a family the past while. As excruciating as the pain has been, I wouldn't trade it for the exquisite joy we've felt. We have truly felt the truth of "opposition in all things." Paul likens it to the process of the refiner's fire. Heavenly Father knows what we need and knows how to help us, and it sure isn't anything we would think of. His path was not one I would have picked – I hesitated to follow it and would have changed the direction many times, but it wouldn't have been right. He is omniscient. He is so loving, caring, and powerful.

God sent us a little piece of heaven and gave us the gift of Zion. "Zion" is generally a state of being, or a geographic location – but now, for us, a member of our eternal family. Our family has forever been changed, and though our little angel's life was short, like the plunk of a pebble thrown into a pond, her ripples are so far-reaching.

We are taught that we need to prepare the earth to receive the heavenly kingdom of God, like Enoch and his people. Many who were around Zion have been given a vision and experience as to how possible it is to achieve heaven here on earth. It isn't easy. I am better capable of maintaining the spirit of Zion when I think to myself, "It isn't about me." Happiness, unity, service, love come best when the focus is on others … Doing good to others, serving, giving, healing – that is the life and message of our great exemplar.

What a great gift God gave to us through His only begotten Son. What a great gift Jesus Christ gave to us all – that we couldn't give to ourselves. God prepared a plan, Christ is central to that plan, and it's all about love.

May we keep the spirit of Christ all year long all our lives through. Thank you for comforting those of us who mourn. We are also grateful for the mission of the Holy Ghost as a comforter. I hope that our broken hearts never mend. We are supposed to have a broken heart and a contrite spirit. A broken heart is a pure heart. May God bless us all to bear one another up – always. And if we fail one another – He will not. He is ever near.

What I Have Learned from Zion

We all learned much from our experience with Zion. During the weeks after she passed away, I wrote down my own very personal lessons, things I did not want to forget. Some of the lessons have been shared already in a general sense, but some things have not been stated.

- I have learned that my wife has an intuition as a mother that I should never forget. I need to listen to her and counsel better with her in the future. I learned that we can have a greater love in our home than I had ever imagined. This love came about because we were united in a good cause, and we turned to God in our greatest need and he blessed us.

- I have seen a deeply caring and sincere side of humanity. If we allow others into our lives, they can be such a blessing and support during times of trial. It is one of the ways God can touch us, through the helping hands of others. I learned from Zion's example. Zion came into this world to do our Father's will at great personal sacrifice – even her life – sacrificing a long and wonderful life on earth to fulfill God's purposes for her. I need to follow her example and willingly give my daily life to Him. As Isaiah has stated: "O Lord, thou art our father; we are the clay, and thou art the potter; and we are all the work of thy hand."[5] God's ways are the paths I want to take.

- I learned that I need to remember to show greater love to each of our children. We do not know how long they will

---

5. Isaiah, 64:8.

be with us. Each moment is precious. Inevitably they will grow up and leave. The time passes so quickly. I want to be a better father and husband and guide this family right. We need to do more things together as a family.

- I learned that God loves my family and is trying to bless us. He sent an angel, in the form of Zion, to show us what can be. He placed Zion in a position to watch over us. Zion is close by and will help us to be a better family.

- We don't need to have a perfect heart to be pure in heart. Zion's heart was symbolically like ours is, not perfect; there are flaws. As we strive to put God and others first in our lives, our motives and desires are selfless and pure and will lead us to a good place.

- I learned that Zion is an answer to my prayers – she is the beginning of change. I don't want to see this purpose of her life wasted and of no effect.

- I have especially learned that Zion's life is meant to be shared with others. Her life is a symbol of love, faith, submissiveness, purity, sacrifice, and grace. The elements of her life are a type of Christ.

The Refiner's Fire

The refining process is one I have come to appreciate and even love as time has progressed. We need to view life from an eternal perspective. As long as we are rooted in the here and now, challenges and difficulties may seem impossible to endure. This will continue until we can see eternal purpose in them. You can endure just about anything and move forward in your life in a more positive way, if you can find meaning and purpose in your trials.

The purpose of life is embodied in Christ's teaching: "Be ye therefore perfect, even as your Father in heaven is perfect."[6] And

6. Matthew 5:48.

further, "Therefore, what manner of men ought ye to be? Verily I say unto you, even as I am."[7] Peter talks in the scriptures about how we should take upon ourselves the divine nature. These qualities include faith, virtue, knowledge, temperance, patience, godliness, brotherly love, kindness, and charity.[8] They are in fact qualities of God. We are charged to become even as He is. In the Old Testament, we read, "...Ye shall be holy: for I the Lord your God am holy ... Sanctify yourselves therefore, and be ye holy..."[9]

This is a lofty goal and purpose. It is not intended to happen all at once but takes a lifetime of growth and refining. The concept of refining is expressed in Malachi 3:2-3, "...he is like a refiner's fire, and like fullers' soap: And he shall sit as a refiner and purifier of silver: and he shall purify the sons of Levi, and purge them as gold and silver, that they may offer unto the Lord an offering in righteousness."

The process of obtaining gold and silver requires a fire that is extremely hot, enough to melt ore (stone and metal). The useless, extraneous byproduct is separated and cast off until all that remains is the precious metal. And yet there are still impurities in the gold and silver, lessening its value and usefulness. To obtain the purest substance, it must be carefully cleansed, and this can be achieved only through a refining fire – even a series of refining fires.

The story is told of a group of women who met in a Bible study group to study the scriptures. They had been reading those verses in Malachi 3:2-3 and felt like they wanted to know more about this process of refining precious metal. One of the women volunteered to visit a silversmith and report back to the group about what he had to say. She went accordingly to a silversmith and without telling him the reason behind her visit, asked him to tell her about the process of refining silver.

After he described the process to her, she asked, "But sir, do you sit while you go through the process of refining the silver?"

---

7. 3 Nephi 27:27.
8. 2 Peter 1:5-7.
9. Leviticus 19:2; 20;7.

"Oh yes, ma'am," the silversmith replied. "I must sit with my eye steadily fixed on the furnace, for if the time necessary for refining is exceeded in the slightest degree, the silver will be harmed."

The lady recognized immediately the beauty and the comfort of the expression in Malachi, "He shall *sit* as a refiner and purifier of silver." God sees that it is necessary and important for the growth of His children to put them into a furnace. But He watches carefully the process of our refining. His wisdom and love are both engaged in the best manner for our good. The trials we have are not random. He will not let us be tested beyond what we personally can endure. If we will trust Him, He will apply the refining fire no longer than is needful for our sanctification.

Before the woman left, she asked one last question of the silversmith: "When do you know the process is complete?"

"Why that is quite simple," replied the silversmith. "When I can see my own image in the silver, the refining process is finished."

What a beautiful concept and truth. We are not finished until we have become like Him, which requires a process of changing and refining. This fits what we are taught in the scriptures: "...have ye spiritually been born of God? Have ye received his image in your countenance? Have ye experienced this mighty change in your hearts?"[10]

We were created, born, with that gold and silver already present within each of us, a genetic inheritance from our Father in Heaven. But it is mixed with impurities, our personal weaknesses. He wants us to have His greatest joys, which come from striving to become like Him. We are to follow the guidelines He has set before us: His teachings and commandments. They teach us how to live well among our fellow men and to draw nearer to God. Personal growth comes at a cost of sacrifice, self-discipline, effort, and dedication. It is never easy, but it is always worth it. Our trials have purpose.

As we become more like Him, we radiate the spirit He gives to His true followers. He urges us to "...pray with all the energy of heart

10. Alma 5:14.

220

that ye may be filled with this love, which he hath bestowed upon all who are true followers of his Son, Jesus Christ; that ye may become the sons of God; that when he shall appear we shall be like him, for we shall see him as he is; that we may have this hope; that we may be purified even as he is pure. Amen."[11]

A friend gave Ruth a gift of a necklace, Zion's birthstone in a setting of silver. The symbolism is very appropriate: the refining growth that came from Ruth's experience with Zion.

My wife once shared with me a poem she found by Ella Wheeler Wilcox titled "Within the Garden's Gate," which is the last stanza of her longer version of the poem "Gethsemane."[12] It was within the garden called Gethsemane that Christ suffered for us an anguish so intense that, as Luke tells us, it caused Him to "sweat, as it were, great drops of blood."[13] It was a suffering that caused him to cry out asking that he not have to endure the pain he was enduring, and would yet endure on the cross, to "let this cup pass from me," and to not have to drink the bitter cup. The poetess brings us into this setting, not as observers, but as participants.

Within the Garden's Gate

All those who journey, soon or late,
Must pass within the Garden's gate,
Must kneel alone in darkness there,
And battle with some fierce despair.

God pity those who cannot say:
"Not mine, but Thine,"
- who can only pray:
"Let this cup pass," and cannot see
The purpose of Gethsemane.

11. Moroni 7:48.
12. Ella Wheeler Wilcox, "Gethsemane", *The Courier-Journal*, Louisville, 28 Aug. 1887, 13.
13. Luke 2:44.

Like Job and Abraham and like Christ, we too must go through our own trials, our own Gethsemanes, and be put to the test of faith. We need to come to the point of submitting our will to His and saying, "Not mine, but Thine."

Our tests and trials are not completely random. They are suited for each of us individually. Paul V. Johnson explained it like this:

Some of the tests of will we face are tailor-made for each of us individually. Since we each have parts of our lives that need to be changed and weaknesses that must become strengths, we should expect the most difficult tests of our wills to be in areas that "wrench our very heartstrings."[14]

We also find the tailor-made experiences of Job in the Old Testament, none of which we would personally care to see dealt to us, yet they sanctified him. If we would be sanctified, we must each expect God will give us what we need to accomplish that end. We must desire growth and change more than we want relief from pain and anguish, a choice which can be a real, even a severe test, of our desire. We must be willing to stay in the refiner's fire as long as He requires it. Whether trials or blessings, they are tailored-fitted to us. Orson F. Whitney said it this way:

No pain that we suffer, no trial that we experience is wasted. It ministers to our education, to the development of such qualities as patience, faith, fortitude, and humility. All that we suffer and all that we endure, especially when we endure it patiently, builds up our characters, purifies our hearts, expands our souls, and makes us more tender and charitable, more worthy to be called the children of God.[15]

---

14. Paul V. Johnson, "Reconcile Yourselves to the Will of God", *CES Satellite Training Broadcast*, August 8, 2006, Joseph Smith Memorial Building, 3.
15. Ezra Taft Benson et al., *Hope* (Salt Lake City: Deseret Book, 1988) as quoted by Howard W. Hunter, "The Opening and Closing of Doors", 13-14.

Anniversary

I wrote in the last chapter that the year after Zion's death seemed to be a series of memories looking back to the milestones put in place by events from the previous year. As we approached September and October, the intensity of that period from the year before swept back into our lives in the form of memories, some difficult and some tender. Ruth wrote about these in her journal:

Sept 30, 2007

I had gone to take Moriah & her friend Sydney to perform a musical number at a Young Women's activity but found myself sobbing during Moriah's violin number. Pres. and Sister Allen had been sitting on the back row, and I was overcome with the memories of a year ago, of how Pres. Allen had joined our family in fasting and had offered such an inspired blessing that was not of healing – but of direction. He wanted so much to be able to bless it all better, but found he was "restrained." I gathered up Moriah's and Sydney's instruments and sat in the van during the rest of the meeting and cried.

And then, a month later, as we approached the date that would have been Zion's first birthday, Ruth recorded these entries in Zion's Journal:

Friday Morning, October 19

While walking [our dog] Yodi and having quiet all around – a gentle mist falling, I sobbed and sobbed – reliving, remembering last year on this day. I went out last night to the front room and looked at the tree through the front window – raining, windy, leaves shaking in the weather.

Friday Evening, October 19

...meeting the institute gang to head out for the annual

leadership conference in Boise. (We missed it last year, Zion's birth). I was driving with Paul telling me the schedule of events and dress. Me, saying I didn't want to be around people right now. Paul asking me why I would not feel up to socializing – pausing, then asking me if I saw something on his forehead. "What?" I asked. His reply, "Bonehead" as he pointed to his head and choked up and said, "I just didn't think." Pres. Morgan had asked if I had a cold, "No, just been an emotional day." I couldn't remember what time Zion was born. Paul said, "I think 4:06 PM." He looked it up on the PowerPoint. 4:02. Paul worked on his presentation on the computer for a bit as I drove. Finally, he set it down and said, "I don't want to repeat last year when I was on the computer and you felt I was not there for you." I told him to go take a nap, freeing me up to weep as I drove. The rain came down heavier and steadily all the way to Boise.

After eating, we listened to the speaker … I walked and held and rubbed the baby of a young couple. My eyes were so dry and tired. Paul wanted to know what to do. I didn't know what to do. So, we went to bed. I didn't sleep well. I relived Friday last year again. How they scooped her away to the NICU, her hands tied with dishcloths – a brief glimpse in the Life Flight carrier, telling Paul to go with her, resting, holding her for the first time Saturday morning.

I miss holding my baby. I am so grateful to have her eternally, well, whole, and saved – sanctified and perfect. I miss her, not experiencing her growing up, but I am so grateful for her watchful care over Adam. Zion was born at 4:02 PM. Moriah at 4:59 PM. I miss Moriah not enjoying a little sister, but know they are both so good. I am so grateful for her sacrifice. I hope my life is better a year later because of her. I will keep trying.

CHAPTER 15

Lessons from Zion's Siblings

Zion's siblings, our children, are normal in most ways. We have endured the trials and travails of their growing up and seeking independence while under our roof, and all the usual challenges that come with parenthood and families. The teenage years have been a real test, too. We have somehow managed to survive it all by constantly trying to do the right things day by day. We are grateful our children have chosen the paths they are now on. They, too, have chosen to learn how to trust God in their lives.

This chapter is dedicated to how our children have been affected by our family's experience. It is presented mostly in their own words. We asked them to share their thoughts about Zion, how it affected them when she was with us, and the effect it has had on their lives in the intervening years. It is interesting to note that each has his or her own version of what happened. Minor inaccuracies may be present in certain details, but the impressions left in the heart are always accurate and the most important. The things that touch our hearts are what shape and change us.

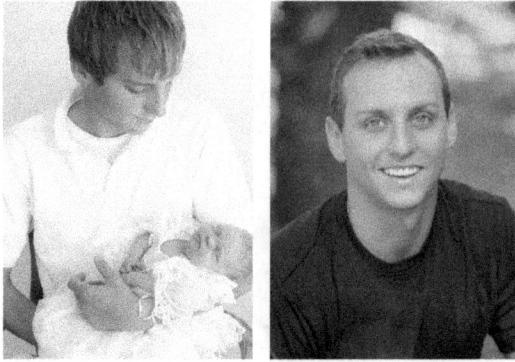

ADAM'S THOUGHTS AND EXPERIENCES WITH ZION

Words fail me when it comes to the brief but amazing life of my littlest sister, Zion. She lived only 11 days due to a combination of defects with her heart.

When I first learned that my parents would be having another child, I wasn't happy. In my fifteen-year-old teenage angst, I falsely thought my parents were being irresponsible. This child would be the last car in the train with a six-year gap after Jacob, my youngest brother; a caboose of sixteen years behind myself, the oldest child. Not to mention the additional financial burden that it could add to our family.

As a teenager, I was just approaching the responsible age of dating, and I was very conscious of my family's less-than-considerable means. I was reminded of this fact almost daily because of my hand-me-down (from cousins) wardrobe and $0 [zero dollar] haircuts from my mom. Girls certainly wouldn't like me for a sleek car and chic fashion. That's what a lot of my world revolved around at that age.

You see, our family vacations were always to visit family members in nearby states. I had never ever flown in a plane (and didn't until I was in college). I was just learning who I was at this point, and I was conscious that our family didn't have much extra. Another child would mean that our family was going to become even less "normal." In that regard, I couldn't have been more right.

I don't have the sharpest of memories, so forgive me if some details are inaccurate in my account. In the months leading up to the birth, I mostly remember that before Zion was born there started to be complications. Whether the heart condition or the Down syndrome was revealed first, I don't remember. But I knew that this was turning into something terribly abnormal, and that impacted me as a teenager. I was powerless to a lot of my circumstances, but I felt acutely helpless in this one.

The reality of having our unborn sister having health problems didn't sink in with me at first. My mom seemed like any other pregnant woman. So, I told myself that the baby would be fine. Doctors can never be 100 percent sure on these things, so there was only a chance of her being born with complications, and bad things never happened to our family! And so, my denial played out for most of the rest of the pregnancy.

One weekend, we were leaving out of town. If my memory serves me, we were just going to our aunt's or grandparent's place in eastern Idaho. My mom opted to stay home by herself because she didn't want to travel in her condition. Before leaving, my friends were planning out their weekend. Back then, we spent a lot of time pranking our friends from school. Many were victims of harmless toilet papering and doorbell ditching. But we were starting to step it up. My friends and I were becoming reckless in our quest to have fun.

Next thing I know, I'm out of town. I'm calling and texting my buddies, and they get the bright idea to use these spent .22 bullet casings I had acquired from working at Scout Camp the previous summer to enact an extreme version of forking at Emilee Williams' home. "Forking" is where you stick a lot of plastic forks into the lawn. In lieu of forks, the bullet casings were spread all over the Williams' lawn. This was a very bad idea. Those bullet casings would take forever to remove from the lawn. They would need to be individually found and picked up. Any stray ones would be a danger. Mowing a lawn could become deadly if bullet shell fragments became shrapnel from the rotating lawn mower blade.

Retaliation came swiftly. Emilee tapped her resources and learned of my bag of bullet casings. Figuring I was the culprit, she talked her older friends into retaliating against me. These older boys came to my house and egged it. They landed a dozen or more eggs on our family's two-story home. That's what my mom woke up to on Sunday morning – all alone. She didn't want the egg to get baked on by the sun, so she had to get out the ladder and clean it up as best she could. My mother – eight months pregnant – exerting herself and climbing a rickety two-story ladder. I still cringe when I think of the stress this must've caused her.

Incidents like this happening and leading up to the birth of Zion made me wonder, "Did my actions lead to Zion having physical impairments?" Was I a source of chronic stress that led to these problems? Did my constant bickering with my siblings diminish her chances of a long, normal life? Was God cursing my family with this difficult birth because of the type of life I was living?

My anxiety grew as the due date approached. Each doctor visit confirmed the worst. Zion wasn't going to miraculously get better. When my parents left, I remember how strong and hopeful they were. They knew that no matter the outcome, we would be blessed. Personally, I couldn't fathom the outcomes. We were going to have a sister with Down syndrome and heart conditions. What would that mean for me? My cousins in St. George had a 20+ year-old Downs cousin on the other side of their family. The stories they told were, in short, hilarious. But that was so distant from me. Up close, a Downs sibling would require so much attention and responsibility. These are the things I remember thinking about as my parents headed to the hospital in Utah.

Next, there was the big news! The delivery went well, but our sister was immediately put into the NICU. Before then, I didn't even know what an NICU was. We kept her in our prayers and got updates from my parents.

My parents decided we needed to come and meet our sister. Even though it was only shortly after her birth, it seemed like an eternity had passed. We made the drive to Salt Lake. Despite all the worrying, the whole thing didn't seem real to me until I walked into the hospital. I began to be anxious as we waited to meet our new sister. Cherish Zion Manwaring. I thought the name was weird for the first while. But later, when I saw the poster that the nurses had made with her name on it, the issue settled for me. It was a little surreal to me that these random nurses knew my sister better than I did. Her likes and dislikes were all spelled out on that poster. I had yet to see the smile that these nurses liked so much. We were brought into the area where my mom and Zion were. I know everyone thinks their babies are beautiful, but Zion was something else. I think I was most shocked to observe that there were no hints of the Down syndrome in her face. I couldn't see it. She looked to me as flawless a baby as they come. And my mom was as proud and loving a mother as could be.

At some point we had a family council. We talked about what the doctors were saying about her heart. We talked about her chance at life. We talked about what the options were. When we came back home, we really didn't know what was going to happen. I went to school, but I expected to get a call to the office at any point. Or one of those yellow notes that the office sent to kids to remind them of their dentist's appointments. Only mine would say that my sick sister was dead or dying. There was a lot of worrying during that time done by me and my siblings. Grandma would get us up to date when we got back from school. But the longer she was in the NICU, the more I worried.

Ultimately, the decision was made to bring Zion to our home. Rather than subject her to who knows how many surgeries which she only had a miniscule chance of surviving, we chose to enjoy her for as long as we could. She would require hospice conditions, but it would be worth it to have her in our home.

The front living room was rearranged to allow for a small crib. I remember when I first held her at home; I put her on my knees so that I could use both hands to play with her grabby little hands. During the first few days, I didn't know what to expect. Would Zion's heart give way quickly? Would she slip from us quietly? How long would we have her? But those concerns were wiped away quickly. Zion cried and fussed and pooped and slept. To me, that made her a pretty normal baby.

Our home was blessed to have Zion. Our family was happy. There was a spirit of kindness and peace. She brought that wonderful spirit into our home. Our home felt inexplicably full, like there wasn't room for even one more little angel. Zion completed our family.

We took family pictures with a child photographer. I remember there was a small miracle that brought the photographer into the picture (pun intended). Those family pictures are amazing and are a treasure to me. Zion was so cute in white. She is the definition of purity and innocence that the white conveys.

The nurses who attended Zion in the hospital after she was born were so great, but my brightest memory is about the story of when they made the plaster casting of Zion's hand. They kept getting it wrong, like Zion would clench her hand or it wouldn't come out right. I think it took them three tries for it to come out, but the result was miraculous. Zion had extended her pointer and pinky fingers and thumb to make the sign for "I love you." When this plaster was shown to us by my parents, it put my family immediately in tears. All but me. I'm embarrassed to say that when I first saw it, I thought that she was giving me the "rock on" sign. I thought it was cool, and I was kind of confused by my family's reaction until it was explained to me.

Sunday came, and we brought her to church in a beautiful long white dress. She was blessed in Sacrament Meeting and given a name. Different as the name was, she was stuck with it forever now! But it is a perfect fit. I remember a lot of our family being there for that: cousins, grandparents, aunts, and uncles.

Though Nyal's birthday was the next day, I think it took back-seat to the new baby. I don't remember a thing about that birthday. But I do remember the day after that very well. Halloween of 2006. I was 15. This was the first year that I didn't trick or treat. Instead, my friends and I watched movies and ran around the neighborhood looking for things to do. We were at my friend Tyler's house, which was on the south end of Twin Falls. I didn't expect this to be the night that I finally got the call. It was so unexpected that I don't even remember who called me. I just remember hearing someone say, "It's your sister. I think you should come home now." I immediately hightailed it back to Tyler's house. I asked his dad to drive me home. I don't think he understood how quickly I needed to get home. And I certainly wasn't going to press him or guilt him by saying, "Can we go faster? My sister is dying." I couldn't imagine believing that enough to say it out loud.

I ran to the door when we arrived. Inside, everyone was so quiet. Much different from the lively environment I had just left, full of laughing friends and loud noises. It was so quiet I hardly felt like I was at my home. Also, the crowd surprised me. I remember my parents and siblings were there. Our stake president, Kent Allen, and I think his wife, along with a couple of other people were also there. Even with all these people, the room felt empty. Without asking, I knew that she had already gone. At first, I couldn't believe it. When they told me, I had to ask if they knew for sure. Zion looked so peaceful lying there. She couldn't be gone! She couldn't leave while I was gone! Then, almost in the same instant, I was angry. How could Tyler's dad have been so slow to react? We should have sprinted to the car, ran every stop sign. This was the one thing that I couldn't be late for. But I was, and it had happened. Slowly, words were said, and the people filtered out. We had the entire night to have Zion to ourselves.

I remember holding her. Feeling her on my knees. But she was empty now. The Zion in her had left. She had left behind her perfectly imperfect body. It was just a shell now. I cried. I held her on my knees and cried. I don't know how long I was there. It felt like half the night.

I don't remember giving Zion up. The last thing I remember about that night is going to my room in the basement. I sat on my bed and cried. I pleaded with Heavenly Father to take care of my little sister. I asked for help to understand it all. Why was she given to us, just to be taken away? I fell asleep eventually.

It is unbelievable to me still how life marched forward normally so soon. The next morning, I woke up and went to school. I don't know how I managed that. Every day that week I went to school. Very few people my age knew what had happened with our family. On Friday, we had a viewing. I think I lost it the most when I saw her little casket. I couldn't keep my emotions in through that experience. I don't remember what was said that day, but I was grateful for the sentiments of all who were there. I felt bad for the family members who had just travelled to be there for the baby blessing and had to return so soon for a funeral. It should be the rarest experience to be present for both of those events for the same person, let alone within the same week.

If my memory serves me, Zion's casket was put into the back of our Suburban. We took her up to Rexburg the next morning. Many of my mom's family that have passed on are buried in a little cemetery in Parker. My mom wants to be buried there, but when my parents bought plots together, they managed to find three plots next to each other. So, they thought to buy all three. We never could have anticipated this use for the third plot, but I'm happy for that small miracle. When we lowered her into the ground, I cried. I cry even as I write this, just the memory brings back those feelings so fresh. I was so sad to say goodbye to our little angel. I was so sad to see my mother and father in anguish, having to bury their youngest child. I naively felt that no one in the world could know the hurt we endured in that moment. But as Zion's body settled into its resting place, I remembered. I remembered that this was temporary. Already, that body was just a shell, just a transitional phase as part of the plan. Already Zion was on to better things, no more weighed down by a broken heart. She was already more perfect than I ever knew her. I think we all felt her close by that day.

Since then, that Parker cemetery has been a special place for me. More special than anywhere else in the world. I go there on occasion to see my sister. In all seasons. I've nearly stranded my old truck in deep snow trying to visit her in the dead of winter. I go there to remember Zion. To Cherish her.

I've made some of my greatest life decisions in that cemetery: to serve a worthy mission, to attend BYU-Idaho, to date certain people, to follow certain job opportunities, to go to Mexico and Jerusalem on study abroad programs. Zion always helps brighten the path. She touches me with a little bit of her perfection each time I visit. She is my guardian angel. I've felt that time and time again.

My dad masterminded the most perfect headstone for Zion. I'm sure he's written a whole chapter about it already, but I can attest to the beauty and thoughtfulness of the piece. I have since been to Jerusalem. I have been on the Temple Mount in Jerusalem, where Mt. Zion historically would've been. I have studied the events that have taken place there throughout time. Israel is a special place, and the Jerusalem stone that my dad included in the headstone has sealed Zion and our family to her namesake. I feel sealed to those biblical events and places because I am sealed to the purity of Zion.

That headstone points straight up to heaven, and I know that's where I can find my sister. Though her body lies in the ground, I know that she is with our Heavenly Father. I feel her close when I am close to Him.

> *"Therefore, let your hearts be comforted concerning Zion; for all flesh is in mine hands; be still and know that I am God. Zion shall not be moved out of her place, notwithstanding her children are scattered. They that remain, and are pure in heart, shall return, and come to their inheritances."* *(D&C 101:16-18)*

MORIAH'S LESSONS FROM ZION

Moriah's Poem

Moriah wrote a poem which I came across while packing up some of the things in her room when she went away to college. She wrote it for a high school English class.

Opposition

I picked her out from 'midst the crowd,
Or maybe she picked me;
She knew I'd known the same ordeal
So very recently.

Her pain-etched eyes, her self-embrace
Said more than words would speak–
I heard the desperate pleading voiced
In droplets on her cheek.

Despondently, she gazed down at
The dirty roadside slush.
In silence (grief won't be conversed)
We let our shoulders brush.

She turned to me. "Why is it so
That tiny babies die
And cancer takes our precious ones?
Was happiness a lie?"

"I understand your pain," I said,
"Your longing for release
From grief and sorrow, coupled with
The dread of hasty peace.

"Although my crisis happened less
Than four short months ago,
I've learned from it. Now let me teach you
Something you should know.

"My thoughts transport me back in time
Back to a fall so bright,
So dark, so warm, so cold, so hard;
As right as day and night.

"I'd waited long – three summer months,
Two fall ones – for this day;
A brand-new sibling (boy or girl?)
Was finally on its way!

"I had four brothers already
And prayed that not a boy
But baby girl be born to us –
A sister to enjoy!

Cherishing Zion

"My prayers were answered: on the phone,
Mom said it was a she!
With flaming joy, rejoicing tongue,
I told all I did see!

"Her name was Cherish Zion, but
As Zion she'd be known.
I couldn't wait to bring her back
Into our loving home!

"But Zion wasn't perfect: though
As pure as she could be,
Her tender heart was faulty, and
She needed surgery.

"The doctors couldn't fix the flaw:
My parents had to make
That choice that every parent dreads;
Both options would hearts break.

"But they were brave! They chose the right
And after one more day,
They brought my sister home, so we
Could Cherish every day.

"What purity! What joy we felt
In holding Zion dear!
And also what great sadness, for
We knew her time drew near.

"(There is a difference, you should know,
Between despair and grief;
While grief is love, despair is wrong
And offers no relief.)

"Thus six more days passed slowly by,
Time mercifully delayed.
On Halloween, we dressed up in
Our costumes, sleek and frayed.

"We trick-or-treated, had some fun,
But never wandered far
From thoughts of Zion. Then the call:
We jumped into the car.

"When we got home, she was still there,
Still live, but ashen white
Our costumes were removed, and then
We gathered close that night.

"Sweet Zion! We all held her,
Tender arms so full of love.
We never knew the passing moment;
It was peaceful as a dove."

"Do you tell me," my friend questions,
"That from sorrow there is rest?"
"Yes," I answer, "and the joy that
Grows of grief is surely best.

"Peace and grief: such subtle siblings!
One without the other's naught,
Just as day without the darkness
Can be comprehended not."

Moriah's Thoughts

When I was younger, I prayed so hard for a sister. It was my greatest wish (besides being able to fly and have magic powers; I was a kid, after all)! Over time, I learned that sometimes Heavenly Father's plan doesn't cater to our wants, and that's okay. His way always works out best in the end. I was 10 when I told the Lord that if He didn't want to give me a sister, I'd accept that because I trusted Him. I even used the Savior's words: "Thy will be done." It felt good to relinquish my will to His.

Two weeks later, Dad told me Mom had had a miscarriage two weeks earlier—and the baby was a girl. I went into my closet and cried, telling Heavenly Father, "You could have let her stay; I didn't mean that I didn't want her." I was sad, but I knew Heavenly Father had perfectly understood and wasn't trying to spite me. In fact, I trusted Him even more because I'd learned that He hears every prayer. As it turned out, waiting to send Zion was perfect since all the kids grew old enough to understand what was going on and remember her.

Fast forward four years to the summer of 2006, when we learned another sibling was coming. I hoped so much for a girl! I imagined everything we'd do, including living in the clubhouse (an awesome outdoor house we'd built with a skylight, loft, and electricity). I was going to teach her, play with her, and love her so much! Even as we learned about the baby's health complications, I hoped things would turn out just fine. I knew the Lord could work miracles if He needed to.

The day Zion was born, I ran straight from the bus stop to the phone and dialed my dad's number (figuring Mom might be a bit preoccupied if she was still in labor). Dad answered, and I barraged him with questions. He couldn't give me a straight answer, and Mom came on the line to say he was bawling. She told me it was a girl, and it was the happiest moment of my life!

Since no one else was home yet, I called my best friend to share the news. When she didn't pick up, I figured it was just as well, since my brothers should be first to know. As soon as I saw Nyal, Sam, and Jacob approaching the gate, I ran out to share the great news, and we couldn't stop smiling!

After a while, our Aunt Maxine arrived from Pocatello with her boys. The next morning, she left the cousins with their friend, Dr. Manning, and drove us Manwarings down to Salt Lake. On our way to the hospital, we stopped by a mall and picked out calla lilies for Mom. (They later became part of Zion's casket spray.)

At the NICU, I was so eager to see Zion but had to let the younger boys go first. After years of yearning, the last few minutes were hard. Holding my sister for the first time was a beautiful moment. It was joyfully fulfilling to finally be there with her. I could see the Down syndrome look in her sleeping eyes at first, but over the days we had her, I couldn't see it anymore. Everything was so pure—and so was the grief that I first felt there when I learned Zion really might not survive. I cried.

We had to go back to Twin that night. Grandma Manwaring stayed with us while our parents were in Salt Lake with Zion. On the day Zion came home, Grandma picked me up from school, and we bought hand sanitizer to keep Zion healthy when people held her. (To this day, I love the smell of that hand sanitizer because it brings back the pure feelings of that time.) It was heartbreaking to know she was coming home to have a peaceful passing. I hoped there'd be a miracle in store—like maybe an amazing doctor with a cure would be visiting our town. Throughout it all, my family and I continued to pray that God's will be done, and we meant it.

Having Zion home was so special. Everything was pure, open, and tender. It's an interesting thing to be so happy and yet grieving at the same time. I think people are their truest selves in that state—and our family was beautiful during that time. So were all the people who came to us with service and comfort. They supported us so kindly and well, and the Spirit of God was in our home and hearts. Our home was a temple filled with love—both joyful and sad. It was a quiet, peaceful atmosphere.

We didn't know if Zion would live for hours or months, so my brothers and I still went to school. I hurried home every day to spend as much time with Zion as I could. As I held her, I memorized her face and motions, her sounds and smell, and I loved her with all my heart. I don't know how to describe that time; there was so much going on in our hearts and our world. I guess the best description would be that it was a time of love—with all the pain, fulfillment, and joy that comes with loving someone with your whole heart. I was guided very closely by the Spirit during this time and the months following, and I'm very grateful for that. I knew what to do and say, when to let someone else take Zion, and how to respond to my emotions with faith and in a way that led to peace. I know what it's like, now, to have the Lord take my hand and lead me. I know He'll support His children in their time of need. I know there is complete peace and hope, even in the middle of the tempest, when we put our trust in Him, and I know there is complete healing through Christ.

Well, you've heard the story from others. The Lord did His will and helped Zion accomplish her mission on earth. The night she left became a truly hallowed evening. We don't know when she passed away, but I was the one holding her when the nurse announced no signs of life. It was such a sacred experience for our family to grieve together there in the night in our living room. Such sacred things can't be shared, only experienced. It was in those moments that I realized we see the clearest when our eyes are full of tears.

Eventually, I went to my room, but I didn't go to bed right away. I sat on my bed and wrote a letter to my sister, expressing my feelings and love. Even that is too sacred and personal for me to share.

Later that week, I put my letter in her casket after the viewing.

Burying your sister is really hard. Some of the most heart-wrenching moments in life are when you see a tiny body that used to move with warm curiosity laying stiff on a dressing table; when the lid is closing over her face for the last time and your little primary-age brother whispers to look as long as you can; when you leave that lonely, precious box on a yellow hillside under the cold November rain; and when you yearn for the future that could have been. That's the purely mortal view. However, there's so much beauty interspersed when you see the bits of eternity peeking through, like the far-reaching effect her precious life has had on people, the tender realizations that she's closer than you imagined, and the glorious future yet to be.

Despite knowing everything was okay, losing Zion still hurt so much—but I didn't want the grief to leave too fast; it was a connection to her. Over the next few months, I obtained complete healing and peace from the Lord. I know death is just a separation, and goodbyes are never for as long as we think. Sometimes, I still have moments of grief as deep as back then, and that's okay. I'm grateful, because it reminds me that I still love her just as much.

Zion has been an immense force for good. She gave our grandpa (who'd hurt/offended some of his family) a chance to serve by providing her beautiful casket and contribute to his family again in a positive, meaningful way. Zion encouraged me as a missionary in Australia when I realized we were doing the same work on either side of the veil, accompanied by the same glory. While there, I brought hope to Priscilla, a young lady who'd lost her son to the same condition as Zion, with the same gospel that gave me hope.

I'm profoundly thankful for Zion. She's our family's anchor to Heavenly Father and His kingdom. Because she's already there, we'll do all we can to be worthy to join them.

NYAL'S THOUGHTS ABOUT ZION

When Zion died, I just felt numb. Like after shooting a shotgun for the first time and your fingers and arm go numb. You know what just happened, but it's like your appendages don't feel like your own. You can still move but it feels like moving through someone else. I felt numbness not from shock or trauma but because of the loss. I didn't realize how much Zion had meant to me until after she died. I knew that she had gotten a lot of attention and made people sympathetic to our family. As a kid, I enjoyed the attention our family got. But then she passed away. I remember walking into my fifth-grade class with Mrs. Noel and telling her, "She's gone." The teacher was confused, but I had to tell someone besides family who knew the story. I've never been one who releases emotion when family is around. It's embarrassing. But I didn't have many close friends, and the one good friend I had didn't share our belief in God's plan of salvation. My emotional release came at the slideshow during the funeral. I remember seeing the picture of Zion's empty cradle with the words "Mission accomplished," and for some reason that triggered within me such a deep sorrow. Sorrow I had briefly felt when I thought I was all alone. This sorrow caused me to burst into tears, and I didn't care about embarrassing myself because my emotions were wack, so deep and overwhelming.

The first few weeks, we didn't seem to talk much. We all knew that it had hit Mom the most, but she seemed to be getting by with all the tasks that post funerals demand. I think that's how she expressed her grief. We seemed to band together. There was a special feeling in our home that had never existed before. I know that most people of our faith desire a heaven in their home and sometimes achieve peace and a place where the spirit resides – but this was completely different. We experienced Zion in our home. I know what it means to be of one heart and one mind with charity for all because we experienced it. People think everyone must be perfect for this to happen. No! We all still had our flaws, but it was like those didn't matter anymore because Zion showed us a higher plain of existence, of living.

After Zion's death, we kids were more obedient. We wanted to make things easier for Mom (and Dad, which could be accomplished by making Mom happy). I wanted to be a peacemaker again like I had been when I was five. I realize now that everyone did their part to help keep that spirit in the home. It was a special blessing, and we didn't want to lose it.

I think that because of our experience with Zion all of us took the gospel more seriously in our lives. I believe the reason all the Manwaring kids have turned out fine wasn't because of Mom's strictness, nor Dad's teaching. Those helped us, but the desire to know and live the gospel (the seed planted by our parents) we began to nourish on our own because of our experience with Zion. I was too afraid to ask God if the things I had been taught all my life were true until I was sixteen, because if I got a negative answer it meant that I would have to leave all I loved and cherished including the comfort that I knew Zion was in paradise awaiting to join God in His celestial kingdom. Eventually, I mustered up the courage to overcome this fear, and I did ask God. I am so grateful He answered me, and I know I can see Zion again.

At first when people would ask how many children are in our family, I would say five, but for the longest time now I say six. Most of my friends know the story, but I feel more comfortable talking to people about her as compared to a few years ago.

In my room at home on the wall was Zion's poster which the nurse or social worker at the hospital had made for her. Sometimes I would lie on the ground staring at it for a long time. I would go over the memories I had of her, of Moriah racing from the kitchen to the fence that had the secret gate where we boys were playing, to tell us she had been born, to visiting her in the hospital in Salt Lake, to having Dad lift up her diaper, and Sam crinkling his nose when he found out what it means to be a girl. I remember Halloween night when we were happily enjoying the evening and after returning home we went outside to say goodbye to some visitors (the stake presidents and their wives). I had grabbed the air horn from his car and blown it. We went in and soon discovered Zion was not breathing or moving. I immediately wondered if I had caused her to have a heart attack because of the loud noise from outside, but according to the nurse, it had been a slow process leading up to then.

Zion made my life more bearable. I hated doing chores all the time, not being recognized for the things I did well, being punished for my misdeeds. I often felt miserable and misunderstood. She helped me look outside of myself for the first time and want to help others. Because of her influence and my character, I always knew I was going to serve a mission for the Lord. It was never a question, just a fact of life.

During my mission in Bolivia, it was hard. I cried so much for loneliness, being in a place far away with no one who could understand me, let alone English. I eventually learned that through the priesthood we have the right to the ministering of angels. Zion was our angel, and whenever I felt overwhelmed and misunderstood and alone with my companions, I would pray that the Lord might allow Zion to watch over me that night as I slept. I remember in La Frontera, a branch [small congregation] I served in on the border between Bolivia and Brazil near Corumbá, I felt her present in the room. I knew she was watching over me. The next morning my companion asked me what I had prayed for during my nightly prayers.

When I told him I had asked for the ministering of angels, he told me, "Elder, I woke up during the night, and when I turned toward you, there was a light over you." I haven't really shared this story before. That was one of my most sacred experiences on my mission.

I know God is real, and I know family relations are retained after the grave and that our love for each other does not die with our bodies. I don't know all the doctrine behind God allowing visits from beyond the veil, but I do know that Zion loves our family very much, maybe more than we all realize. I know our faith and knowledge and obedience light the way before us and can rid the path of impediments for our family, friends, and people around us. For me, Zion, along with God, was a light that kept the darkness at bay, from swallowing me up in my own depression and self-absorption. Knowing that someone was on my side allowed me to get through the day.

While at BYU-Idaho, I've had many a chance to visit her grave. While I don't go as often as I should, the times I do go are full of self-reflection. It's nice to know that while life moves on she can be a stone that never wavers but stays. It's good to see her and converse with her at her headstone. She represents where I want to go, which is eternal life with God. I'm grateful to have had her in our family, and I pray that all our family will join her in God's Kingdom. I'd say the odds are hopeful, since I feel like I'd be the most likely of my siblings to fall away, and yet truly, I could never deny God or the Gospel.

I'm not sure of all that my Dad hopes to accomplish with this book, but if it helps anyone who has ever lost a loved one before their time seems due, trust in God, and trust in your loved one. Things will work out because they're part of God's plan. I know it sounds cliché, but that doesn't make it not true. I know from experience that our lives have been better because of how things went with Zion. If you feel inconsolable, we've been there. While seeking help from others is appropriate, use this moment to live how God wants you to live in order to have the confidence necessary to believe that you'll see your loved one again. 🤟

SAMUEL'S THOUGHTS ABOUT ZION

At the time of this writing, Samuel is a missionary in Quito, Ecuador, serving the Lord and his fellowmen. He wrote us a letter which he felt perfectly expressed the feelings of his heart. Unfortunately, the letter never made it to us. After months of waiting, we determined it must have been lost in the mail. He was hesitant to attempt to recreate that letter because he felt like he could not do as good a job with a new one. He has since sent a new letter, but in the interim, we also were given a copy of a letter he wrote to a friend here at home about his thoughts of Zion. I now have two letters that I will try to present without overlapping too much. To his friend, he wrote:

Being away from my family for seven months or so has really helped me to appreciate them and love them even more. I don't know if I've ever shared with you the story of my little sister. Her name was Zion. My mom was expecting her birth in the year 2006, at the time she was at an "advanced age" to be delivering a child. But my siblings and I were all super excited to get another sister. It soon became evident after a lot of tests that the pregnancy would be complicated. My sister would be born with heart defects and Down syndrome. To me, being eight years old, that didn't matter. I just wanted another sister to love and adore. We sought the best medical advice and facility on this side of the Rockies at Primary Children's Hospital in Salt Lake City, Utah. Her birth went considerably well, and Zion's life was in a stable condition for the time being (hooked up to a LOT of tubes and wires). As my whole family was there at the hospital, we were able to enjoy our new sister's presence. It was a time where my family was more united than ever.

It became apparent that the defect in Zion's heart had to be corrected or she would have a short life. The doctor said there was a medical procedure that could be performed, but due to my sister being an infant, it had an extremely, extremely high mortality rate.

Our family decided then to enjoy my little sister's company as long as we possibly could without surgery. After a little less than a week of being in the hospital, we took her back to the comfort of our home in Idaho. I remember going down to her cradle at night and just thinking and enjoying her peaceful company.

At this point the narrative of Samuel's letter to his friend is followed by the (second) letter he sent us for inclusion in this book:

On this day in September, almost eleven years after Cherish Zion's coming to this world, I find myself looking at some photos of her and reflecting on my feelings and the experiences I shared with my sister. We nicknamed her "our littlest angel," as appears on her headstone. I think it was because she was always so incredibly peaceful. I would say it's also because she brought a certain, almost palpable tranquility into our home.

My most cherished memories with my little sister Zion all happened in our family home in Twin Falls, Idaho. One such experience was after spending some time as a family (scripture study?), and I distinctly remember walking into the darkened room where Zion was sleeping in her crib. Being eight years old at the time, one could say I wasn't spiritually mature. But I do know I was very spiritually receptive and tender to the comfort brought by the Spirit. As I stood over Zion's crib for a long time (I don't remember if it was a handful of minutes or nearly an hour), I felt the comfort of the Holy Ghost. I enjoyed being alone with my baby sister because I could feel the presence of her pure spirit seemingly radiating from her. To this day, it impresses me that I was able to recognize this so clearly, having been recently baptized just a few months before her birth, and given the gift of the constant presence of the Holy Ghost. It impresses me even more that a newborn baby could bring such an overwhelming tranquility to our home, even to my very soul.

Another experience I clearly remember was coming to my dad with a tender question: "Why can't God heal [Zion's] heart?" There are two ways one can interpret this question. The first puts God's power, might, and capability into question – at the same time acknowledging that He has the power to heal. The second questions His will, His plan. At my young and tender age, maybe it was a mix of the two. I had never had anything test my faith to such a degree before. I wanted my dad to help me find an answer. My dad, Paul Manwaring, is a just man of great faith who has a profound understanding of Christ's doctrine and the nature of God. But when I asked him that question, he simply hugged me, and said, "I don't know." We just sat there and had a "good cry," as my dad described it. It was one of the most tender moments of my life there with my dad as I realized what it meant to turn over one's will to the Lord, and trust him that whatever happens, it's for our own good, our own benefit. It's important to understand that I love my little sister, and I wanted so badly for her to not be in this condition, and just be a normal baby and live a normal life. But, as an eight-year-old, I learned a very sobering lesson, the same that Jesus learned (Mark 14:36): "Abba, Father, all things are possible unto thee; take away this cup from me: nevertheless, not what I will, but what thou wilt." It's heart-wrenching but comforting at the same time. "Not my will, but thine be done..." It helped me a lot to accept God's will, no matter what would happen. This was a grand and priceless lesson for me.

On October 31, 2006, my siblings and I went every which way to celebrate Halloween and load our candy stashes for the following few months. If I remember right, it was very cold for being October, and everyone in my family ended up returning home a little earlier than we might have. That, in and of itself, was a miracle in my mind. My little sister had started to fade away as we all gathered in our living room. It was incredibly heart-wrenching as she drifted away from us, her beloved earthly family, and returned to the presence of her Heavenly Father. I will forever remember what the nurse (Ann Babble?) said when she soon after listened for a heartbeat that wasn't there. "Poor little girl" was the simple, poignant, and teary-eyed statement that was left in the official moment of her passing.

I remember holding Zion's body for an instant and weeping because her pallid frame was all that was left behind. It was incredibly tough for me, and I remember crying myself to sleep that night, probably the only time in my life I've ever done that. At this moment, I can't keep tears from coming as I relive in my mind this incredibly tender experience – so key in my spiritual development. A pain so deep like this can only be filled by the peace of the marvelous gospel of Jesus Christ.

Cherish Zion, in her short eleven days here on earth, was

never able to walk, nor talk, nor have much experience in life. But in those eleven days, she must have felt more love from her family than most people would have in a lifetime.

I love this gospel of Jesus Christ because I don't have to keep those feelings of loss and sadness in my heart from when my little sister passed. I <u>know</u> I will see her again. I <u>know</u> there will be a resurrection in which she will receive a perfect and glorified body. Above all, I <u>know</u> that families are made eternal through the sealing power of the Holy Priesthood in God's sacred temples. The Holy Ghost has confirmed this truth to me many times, and I'm infinitely grateful that my parents are sealed in the temple to each other and to all my brothers and sisters. I know that in God's presence, we will be able to enjoy Zion together for an eternity and be infinitely happy.

From that experience I learned that death really has no lasting sting if we are sealed together as eternal families. I love my sister Zion so much, and I can't wait to see her again and give her a big hug. In the name of Jesus Christ, Amen.

Sincerely,
Elder Samuel Manwaring 2017

I am grateful to Samuel for those personal and tender thoughts he shared in his letter to us. In his letter to his friend, Samuel closed with the following thoughts:

After my sister's funeral, I was sitting in the very back of the car with my cousin just kind of staring off into the night. I remember promising to myself with fresh tears rolling down my cheeks that no matter what, I would always remember Zion in whatever way I could.

JACOB'S THOUGHTS ABOUT ZION

Because Jacob was so young when we had Zion with us, we were still in that stage of his life when we would say prayers with him each night before he went to bed. I remember that for at least the next two years after Zion passed away, Jacob prayed for his sister. Ruth wrote the words he offered in one of his prayers only a couple of weeks after Zion was gone: "I'm thankful for my little sister. That Zion could be in my family – that she could bring love to our home. I'm glad she could be in my life."

Jacob says he does not remember a lot of detail, but he recalls how the experience influenced him. He shares the following:

I was excited for a baby sister! The addition of a little sister to the already large Manwaring family would mean that lots of family was going to visit us, which was always exciting as a little kid. This meant that my favorite cousins, who were all my age, would be there to celebrate her birth. Although I did not understand the full gravity of the situation, I was still excited to welcome a younger sibling into my life.

The spirit I felt that first day I met my little sister in the hospital was undeniably extraordinary--one that I have trouble describing but no trouble remembering. In the mortal vocabulary, I doubt that there will ever be a word to describe this sensation, only in God's dictionary can it be found. I'm sure God uses this word every day to describe His love for each one of His children. I'm very grateful for my sister and for the love I've been able to feel every time I think about her. Although I don't have a perfect memory, I know that she has changed my life, and I know I will be able to return to her once more, in a better world with all those I love.

What I remember most from my scattered memory of my childhood is the family pictures, especially the pictures with just her and me. When I would hold her, I would feel a connection I've never felt since. I believe such a connection has to do with the thinning of the veil, a close connection between her perfect spirit and my sometimes-tattered spirit. I truly do believe this because every time I think of her and these memories, I can feel her closely as if her true spirit is next to me, the same as it was that day in the front room. That was a day to remember, the calm and reverent quiet family atmosphere, and just an overall feeling of happiness. My memories of my little sister could best be described as standing in a room full of light, holding a crystal bowl filled with water, peering into that bowl and seeing images about our time together, while simultaneously being surrounded by those scenes and enveloped by light. Though the brightness can be physically discerned with my eyes, it is best seen with the heart. I try to remember if there was ever a time when I was with my little sister that I was not overjoyed or unceasingly happy, but that memory does not exist. Blame it on the innocence of a child's mind, but the eye of a child can only see the purity and beauty of life.

I feel impressed to add my testimony about the Second Coming of Christ. I have a strong testimony of the Second Coming, the Resurrection, and life after death. I believe that if you have a strong testimony of these things, everything else will fall into place. This is because everything we do, every choice we make, and every word we say, we must do with an eternal perspective. Where many get stuck is in the past and present. They don't care for those things which will truly bring them happiness in the long run, but are seeking after instant gratification. That is why I am blessed to have a sister that helps me to keep an eternal viewpoint. She has helped me to become stronger. She has helped me to become more kind. She has helped me not give up. But most importantly, she has helped me become who I am today. For that, I can only say thank you to my dearest and only little sister, Zion. We love you. I am imperfect, but I am trying to be better, to make you happy, and to make myself happy. Thank you for your constant reminders and for sticking close and not giving up. You are missed, but you are not forgotten.

Zion, I love you.

Jacob wrote the following poem about his sister Zion:

My Fellow Kin
I feel her 'round me day by day,
Wondering, when I meet her, What will I say?
Will I recognize her? Where to begin?
What if I forget about my "fellow kin?"

Every day, I'm enlisted in a battle
To begin, live, and endure – free of sin
And when I emerge victorious, though tattered
I will be reunited, with my fellow kin.

CHAPTER 16

"Your Life Will ... Influence Many"

For many years, I have known this was a book we needed to write. I have felt it was important in fulfilling the part of Zion's blessing that said, "We bless you that your short life will accomplish great good in this world for a long time to come, and that there will be a rippling effect which will influence many and be the means to build faith, testimony, and a deep and abiding trust in a loving Heavenly Father and His Son Jesus Christ."

I have felt guilty at times for letting so much time pass, but I am glad for the perspective the intervening years have given me. I am now able to share a couple examples of how this statement has begun to be fulfilled.

Many Hearts are Touched
It wasn't until I began accumulating the various journal entries and other writings that I noticed something Ruth repeated often: She

didn't want Zion's life to be forgotten. It was her heartfelt desire that Zion's life would matter to others beyond herself.

Ruth has been gratified by evidence that Zion's life indeed has made an impact on others, and that she is remembered by many. In Ruth's words:

> *The cards we received then and in the weeks and months (and years) that followed would warm our hearts and souls. As Paul describes it, each card was like a hug from Heavenly Father. Through other people, God was showing us that He loved us and Zion and that she had mattered and her life had been a force for good for many besides us. We truly are His hands when we reach out and care for one another. That was made manifest to us before, during, and after Zion's journey with us.*

There were literally dozens upon dozens of cards that were given or mailed to us. Many cards came during or after the funeral. Most of them were addressed to the family, some of them to individual children. There were cards from people we know, and many from those we did not know, random people who read the obituary or heard about our situation from a friend. The cards came randomly in the following months. The following is a sample of what was received.

❦

"For one who lived such a brief time, her life has touched so many."

❦

"Maybe a 'Thank You' note seems odd at this time, but our family would like to thank yours for sharing your little baby girl with everyone before her journey back to heaven. Your family is truly an inspiration to us and always has been in facing our own trials."

❦

"The name she was given is what she radiated. Cherish the memories you had with her. I know she touched my life ... Thank you for sharing a tiny portion of her life with us."

❦

"My parents sent us the funeral program of your beautiful little angel Cherish. Even from the program her huge spirit emanates and makes my heart tender."

❦

"Cherish Zion – what an awesome name!"

❦

Adria's Dream

In an earlier chapter, I referred to the dream of Adria Sumsion. She had that dream while Ruth was struggling with accepting the pregnancy. Even though she told Ruth about it at that time, she wrote it down and gave it to Ruth after Zion had passed away. It was another tender mercy, both as a premonition and as a postscript. Zion had a powerful influence on Adria, who has continued to express as much in the years since. She addresses her letter to Zion:

Dear Zion,

I am writing to you in spirit today to add a little to your life story. It's a beautiful story with a forever ending...

I first became acquainted with your mother while serving with her in Primary. How blessed I am to be influenced by her faith and testimony of this true gospel. She is faithful, committed, and knowledgeable as she serves the Lord – she shared with you the same light and countenance that I recognized in you. "The magic" that was missing after your passing is the same magic she emanates now. What a gift to have chosen each other as mother and daughter.

Your mother and I were making Primary visits one Sunday afternoon when I decided to tell her about a dream I had – It was about you, Zion. For some reason, I was made aware that you would bless this family with your coming. I remember seeing you in your mother's arms. You were sleeping and peaceful. Your hair was dark and golden, your features perfect. You looked like a Manwaring with your almond shaped eyes, and your little hand was wrapped around your mother's finger. We had a brief discussion and then I remember coming into your home where, all of a sudden, you were a little older – able to walk and run through your house. As I approached your mother to visit with her, I remember you went running, almost dancing by us through the living room and then quickly up the stairs. You were so quick, in fact, I only saw your hair bouncing behind you and that you had a dress on with a beautiful ruffle on the bottom. The only other detail I remember is your mother saying, "She fills our home with happiness" – and of that I have no question.

We miss you, but nothing like how your family misses you. Most of all your mother. You do fill your home with happiness, and although I did not know how your earthly story would end, I do know how your heavenly one will. You are special – your family is special, and I cannot wait to meet you in your true spiritual stature.

Lovingly,
Adria Sumsion - Family Friend

"I Love You"

I share with you now something I could have related much earlier in this book, but it seems more appropriate here. It has to do with my hand after I lost my fingers in the snow-blower accident. The configuration of my hand after the trauma is very interesting. I lost the end of my index finger at the first knuckle, which left it about as long as my pinky finger. The middle two fingers were lost at the middle knuckles. When I hold my hand up with my thumb out, it looks very much like Zion's hand cast – the American Sign Language symbol for "I Love You." I share this feature with my daughter: a message of love from my Heavenly Father. Like the message Zion left us, and the message that God also left us through Zion, my hand is a constant reminder of Him, of His love, of Zion, and the blessing she is to us.

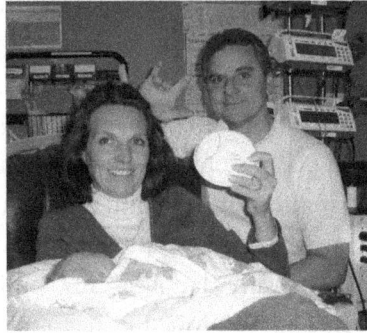

I did not realize this resemblance right away. There were certain children I knew before my accident that I had always "high-fived." After the accident, I couldn't say, "Give me five." So, I said, "Give me two and three halves." It was amusing to see them try to shape their hand into something similar to mine. In the process, we saw what they created through this effort. It was the ASL sign for "I love you." I eventually just said, "Give me some love," as we greeted each other. I have told people when I wave at them, I am just saying "I love you."

The physical symbol of Zion's life, for us, has become the hand cast and the ASL message, "I love you." Because of this connection with Zion, this has also become a constant in our communication with our children. As they have been away at college, we video chat with them each week. Every conversation ends with holding up my hand to say, "I love you." They, in turn, sign the same as their farewell. This is a natural reminder that always draws the memory of

Zion into our conversations. We are perpetually reminded of the love we shared with her when she was alive, and her continued influence in our lives as we strive for that high-water mark of love one for another. To me, this is another miracle and certainly a great tender mercy from a compassionate Father in Heaven. It lends meaning and purpose to the accident I had. Was there a divine intent in the formation of my hand through that accident? Perhaps. But all the same, I am grateful for the hand I am left with and how it connects me with my daughter, my family, and the rest of humanity. Every day, I am reminded of her, and I am grateful we had her in our life. Every day, I am reminded to love my fellow men. Every day, I am also reminded of the love that God has for me.

My brother Mike sent a piece of art to me. It now hangs on our wall next to photos of Zion. It is one of my favorites. It is a picture of Christ's hand, with the message he left for us through his suffering and sacrifice. It is entitled "Greater Love," in reference to the scripture that states, "Greater love hath no man than this, that a man lay down his life for his friends."[1]

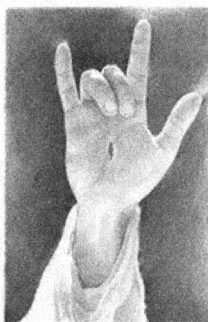

GREATER LOVE

Charity Anywhere

We have tried to use our memories and lessons of Zion to become better people and to serve others. As the next year progressed and

---

1. John 15:13.

we moved forward with our lives, we were grateful for the opportunities we found to serve others. I had become acquainted with a wonderful couple living in Twin Falls, Gordon and Susan Carter, who had formed an organization called the *Charity Anywhere Foundation.* They had come a couple of times over the years to speak to the college-age students about service opportunities and to share the work they were doing through their foundation. One of the annual volunteer opportunities for students was to travel to Tijuana, Mexico, over the Christmas break, to build homes for people in need. Because this was a charity, the participants provided their own funding. The cost was not much, but it covered travel to Mexico, room and board, and the cost of the materials for building the homes. Knowing the scanty means of most students, Gordon made the suggestion to the students that if any of them were interested and they lacked the funds, perhaps the students could tell their parents they did not want any Christmas presents that year but preferred their parents use the money they would have spent on gifts for them to pay for them to go serve others. I thought this was a great idea. What an opportunity to develop greater selflessness. In talking with Gordon, I also found out they accepted the help of families as well.

Because we felt so blessed to have had Zion in our lives, we wanted to say "thank you" to God for His kindness and all the blessings we had received through that experience. These thanks were offered daily in our prayers, in fact, in every prayer. When we knelt with the younger children every evening beside their beds, this was always stated by each of them, "Thank you, Heavenly Father, for letting us have Zion in our lives." There are so many ways to say thank you, but I learned a long time ago, as a young adult, a phrase I have remembered and repeated often over the years: "If you would love God and desire to show Him that you love Him, then you must learn to love and serve your fellowman. For only by so doing can you truly show your love for God."

I thought, "Let's suggest to the children that we show our gratitude to our Heavenly Father by not having presents for ourselves this
next Christmas but use the money we would have spent on ourselves
to help build a house for someone in Tijuana, Mexico." I defer to Ruth
to tell what happened at the end of the 2007. This is what she wrote in
our annual letter to family and friends at the beginning of 2008:

New Year 2008

*Knowing our Christmas would be different this year, we didn't
stress about getting our traditional letter out until after the
holidays.*

*About four years ago, Paul came home and told me about
an annual trip to Tijuana each Christmas that Charity Anywhere sponsors to build "homes" for needy families, and Paul
said how much he wanted our family to do this some Christmas.
At that time, Jacob was three, and I thought Paul had lost his
marbles. "There is no way you're going to get the kids to give
up their Christmas to charity," I solemnly proclaimed. But Paul
persisted and earlier in 2007, we determined as a family this was
the year to travel to Mexico. Seven passports later, we arrived
early Christmas Day in San Diego and then left the comforts of
the United States and crossed the border into Mexico.*

*A little background: The Catholic church built a hospital
in the Tijuana suburb called Miramar but have been unable
to maintain it as a working hospital. Gordon Carter made
arrangements with the Padre for his Charity Anywhere groups
to stay at the hospital in exchange for paying the monthly utility bills. Our group was about eighty people, mostly college
students. There was a large group of high school seniors and
then various families.*

*After our arrival at the hospital, we unloaded our very
jam-packed van (we had gone through our house and found*

MUCH we wanted to give away) into two different rooms, and Gordon walked us down the hill into "the valley of the shadow of death."

We spoke to Rosa. Rosa had approached Gordon earlier and shown him a "lot" she owned and wanted to have a home built on for her family of five children. Gordon thought this was a great project for our family and began negotiations with Rosa. Think with me ... Gordon doesn't speak Spanish, Rosa doesn't speak English, I can understand un pocito (muy marlo), and Moriah is in her second year of Spanish and very timid. They sent for Victoria to translate. She was a neighbor in this little "village," had three teeth in her mouth, and did help us to make very basic arrangements.

"Yes," they did own the lot; "Yes," they would have the old rusty food concessions trailer moved by tomorrow; "Two rooms with a cement floor"; "Yes, they could get water for mixing cement"; and "Yes, we could use the sand pile by the lot for cement."

Well, after we climbed back out of the valley, Gordon then had us drive down to our "site" so Paul would be able to give directions to the building supply driver to get our materials delivered. We were scraping the bottom of the van on the rocks of the gully we were driving over. We headed back to the building supply to place our order for building materials for tomorrow. I hadn't thought to pack hammers or other tools, but we did have gloves.

I was beginning to see how full of faith Gordon is. He fully expected our family to build Rosa's family a house. I don't build homes; I clean them. My kids don't build homes; they mess them. Paul seemed undaunted and quickly came up with a rudimentary floor plan and rough estimates of materials. And he had the foresight to rent a cement mixer.

...Friday morning, we all hiked down and found lines scratched in the sand of Rosa's lot in the dimensions the father wanted (12 feet by 24, it would have fit in our living room back home). The trailer was still there so we worked around it. Paul started laying the forms.

Gordon explained to Rosa and her husband they would need to pay fifty dollars a month for three years, "like Habitat for Humanity." "Yes, we can do that. No problem." Gordon is happy too, because this family is benefitted by owning their home instead of paying someone else fifty dollars a month in rent for a one-room shack with a dirt floor.

Rosa's oldest son, Jorge, was my "bien, travajo cabello" (my good work horse). When we got to the site, we found we needed shovels, picks (pickos), wheelbarrows, etc. Jorge would disappear for a few minutes and then reappear with the needed items. Whatever you needed, someone had it. They knew who had what, and they shared it.

While those of us who could wield shovels and move wheelbarrows worked, the little guys got acquainted with the kids

who congregated to our "site." I asked the natives to teach my kids Spanish and began with some simple words. "Rabbit, como se dice rabbit en Espanol?" "Conejo" "Oh yeah, y teeth?" "Dientes" "Tongue?" "Lengua", etc.

After getting the pad poured, most of us rounded up our tools and things and headed back up the hill to clean up and wait for dinner. But those energetic teenage boys were challenged to a game of soccer with the locals, on their turf – the street. I understand it was a good match, and the gringos learned from the natives some slick moves.

The next day (Saturday), the frame began to go up. The gang worked long after dark trying to get up all the wall frames. A college student, Justin, and his group joined up with us to speed the work along. They were prepared and had brought their own hammers and tools from the States.

Our last day of good labor was New Year's Eve (also Adam's birthday). Our group headed down to the site, and Myrna and I headed off to Costco to get Adam a birthday cake. Unfortunately, we got there too early, and I took the first and only sheet cake they had ready, which read "Happy New Year" instead of "Happy Birthday." But I figured they both applied.

Monday ... that was the day they got the roof on. Gordon had given some of us a ride down, and as we headed back up, he offered a ride to whomever and Nyal took him up on it. Gordon shared with us a bit of their conversation. When Gordon asked Nyal what he thought about the neighborhood, referencing the sewage running in the street, the small shacks, the garbage in the gully they'd been playing in for days, the squalor, lack of running water, electricity, etc., Nyal surprised him with his response. "Oh, I wish my neighborhood was like this back home. There are so many kids my age to play with.

It's great, I don't want to leave!"

The next morning after getting the van loaded up, we made our final trip into the valley of the shadow of death for the home dedication. Because it was New Year's Day, many of the local men were home. Rosa's husband was there, and Myrna had come to translate the events and explain the dedication/blessing.

Paul took a moment to explain why we had determined to spend our Christmas here, away from home and hearth and loved ones. He explained how a little over a year ago, we had a little daughter born into our family. Quite an unexpected arrival, but with some surprises come quite unexpected challenges and blessings.

Paul told them about Cherish Zion and her heart problems that only allowed her to stay with us a short time. He related how she changed our lives and God blessed  us in so many ways with her short life. We felt we wanted to show our gratitude to Him for our littlest angel and chose to serve others this holiday season. Just as so many had lifted and shared our burdens and joys, we wanted to do the same for someone else. Paul explained the matching shirts we had printed up and that all our family were wearing that day. The saying on the back came from an Institute council theme a student had come up with years earlier. I had not understood the sentence until Zion entered our lives.

"LIVE BEYOND THE DREAM ... TOGETHER
IT'S A ZION THING"

This has become a family motto.

On the front of our shirts was an outline of the shape of Zion's hand from the plaster mold in the perfect ASL sign/shape for "I love you." This sign has become particularly significant to our family when just eleven months before Zion's birth, Paul's hand had been chewed up in a snow blower accident that left it permanently in that "I love you" shape. Her little hand mold is now our family symbol. Hence, we had on our Zion shirts in her memory at this little 12 X 24 structure Rosa's family would soon call home.

As we gathered that last night in a Tijuana chapel and shared with one another what projects we were all doing, I will never forget Gordon's words to us upon returning to our homes that we might feel "dirty guilty" to walk into our walk-in closets which were bigger than the homes we were building for these families. Our family felt it a privilege and blessing to share so little of all we have been blessed with. We have the gospel, a temple marriage, comforts beyond our needs or wants, and freedom to do whatever, whenever. We hope we never feel ungrateful again.

I am so grateful to Gordon and those who go and do what they can with what they have and bless a slight number. "We *can't do everything for everyone everywhere, but we can do something for someone somewhere."[2]*

The motto for the Charity Anywhere Foundation is "Be Good, Do Good." We love that phrase and often repeat it or use it in written communications.

Samuel's Mission Experience

One sample of how Zion's life has continued to influence others comes from our son Samuel, through an email we received from him as a missionary in Ecuador. He shared with us the story of a young man, Maikol. They had been teaching him along with his girlfriend Evelyn, who was expecting a baby. Maikol's life has been very difficult. He grew up in extreme poverty with a drunken father and abusive parents. As a child and youth, he never really knew happiness. He would often sleep on the side of the jungle road instead of going home to sleep. One time, he was taken to the police station because the neighbors got mad that he was always picking their fruit, driven by desperation and hunger. The only bright spot in his life was a little sister whom he dearly loved. When he was a teenager, his little sister suddenly died. It totally devastated him, so much so that he turned to a self-destructive, promiscuous, and drunken lifestyle. He continued on that path for years. After meeting my son and his missionary companion and listening to their message of hope, Maikol was deeply touched and has embraced what he has been taught. He is making much different decisions now and acting in accordance with a newfound faith. His life dramatically changed.

I think about how Samuel has had life experiences that allow him to be understanding and compassionate in his acceptance and teaching of others. I could almost see him intently listening to Maikol tell his story, see his empathy for Maikol having lost a sister, and understanding the resulting pain and effect it had on Maikol's life. After Maikol finished sharing his story, Samuel writes: "With tears

---

2. Richard L. Evans, *Quote Book* (Publishers Press, 1971), 51.

in his eyes he told us, 'Thank you! You are my best brothers, my best friends. Without you, I would still be very sad and desperate. Thank you for helping me change my life!'"

As I read these words of appreciation for my son, I was deeply touched and very grateful that he has had this privilege of having such a profound effect on others. Those are significant words – "my best friends, thank you for helping me change my life." Samuel was deeply touched by the love he felt for this young man and his family. He continues,

> *When he said that, I felt the Spirit so strongly and tears came to my eyes as I felt God's love so powerfully for Maikol and Evelyn. It really helped me to recognize WHY I am here in Ecuador. I know that it isn't by coincidence that I was sent here and found this wonderful family. It was one of the most meaningful moments I have had in my whole mission, for that matter, my whole life. After Maikol finished telling us his story, we sang together one of my favorite hymns, "Families Can Be Together Forever," and helped them to understand that he'll be able to live with his sister again. I love the gospel, and I love the power of the Holy Spirit that influences God's children to act, to change. I know that my companion and I haven't done anything special or anything of our own accord. We simply follow and teach by the Spirit. Miracles have happened.*

I feel this is another ripple that extends outward from the formative experiences of Samuel's young life, of which, as you have witnessed, Zion was an important part.

Dad

Zion had found a soft spot in my father's heart. He was a loving and caring grandfather to her in the few days we had with her. As I look back on the hospital pictures, I realize this even more. He attended each major event of her life and death. He took it very hard when she passed away. He sought out and purchased written material on dealing with the death of a grandchild.

My father had made certain poor choices over many years causing significant and lasting harm to family members. His grave mistakes also caused him much personal pain and regret. The price he paid in terms of remorse, repentance, and restitution was measured, not just in months or years, but in decades. In fact, he spent the rest of his life trying to set things right to the best of his ability. I watched him change ever so gradually as his gratitude for and reliance on the Savior's Atonement deepened. He was grateful when he had opportunities to do something for his family.

My father developed kidney disease, which progressed in the following years. As his kidneys deteriorated and became less and less effective in filtering his life's blood, he was given his options. He could go on dialysis, or he could forego any treatment. My dad is a very meticulous planner, and he did all the research he could on dialysis. He asked the right people pertinent questions and studied out his options. In the end, he decided he did not want to do dialysis. From his research, he saw that his whole life could revolve around dialysis. He felt like he was ready to meet God whenever it was his natural time. He had lived over eighty years and did not fear death or what was on the other side of the veil of mortality. His doctors told him he would have about a year and a half of life if he chose to forego treatment. He had time to prepare. Part of that preparation included divesting himself of his worldly goods.

In June of 2012, I decided to spend some time with my father. The doctors figured that he might pass away in the early fall. With this knowledge, I valued the time I spent with Dad in Salt Lake City. I found him at peace with his situation. We went through some of his belongings to decide what to keep and what to give to charities, what would be valuable for family and what would not. We were able to visit and reminisce about important things. He told me about his own father, Paul Walker Manwaring, who had died just months before I was born. I was named after him. He spoke of how his father had been injured on army training maneuvers during World War II and then years later suffered a stroke related to that injury. My father was serving in the military in Oklahoma when he was notified that his father was not doing well. He obtained leave and was able to get to the hospital in Utah just in time to be there for his father's last few breaths. As he shared the details of his father's death, he was filled with emotion and cried as he relived that moment of passing. I saw my father as a son that day and gained a new perspective of him. I am so glad I took the time to be with him.

A month later, my family was planning a vacation that would take us through Salt Lake City. Ruth was already there, and the kids and I would pick her up and continue our vacation together. While Ruth was in Salt Lake, my father experienced major physical set-backs that hastened his decline. Ruth called me and said the doctors were giving him only a few weeks to live. During our drive to Salt Lake, she called again. The doctors had reassessed his status and now gave him only a few days. I arrived with the kids and found my father very weak. He was in and out of sleep. I was able to sit and talk with him for a few minutes. He was aware of my presence, although he was able to speak but very little. He then lay back down and went to sleep. My mother was there also, and so was a hospice nurse. When we first arrived, the nurse told us he had only a day or two left to live. Things had changed rapidly, and he was on a downward spiral. After being with my father for only a few minutes, the nurse updated the diagnosis. She said that he would pass away within the hour. Dad was resting peacefully, but the signs of an ebbing life were evident to her trained eye and experience.

My mother looked at me and asked, "Can you give your father a blessing?" My dear mother had been my father's primary caregiver in his final days. These two good people had raised a large family of seven boys together and had been through so much in life. Would

I give my father a blessing? "Of course," I replied. And so, I knelt on one side of my father, my mother was on the other side holding Dad's hand. I laid my hands upon his head and gave him a solemn blessing.

I told my father that his mortal life was coming to a close. I expressed to him my love and appreciation for all the good he had taught me, lessons that will always be treasured. I felt that he could hear my words. I assured him there were many others just beyond the veil who were waiting for his arrival: his father, his mother, and many other relatives. I then said, "Dad, there is also a little girl who is waiting to welcome you – our daughter, your granddaughter Zion. It is her privilege to greet you. Please give her a hug from us." I then said, "Dad, it is okay to let go. I release you from this mortal life."

My father passed away quietly under my hands as I completed the blessing. Once again, I felt a peace that accompanied this moment of sadness and loss. I am so grateful for the comfort God grants us when we need it and ask for it. "Sweet is the peace the gospel brings."

My children were present at my father's passing. It happened all so suddenly that no one had time to ask if anyone wanted to be excused. We were together as a family. In fact, there was a lot of family present, including those unseen, but not unfelt, on the other side of the veil. I felt amazingly close to Zion at that bittersweet moment. I literally passed my father on to her, practically touching each other through that veil that separates us all from our loved ones for a brief period. At times like this, the veil of death – where time touches eternity – seems very thin indeed. Death brings us all to this threshold. In Zion's blessing she had been told, "We bless you that you will become our family's guardian angel to watch over us, to bless us to come and join you in our [Heavenly] Father's presence. You will be blessed to greet your grandparents as well." This part of her blessing was being fulfilled. I am sure it was a happy reunion. I can just picture my father being led by a little girl holding his finger and showing him the wonders of a paradise she has already become very familiar with.

We had arrived only forty-five minutes before my father passed away. As I look back on it, it was an honor for me to be there for him and to represent my six brothers who were not able to get there soon enough. It also seemed right that I had the privilege of helping him reconnect with his mother whom I had been very close to in her life and with his father, my grandfather and namesake. Ironically, it was a repeat in some respects of the death of his own father – a son arriving just moments before his passing.

Future Generations

In the past few years, my mind has turned more and more to my future posterity, to the generations yet unborn. My great desire is for my children to be faithful to the principles I have come to understand, believe, and cherish. I would not spare them the challenges of life, but I wish for them to have the strength, ability, and the keys of knowledge to meet those challenges and in the process become more like Christ. It is my heart's greatest desire that my posterity be happy – not just my children, but my grandchildren for multiple generations. I believe this can be realized if they will embrace the principles of faith upon which true happiness is based. I believe there is a greater likelihood of this happening for each succeeding generation if the children are taught while young and have their own validating experiences. If they have these truths firmly planted and nurtured in their hearts, then our children will teach them to their children, and so on. I also know it is only possible to personally pass these truths on if we sincerely believe them, love them, and live them ourselves. If our children see that we love something, and it has been a blessing to us, then it becomes more likely they will love it, too. We must teach them and share with them our thoughts and our feelings.

I acknowledge that we cannot force our beliefs on our children. They must choose for themselves. Sometimes they choose counter to our wishes, despite all our best efforts. All we can do is follow the admonition of the scripture to exercise our influence over them "by persuasion, by long-suffering, by gentleness and meekness, and by love unfeigned; by kindness and pure knowledge … that [they] may know that thy faithfulness is stronger than the cords of death."[3]

This book is a legacy that I hope will connect me with my future generations and in some small way fulfill the words of the Old Testament prophet Malachi: "And [the lord] shall turn the heart of the fathers to the children, and the heart of the children to their fathers…"[4] Zion's life, the lessons we have learned, and the concepts surrounding the meaning of her name are the very things I cherish and would have my posterity cherish, too. How will they know about any of this unless I write it down for them to be read from generation to generation?

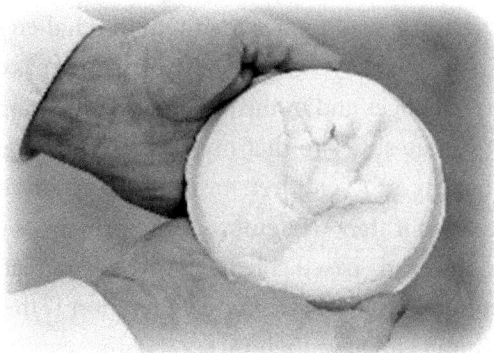

---

3. Doctrine and Covenants 121:41-44.
4. Malachi 4:6.

CHAPTER 17

Cherishing Zion

Each of our children's names has a story and a special meaning. This was important to Ruth and me as we considered naming children. We did not want to select names just because they sounded nice or unique. We wanted our children to have names they could be proud of, something to live up to. For example, our son Adam's name is actually Adamson Paul Manwaring. The name Adamson is my mother's maiden name (and my middle name). We have always told him that the name Adamson should remind him of his grandmother, my mother, who is a wonderful, extraordinary woman full of wisdom and charity, and he should strive to become like her, to live up to the name. Like Adam in the Bible, he is also the first born in our family.

Here is the background on each of our children's names:

- **Moriah** is a place name derived from the Bible; it is the mountain where Abraham went to offer his son Isaac as a sacrifice to God (Genesis 22:2). Later in the Bible, Mount Moriah is identified as the place where the Temple of Jerusalem was erected by Solomon (2 Chronicles 3:1). We have always told Moriah her name should remind her of the temple, and that she should always keep herself worthy to be able to enter there.

- **Nyal Ephraim.** He was named after his uncle Nyal who passed away as a child, who was in turn named after another uncle who generously provided Ruth's father the means to begin farming. Ephraim has multiple meanings to us. First and foremost, Ruth's great-great-grandfather, Ephraim K. Hanks, was a rugged pioneer with an adventurous spirit and colorful personality. He was a man of tremendous faith and compassion. Through his instrumentality, God performed many miracles. He was a hero who was one of the first to respond to the call to help rescue hundreds of handcart pioneers caught in the severe snow storms of an early winter. Ephraim was also the birthright son of Joseph who was sold into Egypt. Ephraim was one of the leading tribes of Israel. Nyal has already done much to live up to his namesake.

- **Samuel Hanks Manwaring.** He was named by a voice that came to Ruth in the night. That story has already been shared. We joke that he named himself. The name Samuel means, "God hears" or "Heard of God." It is the name of more than one prophet of God. He also bears his mother's maiden name and my surname. He is admonished to take the best of these elements and incorporate them into his life.

- **Jacob Joseph Manwaring.** This is a powerful name. Jacob was the father of the 12 tribes. His name was changed by God to Israel. His son Joseph was a great leader who always rose to the top of any situation or challenge he might be in. These great prophets, and other prophets by the same names, provide wonderful examples of goodness and godliness for our Jacob Joseph to follow.

The name Zion has profound meaning. We have come to cherish more deeply the concept behind the meaning of her name. Its significance carries us into some of the final thoughts in this volume.

The Meaning of Zion

We first find Zion mentioned in the scriptures as a location, a hill or high prominence in Jerusalem acquired by David when he conquered the Jebusites.[1] Zion was renamed the City of David. But the name "Zion" did not stay there. It would almost seem as if the name was extended to the Temple site (Mt. Moriah) when the ark was carried there – the place upon which Solomon built the temple.[2] And so, Moriah and Zion became synonymous with the Temple, the dwelling place of God.[3] In later books of the Old Testament, the name Zion was sometimes used to denote Jerusalem in general[4] and sometimes a collective term referring to God's chosen Israel.[5] In the New Testament, it is also used to denote the Church of God,[6] and sometimes the "heavenly city."[7]

The literal translation of Zion is "fortress." When I was a youth living in Bamberg, Germany, my parents took us to various places of interest. One of those was a town called Coburg. The central feature of interest in the city is the Coburg Castle, set high on the hill overlooking the town. As we toured the castle, we learned that Martin Luther took refuge here while considered by the Holy Roman Church a heretic and an outlaw, because of his opposition to some of its doctrine and practices. Martin Luther wrote a majestic hymn that became the anthem of his movement: "A Mighty Fortress is Our God." God is like a fortress. He can protect us and give us refuge from danger and adversity. The prophet Isaiah writes of Zion: "[It] shall

1. 2 Samuel 5:7.
2. "Zion", retrieved from https://www.biblestudytools.com/dictionary/zion/.
3. Isaiah 8:18: "...the Lord of Hosts, which dwelleth in mount Zion".
4. Psalms 87:2; 149:2; Isaiah 33:14; Joel 2:1.
5. Psalms 51:18 ; 87:5.
6. Hebrews 12:22.
7. Revelation 14:1.

be a defense …a place of refuge…."[8] Over time, the word Zion has taken on several other significant meanings. It is much more than a geographic location or a fortress. Zion is a divine, motivating concept, an attainable ideal to strive for:

> *"Surely, Zion is the city of our God, and surely Zion cannot fall, neither be moved out of her place, for God is there, and the hand of the Lord is there; And he hath sworn by the power of his might to be her salvation and her high tower. Therefore, verily, thus saith the Lord, let Zion rejoice, for this is Zion – The Pure in Heart."[9]*

Zion – The Pure in Heart

The foregoing scripture describes Zion as "the city of our God." How can one have a heavenly city unless the people who inhabit it are also heavenly? It is not just the presence of God that makes heaven wonderful and peaceful. It is the sanctified presence of those who reside there, a holy people who are inclined and well-practiced to live in peace and harmony with each other. The kernel of Zion begins with the individual. It centers in the idea that we must attain certain qualities within ourselves before we can truly be considered a "Zion" person. Those who qualify are what the scripture calls "the pure in heart." The teachings of Jesus in the Sermon on the Mount include this promise: "Blessed are the pure in heart, for they shall see God."[10] The other qualities found in that great sermon are ideals we can personally work on to become the kind of people who qualify and are prepared not only to see God, but to *live* with Him. The qualities Christ describes in the Beatitudes (meekness, humility, merciful, hungering and thirsting after righteousness, peacemakers, etc.) will lead us back home to God, our Father in Heaven. This has been a constant theme throughout this

---

8. Isaiah 4:5-6.
9. Doctrine and Covenants 97:20-21.
10. Matthew 5:8.

book: Let us learn and grow from the experiences we have through-out life, and trust in a loving God, our Heavenly Father, to help us improve and *become* more like *Him and His Son.*

Each of us must become a "Zion" person, pure in heart, willing to do good, to love our fellow men, and to unite under one common standard that will bring us into harmony with one another. That standard is God and all He stands for. When you consider what He has asked us to do by living His teachings and keeping His commandments, it is all intended to bring about a unity among mankind, His children, and to guide us home to Him at the end of our test in mortality. Jesus was once asked, "Master, what is the great commandment in the law?" He answered, "Thou shalt love the Lord thy God with all thy heart, and with all thy soul, and with all thy mind. This is the first and great commandment. And the second is like unto it, Thou shalt love thy neighbor as thyself. On these two commandments hang all the law and the prophets."[11] In other words, it all boils down to these two ideals: Love God and love your fellow man.

The heart is often used as the symbol of who we truly are as a person. We can be hard-hearted or soft-hearted, etc. The same challenging circumstances can have different effects on us depending on how we choose to react to what we are experiencing. The same boiling water that hardens an egg, softens a potato. The wonderful thing about hearts is, they can change. The heart encrusted with doubt and rebellion can become full of faith and charity. The heart which is impure can become pure. I love the beautiful teaching about the heart by the prophet Ezekiel:

Then will I sprinkle clean water upon you, and ye shall be clean: from all your filthiness, and from all your idols, will I cleanse you.

A new heart also will I give you, and a new spirit will I put within you: and I will take away the stony heart out of

---

11. Matthew 22:36-40.

your flesh, and I will give you a heart of flesh.

*And I will put my spirit within you, and cause you to walk
in my statutes, and ye shall keep my judgments, and do them.*

*And ye shall dwell in the land that I gave to your fathers;
and ye shall be my people, and I will be your God.*[12]

The condition of our heart not only determines the quality of our mortal lives, but how and where we will live in eternity.

I am so grateful for the concept of Zion that is reflected in the name of our daughter. It is a reminder to us of what we are striving for, to be pure as she is pure. Though her heart was not perfect physically, what heart can be more spiritually pure than the heart of a beautiful, innocent infant?

Zion Families

The concept of Zion does not stop with the principle of individuals being pure in heart. In fact, that is the starting point – it grows outward from there.

The Heavenly City is not made up of individuals alone, but also of families. Families are ordained of God. It has been so since the beginning. Adam and Eve were created in the image of God, their father, and given to each other (married) by God and told to multiply (create a family) and replenish the earth (replicating the process with many families). The building block of society is the family. In fact, the concept of family is eternal. We are God's children. Each of us is a unique beloved spirit son or daughter of heavenly parentage. We lived with our Heavenly Father as a family before we came into this life. We continue the pattern here in mortality. Our ultimate goal is to return to the presence of our Heavenly Father and our home with Him, our heavenly family. Families are indeed meant to be forever. We, each of us as God's children, have inherited a divine nature and have a divine destiny. On this subject, C.S. Lewis, the

---

12. Ezekiel 36:25-28.

great Protestant philosopher, said the following:

"It is a serious thing to live in a society of possible gods and goddesses, to remember that the dullest most uninteresting person you can talk to may one day be a creature which, if you saw it now, you would be strongly tempted to worship ... All day long we are, in some degree helping each other ... There are no ordinary people."[13]

What is the purpose of the family? Aside from the obvious purpose to bring children into the world, the family exists to help each family member through nurturing, teaching, discipline, and love. In the family, we learn how to associate with each other and thereby how to relate to other people. It is where we receive our first lessons in life. Everything begins in the family. This is where the patterns of our life begin to form.

This unit of the family is sacred and deserves to be protected. It is under attack in so many ways today. Husbands and wives need to be faithful to one another and to care for each other. It is God's intent that children come into a home where a husband and wife have a commitment and loyalty to one another and honor their marital vows. Marital covenants between a couple and God are a great blessing. They help us to keep our feet on a path leading to greater happiness. God entrusts his spirit children into our care, therefore, parents are under a solemn obligation to train and care for the children God gives them. From an inspired document about families I quote the following:

"Parents have a sacred duty to rear their children in love and righteousness, to provide for their physical and spiritual needs, and to teach them to love and serve one another, observe the commandments of God, and be law-abiding citizens wherever they live. ...Happiness in family life is most likely to be achieved when founded upon the teachings of the Lord Jesus Christ. Successful

---

13. C.S. Lewis, *The Weight of Glory* (San Francisco: Harper, 1949/1980), pp. 45-46.

marriages and families are established and maintained on
principles of faith, prayer, repentance, forgiveness, respect, love,
compassion, work, and wholesome recreational activities."[14]

Another great quote on the subject, attributed to C.S. Lewis states,
"The homemaker has the ultimate career. All other careers exist for
one purpose only – and that is to support the ultimate career."[15]

It requires much of us to overcome the baser tendencies of the
natural man and to become the person God asks us to be. There are
times when we just don't feel capable of becoming that good. Then
is when we must reach out to others and reach up to God and hum-
bly ask for help to change. God intended our families to be the first
resource to help us and teach us. His hand is often manifested in
our lives through the efforts of good and loving parents. This is how
He designed it. It is up to us as parents to fulfill His intent. I know it
does not always work out perfectly because of people's agency – the
power to choose – a freedom God respects so highly that He will
never take it away from any of us.

It is unfortunate and sad when families do not fulfill this divine
purpose. This is also why it is so important to reach beyond the
bounds of our immediate family to extended family, and to the family of God (our fellow men). When we truly love our fellow men,
this is what we do: We serve them and minister to their needs. I love
the following quote:

"A man filled with the love of God, is not content with blessing
his family alone, but ranges through the whole world, anxious
to bless the whole human race."[16]

---

14. "The Family: A Proclamation to the World," *Ensign*, Nov 1995. 102.
15. "Letter of C. S. Lewis" (1988 ed. P. 447) The actual quote is a bit different but contains the
same idea: "...*a housewife's work ...is surely in reality the most important work in the world. ...[it] is the*
one for which all others exist."
16. Joseph Smith, *History of the Church*, (Salt Lake City Utah: Deseret News, 1908), 4:227; from a
letter from Joseph Smith to the Twelve, Dec. 15, 1840, Nauvoo, Illinois, published in *Times and*
Seasons, Jan. 1, 1841, p. 258; this letter is incorrectly dated Oct. 19, 1840, in *History of the Church.*

The family also becomes the laboratory in which we learn how to deal with other people up close and to practice the virtues we have talked about again and again, until we begin to get it right. What we learn in the family is what we apply in our dealings with our fellow men.

The following scriptural teachings have always impressed me as a great guide for families:

> *And as all have not faith, seek ye diligently and teach one another words of wisdom; yea, seek ye out of the best books words of wisdom; seek learning, even by study and also by faith.*
>
> *Organize yourselves; prepare every needful thing; and establish a house, even a house of prayer, a house of fasting, a house of faith, a house of learning, a house of glory, a house of order, a house of God;*
>
> *That your incomings may be in the name of the Lord; that your outgoings may be in the name of the Lord; that all your salutations may be in the name of the Lord, with uplifted hands unto the Most High.*
>
> *…Let not all be spokesmen at once; but let one speak at a time and let all listen unto his sayings, that when all have spoken that all may be edified of all, and that every man may have an equal privilege.*
>
> *See that ye love one another; cease to be covetous; learn to impart one to another as the gospel requires.*
>
> *Cease to be idle; cease to be unclean; cease to find fault one with another; cease to sleep longer than is needful; retire to thy bed early, that ye may not be weary; arise early, that your bodies and your minds may be invigorated.*
>
> *And above all things, clothe yourselves with the bond of charity, as with a mantle, which is the bond of perfectness and peace.*[17]

---

17. Doctrine & Covenants 88:118-125.

Because our Father in Heaven has asked us to do this, we can be confident that He will help us. We can turn to Him with a great degree of faith, as we are assured so many times in scripture: "Ask, and it shall be given you, seek, and ye shall find; and to him that knocketh it shall be opened."[18]

Zion families are not perfect, and the process of getting there is not without its bumps and bruises as we stumble along doing the best we can. As parents, we have felt like we were failing at times when fighting and quarreling has been part of our home scene. This has been especially evident during the teenage years. Zion must have been shaking her head on numerous occasions if she witnessed some of those moments. I believe she has had faith and confidence in us to work things out. We have always tried our best to do that.

Zion Societies

Societies consist of both individuals and families. There are many different types of communities in the world. Some we would be happy to live in, while others we would be fearful of crossing into their borders. On occasion, I have asked people to describe what kind of society they would like to live in, or, if they could create any kind of society/community, what would it look like? The answers are always similar and even somewhat predictable: no crime; people care about each other; no selfishness, greed, or violence; no poor, no class distinctions; everyone treats others as they would be treated – they live the golden rule; people keep their commitments and promises, they are reliable and self-reliant, honest and hard-working; there is no contention, arguing and fighting, but mutual respect; people think more about how they can contribute to the well-being of others rather than just themselves.

Certainly, this would be a wonderful place to live. There may be communities right now that are closer to this ideal than others. I have seen such communities that have developed a culture

---

18. Luke 11:9.

approaching this ideal. We have lived in such a community, as you have witnessed in the reading of this book. As you can imagine, it is hard to maintain such a culture with the destructive influences of the current world constantly creeping in. But it is possible to have such communities when its members are continually trying to live good and wholesome lives. They are committed to God and trying to keep his commandments. They are trying to follow the pattern set in this scripture:

And the Lord called his people Zion, because they were of one heart and one mind and dwelt in righteousness; and there was no poor among them.[19]

How can we achieve such unity with such diversity? Is it even possible? These are pivotal questions. First, God assures us it is possible. To achieve it, I believe the answer is to share the worthy goal of following the example Jesus Christ laid before us, and to be united under a common righteous standard: To love God and to love our fellow man.

If we have enough Zion people and Zion families, we can have Zion societies. It is a high ideal, but isn't it what we all want to ultimately achieve, to live in peace and happiness with those we love and cherish? The only way to change society is to begin with ourselves. There are a few simple concepts that can contribute in a big way to this end:

1. Eliminate selfishness from our lives

2. Cooperate completely and in harmony with others

3. Sacrifice our time, talents, and means

4. Love God and trust him.

The title of this chapter is "Cherishing Zion," but it entails much more than cherishing the memory of a little girl who blessed our

19. Moses 7:18.

lives in so many ways. It incorporates the idea that we should cherish the concept of Zion as it has been expressed here. We hope to always cherish Zion, in every way. We are striving to become Zion individuals, working together to become a Zion family and contributing in our own small way to building a Zion society. We have faith that as we continue to do so, one day we will all be reunited together in a heavenly place often called Zion.

Zion's Headstone

The story of Zion's headstone is an inspirational story and very meaningful for our family. It is another tender mercy.

As you will recall, while Ruth and I were in the hospital with Zion that first Sunday after she was born, we had just received serious news from the doctors. They were gently letting us know that surgery may not be a good option, depending on what happened in the next day

We went to the hospital chapel directly from speaking with the doctors, since a church service was about to begin. It was an emotional meeting for both of us as we contemplated the news and tried to process it. We were grateful to have this time in a sacrament meeting. It gave us much-needed solace, peace, and comfort.

During the meeting, I began to have some thoughts about the future. I realized that the direction things were going was in many ways out of our hands. That very morning, I had an inspired moment where I had seen our family together at home and saw Zion with her siblings surrounding her. For some reason, my thoughts turned to a grave marker, a headstone. I remember thinking about the Holocaust museum (Yad Vashem) in Jerusalem, Israel, where we had visited a few years before. Outside the museum was a series of white pillars that had been erected and were broken off at various lengths. It was explained that these pillars represented the young who had died in the Holocaust, whose lives had prematurely been cut short. As my thoughts progressed, I thought of Zion and how

her life might be "cut short." I thought of her little body that was in
trouble because it was not born perfectly whole, but that her spirit
was in fact perfect, pure and eternal. A thought began to form in my
mind that her headstone should incorporate these same ideas – a
rough, unfinished, unpolished, imperfect body – but a spirit that
was the opposite of all of that. I sketched out what I was thinking as
a rough draft. I could see a smooth and polished shaft rising out of
a rough base: The base representing her earthly body and existence,
and the shaft representing her spirit. My notes included this simple
statement: "A monument – a life cut short, a life eternal."

I put my notes away, but the time eventually came, many
months later after Zion had passed away, when we were able to
turn our thoughts to the necessity of providing a headstone for her
grave. I thought of Zion's name and what it represents. I thought
of the different Zions of the latter days. Of course, there is the pure
in heart, a Zion people. There are significant places that have been
called Zion. There is the Zion of the eastern hemisphere in Jerusalem. The temples of Solomon, Zerubbabel, and Herod were all built
on Mt. Moriah, also referred to in scripture as Zion. Then there is
the Zion of the West. The Church of Jesus Christ of Latter-day Saints
has its headquarters in Salt Lake City, Utah. This has always been
considered a Zion by the Latter-day Saints – a long time gathering
place. The pioneers who trekked westward were "gathering to Zion."
And finally, there is another Zion, a third geographic Zion. It was
the original gathering place of the Latter-day Saints in the city of
Independence, Missouri, in Jackson County. The Saints were driven
from their homes in Jackson County, but it is considered a future
gathering place, a future Zion.

As I thought about these Zions, I especially thought of SLC and
Jerusalem. I knew there were two different types of stone representative of the temples built in both of those places. The Zion in the
Rocky Mountains has the Salt Lake City Temple. The stone that was
cut out of the granite quarries and used to build that temple would

be perfect to use as the base of the
headstone for our Zion. The other
stone is Jerusalem limestone. We
had become acquainted with this
stone on our many trips to Israel. I
came to appreciate that this stone
was used in the construction of
those temples built on Mount Zion. It is a beautiful white limestone.
Many structures in Jerusalem today are built of this material. It was
also the material of the pillars at Yad Vashem representing the lives
of the young cut short. This would be perfect for the shaft that would
represent the spirit of Zion, pure and perfect.

On a subsequent trip to Salt Lake City, Ruth and I visited the
stone quarry from which the stone was cut for the Salt Lake Temple. We eventually found a piece of stone that we thought would be
adequate for the base of the marker. It must have weighed about
250–300 pounds. If you can imagine Ruth and me wrestling that
stone in the snow of winter, then you would have to imagine a rather
comical scene as we pushed, pulled, tilted, tugged, lifted and lever-
aged that beast until we finally had it in the back of our van.

We selected a monument company in Idaho Falls to do the work
and delivered the stone to them. After sharing my ideas and showing them my sketches, they began to work on the base. After a short
time, they called me and said the stone we brought them for the base
would not work. They told us however that they had a lot of granite
leftover from when they were contracted to do work on one of the
temples the church was building. Their stone had also come from
the same quarry we had gotten ours. Perfect.

Obtaining the white Jerusalem limestone was more difficult. I called Bonnie Belkin, a tour guide we had used in Israel,
and asked if she could connect us with people in the construction
industry in Israel. She said she would see what she could do. Eventually we learned that the cost of shipping a piece of stone with our

specifications was exorbitant, more than we could afford. It was suggested we look for a piece in the United States that had come from Jerusalem, something already here and more affordable. I searched the internet and eventually found two Jewish brothers in the stone industry in Kansas City. They had pieces they were thinking of using as table legs for a stone table. The size was perfect for our design. We ordered the stone and had it sent to Idaho Falls, where it would be cut and shaped into the form of an obelisk. We had learned on a trip to Egypt that the obelisk was considered by some to be a symbol of eternal life. Like a church spire it points to the heavens, toward God. For us, it was also a symbol of upward, eternal progression. It was perfect for our purpose.

On one of our trips to see Ruth's folks, we stopped by the monument company in Idaho Falls to see how things were going. They had carved the base and the shaft but had not put them together yet. I really wanted to see the shaft, so they sent a man into the stone yard to get it for us, and after a long time, he came back with bad news. The shaft was gone. They had no idea what had happened to it. Eventually, it was determined that someone must have stolen it. Fortunately, the stone dealers in Kansas City still had a couple pieces in the same size. This time I asked them to send me both pieces. I decided to use one of them in Zion's memorial garden that I was going to build at our home in Twin Falls.

I don't know how I missed it when I ordered the first piece, but in reordering, I saw the address of the stone dealers was actually in Independence, a suburb of Kansas City, in Jackson County, Missouri – the future, third Zion. This was yet another of the tender mercies and little miracles we added to Zion's story. Her marker would be represented by all three geographic Zions that are of great significance to us.

We learned of a business, also in Idaho Falls, that had the ability to put photographs on porcelain. These images were often used on headstones. We had originally wanted Zion's hand (ASL "I Love

You") etched on the stone, but instead we had a porcelain plaque with a picture of the actual plaster cast of her hand put on the headstone above the inscription. This image, we are told, will never fade.

The headstone turned out well, though not as perfect or aesthetically pleasing as I had imagined, but all the symbolism is present and is perfectly preserved. It is certainly unique. Ruth's brother and his sons installed the headstone when it was finally delivered. They formed and poured a concrete slab for its placement. We are grateful for their service. We gathered as a family at the cemetery for the placement of the grave marker. We took with us the original temporary brass marker, which we now have in our garden. We also were given a granite shaft by my brother Richard. It came from the Temple quarry in Salt Lake City. We now have the two stones, Salt Lake Granite and Jerusalem Stone (via Jackson County, Missouri).

In the years since Zion passed away, the wisdom and further inspiration that guided Ruth to buy the third burial plot in Parker, Idaho, have become evident. Initially, Ruth had misgivings about burying Zion so far from our home in Twin Falls. She shares the following:

> We had settled in to live there (in Twin Falls) forever, but it didn't seem right to bury Zion there. As hard as it was to know I couldn't go and visit her grave whenever I wanted, I can see the wisdom these many years later.
>
> My parents faithfully decorate her grave along with their son's and my grandparents and other family members who are buried there. The cemetery is frequently visited by my sons as

they attend the university in nearby Rexburg. I hope that all my boys who attend school here will take the opportunity to visit her grave. I noticed this past summer when I stopped by to place a little memento on her gravestone that there were many pennies lying on the cement base. I found that Nyal, my second son, had placed those there on his visits to the cemetery.

We visit Zion's grave whenever we are in the area to see family, rain or shine, winter or summer. Ruth always makes sure to leave a gift appropriate for the season: A pink Santa hat at Christmas time, flowers in the spring, balloons if it is close to a birthday, etc. We often receive, by email or text, pictures from extended family members when they visit and leave a remembrance at her gravesite.

As our children visit Zion's grave and watch over her, she in turn watches over them. She has had her work cut out for her. She is doing a good job.

CHAPTER 18

The Highway of Submission: Moving On

I had always wanted to do something with the eastern edge of our property. On a couple of occasions friends and students approached me about the possibility of using our home to host their wedding reception. I envisioned making part of the property into a garden with a path leading to a covered area where a wedding party could receive guests. I would include a beautiful gazebo, fountains, and terraced gardens connected by steps and retaining walls. The concept was all planned both in my mind and on paper and would be beautiful. Moriah could use it for her wedding reception some-day. I had determined to call it Zion's Garden.

We started construction that summer. Adam worked for a man who was skilled in operating earth-moving equipment. We hired him to carve terraces and paths to my specifications. I began to build retaining walls and steps between levels, and laid piping for fountains and a drip system. We made a lot of progress through the

fall. When winter came, we suspended work, intending to continue when the weather improved the next spring.

It was in February of 2008, a couple of months after our family had returned from our Mexico trip, that I received an unexpected phone call while in my office one day.

"Paul? This is Richard Hawks."

I knew Richard Hawks. He was the person my area director answered to in the central office. It was very unusual to get a phone call from the central office. I wondered what he could be calling about.

"Yes, Richard. What can I do for you?"

We exchanged a few pleasantries, and he asked about Ruth and my family. Then he said,

"The purpose of my call is to ask you if you would consider a change of assignment.

Would you consider moving to another location?"

At that moment, my mind and body had a physical reaction I have rarely experienced in my life. I was in shock. My head was reeling, and my heart literally began to race – it felt like a million beats a minute. This proposition was so unexpected, so out of the blue. I'd had no anticipation of a move. We have annual interviews with our area director in which we are asked various questions, including our disposition about where we are located and if we have any need or desire for a new assignment locally or elsewhere. I had expressed no interest in relocating. All I remember thinking at that moment, and repeatedly thereafter was, "Why would I want to move!? Why would I want to be anywhere but here?!"

I don't recall much of our conversation after that, but I do remember the feeling of complete shock. I must have conveyed my surprise in the way I responded to him. I asked where he had in mind, and he said California. There were a couple of possible locations, one in the Bay area and the other in Southern California. At some point he said, "Why don't you think about it and talk to Ruth and get back to me."

Throughout my career I have been open to new assignments, and I have always been what I would consider "a good company man." I have seen these changes as opportunities for growth. I have believed such requests were inspired. But now, I was shocked and disoriented and could not concentrate on anything. The questions flooded my mind: "Why would I want to move anywhere? Our lives here are perfect. Our family is well situated. The kids have their friends, their music programs, their good teachers. We have so many good friends and people we love. We love the lifestyle we have with the daily chores, the animals, the paper routes, the work ethic. We love our home, our orchard, our vegetable gardens, our horse property, our barn, our cows and chickens. I have built up a very successful program here at the institute. This is all perfect. Why would we even consider moving anywhere else?"

I could not concentrate at my office and needed to get out and do something else. I had to walk. I had to think. I needed Ruth. I wanted to talk with her. So, I went home. It was the middle of the afternoon. When I entered the house, I called out Ruth's name. No one answered my call. The kids were all in school, and Ruth was

gone. My main recollection is that I went to the dining area, which opens onto the back porch, and stood there looking out over our property, the spacious backyard, our pasture beyond. My gaze drifted to the right, and I looked at the area I had been working on last summer and fall, Zion's Garden. I thought of all the effort that had gone into having the land contoured and carved to fit my plans; the retaining walls and steps I had put in, the work in progress; but it was an unfinished work!

I continued to look over our corner of Heaven. A little further to my right was the "tree house" Adam and I had built over a couple of summers. It was a crown jewel on our property. Adam had wanted a treehouse, but there were no trees large enough to sustain one when we moved here. He was ten years old then. I eventually came up with the idea of building an elevated platform, then building on top of that, and planting trees around it so it had the appearance of being in the trees. Adam loved the idea and sketched out the "tree house," our first blueprint. The concept grew as construction progressed. The finished product was amazing and wonderful. It was a small house perched on a platform with a porch and steps leading up to it. It was insulated against heat and cold, had drywall, electricity, custom windows and door, a loft, a skylight, and siding to match the house. There was a zip line from the porch of the tree house down to the pasture, about 70 yards away. Ruth had named it, appropriately, the "Kid's Condo." It was a wonderful source of fun and enjoyment. Underneath the tree house was a sandbox where the kids could play. All of this was part of the good life we had created for ourselves here, full of wonderful memories from the past with great memories yet to be made.

As I stood there looking at this scene, agonizing over the proposed relocation, torn in my thoughts about what was the right thing to do, I prayed for insight and inspiration. In response, a single powerful impression quietly entered my mind and heart: "This is right!" Meaning – "This move you are asked to consider is right." My mind began to settle, and a peace began to work its way into my soul. I say 'began,' because it was not a full and immediate resolution, but it was a beginning. I marveled at this because it ran counter to the initial direction of my thoughts. Everything within me, as I surveyed the physical evidence of our good life, was centered around the singular thought "How can we even think of leaving all of this and going somewhere else?" But here I was, now beginning to open up to the possibility.

My gaze drifted back to my left, to the barn and corrals, the garden, the orchard, and then beyond to the temple, only a block and a half away. Majestic and beautiful, the new temple rose above the houses and neighborhood that lay between it and our home. Still under construction, it was due to be finished and dedicated in the upcoming summer. We were so excited to have a temple in our city, especially so close to our home and visible from our back porch. Temples are symbols of our faith and devotion to God. Our willingness to consecrate our lives and conform our will to His is integrated in the covenants we make in the temple.

It was not until later in the day that I was finally able to talk to Ruth. I could not predict how she would react to Richard's request, but I believed it would be similar to mine. As I related to her the conversation I had with Richard Hawks, her reply completely surprised me, "That sounds exciting!"

"What? Are you serious?"

Ruth was excited by the prospect of a new adventure, especially the possibility of moving to the Bay area. This was not what I had anticipated. The excitement turned out to be only her initial reaction, however. This sentiment did not remain at the same level of enthusiasm over the next few hours, let alone months, but it did shift everything to a new realm of possibilities. We talked about the decision before us. I told her about my reluctant thoughts earlier in the day and my subsequent impression that this was the right thing to do. It certainly was not my preference to move, but maybe it was what God wanted for us. We decided to talk to the kids about it and hear what they had to say. When we presented this prospect to the kids, they were not convinced it was a good idea. They said they did not want to move, but they did want to do what was right. We all decided to fast and pray as a family on the coming Sunday and then have another family council on the matter. Ruth said the only way she could ever feel completely okay with this decision was if the children were at peace with it.

Sunday came, our family fasted, and then we met together and had a prayer. We asked the kids what they had been thinking throughout their fast and each of them expressed their feelings. It was unanimous: we all loved living in Twin Falls, but if it was God's will for us to move, they would support that decision. A couple of them said they felt it was the right thing to do. The final decision then rested with Ruth and me. The feeling that this was right had only grown within me. Now, with the family unity that came from our fasting and prayer, we felt like we could move beyond our own personal desires and adjust our focus to a new direction in life. So, the decision was made to move to a new assignment in California. We called Richard Hawks and informed him of our decision.

This was not an easy thing for us. It was a move done purely on faith. We had absolutely no other motivation than to do what was right in the eyes of our Heavenly Father. On a personal level, it only made sense to stay where we were. All the lessons we had learned in life, the lessons we had learned from Zion, were now coming into play. Trust God. He knows what is best. You can't see what He can see. Trust God. Have faith.

This evolved into a greater exercise of faith than we had imagined. Everything began to stack up against us to test our resolve to go through with this move. It is impossible to convey all the challenges which came our way. The path forward was fraught with every obstacle imaginable. If this was the right thing to do, why wouldn't it go smoothly and without a hitch? But hitches there were, and plenty of them. I think that we, meaning people in general, often have the misconception that if we choose to do the right thing and follow God's will, everything will go well, and He will pave the way with rose petals. This can be the case if it is His will and suits His purposes for us, but sometimes the real test of faith comes after we make the decision to follow Him. Such was the case with this change of assignment we had accepted. I have often quoted (actually misquoted) Shakespeare as saying, "When troubles come, they come not single file, but in armies."[1] As we made arrangements for this major change in our lives, a legion of adversity came against us.

The "hitches" I mentioned earlier began with a house fire. Ruth took a phone call while cooking in the kitchen and left for a couple of minutes to take care of a matter related to the call. During her absence a grease fire erupted. She tried to put it out, but in her panic, she had a hard time getting the fire extinguisher to work. I was upstairs when the house began to fill with smoke and alarms started going off. I ran downstairs and found our kitchen well in flames. We finally got the fire extinguisher to function and were able to put out most of the fire before the extinguisher emptied out. Thankfully, the spray nozzle at the kitchen sink had enough pressure to reach the last of the fire. Literally, if we had been five seconds later in our attempts to put out the fire, it would have gone beyond our control to extinguish. Smoke penetrated every corner of our home, blackening and infusing

---

1. William Shakespeare, *Hamlet*, Act IV, Scene V as spoken by Claudius. The actual quote is: "When sorrows come, they come not as single spies, but in battalions."

everything with noxious soot. When the insurance agent and the restoration specialists came to assess the damage, they found it was more extensive than we had imagined. There was a lot of smoke damage. It required getting rid of appliances, a complete kitchen reconstruction, dry-cleaning all our clothes, cleaning and repainting much of the interior of the house, etc. Dealing with all the restoration on top of preparing for a move became a true challenge.

In the meantime, we decided to take the assignment in southern California. Our new home would be in Moorpark in Ventura County. We were not unfamiliar with Southern California. We had left Glendale, California, only eight years before to come to Idaho. In fact, all our children except for Zion had been born there. When we relocated to Twin Falls, it had been a good move for us in all ways, including financially. We were able to realize good equity from the sale of our home in Glendale and used it to buy the property in Twin Falls. Moving back to California was a different matter. Home prices had skyrocketed. Our home in Idaho was large, with outbuildings and a couple of acres, and would be paid off in a few years. Now we would have the challenge of buying a smaller and more expensive home than the value of our entire property in Twin Falls. We would need to take out a thirty-year mortgage in order to have payments which would meet our monthly budget.

Our initial house-hunting trip to Southern California did not go very well. We found the economy in California had begun to deteriorate with the onset of the Great Recession and home prices had begun to drop, but they were still inflated. Ruth had a hard time finding anything affordable that she liked. Each night as we returned to the hotel after seeing numerous properties during the day, she just cried. She asked, "Are we sure this is the right thing?" At one point, we talked to Richard Hawks, somewhat discouraged, and he shared with us a speech given by Jeffrey R. Holland: *Cast Not Away Therefore Your Confidence.* The message was helpful and applicable to our situation, one we would need to read more than once throughout the next few months. Following are excerpts from the talk:

I wish to encourage every one of you today regarding opposition that so often comes after enlightened decisions have been made, after moments of revelation and conviction have given us a peace and an assurance we thought we would never lose. In his letter to the Hebrews, the Apostle Paul was trying to encourage new members who had just joined the Church, who undoubtedly had had spiritual experiences and had received the pure light of testimony, only to discover that not only had their troubles not ended, but that some of them had only begun.

... Paul said to those who thought a new testimony, a personal conversion, or a spiritual baptismal experience would put them beyond trouble,

> *"Call to remembrance the former days, in which, after ye were illuminated, ye endured a great fight of afflictions" (Hebrews 10:32; emphasis added).*

Then came this tremendous counsel, which is at the heart of my counsel to you and the title of my remarks this morning:

> Cast not away therefore your confidence, *which hath great recompense of reward. For ye have need of patience, that, after ye have done the will of God, ye might receive the promise. ...*

Of course, our faith will be tested as we fight through these self-doubts and second thoughts. ... After you have gotten the message, after you have paid the price to feel his love and hear the word of the Lord, "go forward." Don't fear, don't vacillate, don't quibble, don't whine. ... If God has told you something is right, if something is indeed true for you, he will provide the way for you to accomplish it. [2]

---

2. Jeffrey R. Holland, "Cast Not Away Therefore Your Confidence," *Ensign*, March 2000.

This is the test of faith: remaining true to a conviction when the evidence of it no longer exists, when the emotion of the point of decision has faded and all you are left with is its memory, which carries only so much weight in the face of present realities. It is so easy to second-guess ourselves when the refining heat is turned on. It is just so easy to doubt when all the evidence seems to run counter to that initial conviction. And *our* conviction *was* put to the test – again and again! I have heard it said that "character is the ability to follow through on a resolution long after the emotion with which it was made has passed." The strength of our character was sorely tested during this transition.

Looking back on this period of our lives makes me tired even now. It wore us out, physically, emotionally, and spiritually. I want to give an accurate and complete idea of the difficulty and stress we experienced, and how our resolve was tested, but I realize that I could write another book on that topic alone; and it does not suit the purpose here. Perhaps it is sufficient to just briefly mention a couple things.

The challenge of getting our property ready for sale was multiplied by the size of our property and what we needed to do to get the best purchase price. Added to this were all the many decisions we needed to make with remodeling the kitchen and other repairs and upgrades to be done, not to mention living without a kitchen for months. Putting the home on the market could not happen until everything was completed and ready for prospective buyers. This set us back a few months. When we finally put the house on the market, we found there were very few qualified buyers for a property in our price range. But before long, a dentist from Florida, who was relocating to Twin Falls, made an offer. After counter-offers and negotiations, we agreed on an acceptable price. We were grateful. Ruth felt so relieved, like a huge burden had been lifted. Two days later the real estate agent called and told me the buyer had backed out.

I remember that morning when I broke the news to Ruth. We were standing in the garage. She was wearing her work clothes and had been happily engaged in gardening. When I told her that the buyer had backed out, she literally sunk to the floor in disbelief and despair, frustrated and heartbroken. She cried and cried. I had not ever seen her like this. It was the last straw in a series of difficulties. All I could do was put my arms around her and try to console her, even as I was feeling deeply discouraged. Why couldn't things go more smoothly? Why so many challenges? How much more could we endure? It did not help when almost no one came to see our home when we put it on the market again. I had to give Ruth a break from all of this, so I sent her to her sister's home in Pocatello for a few days. Eventually, a few very stress-filled weeks later, the real estate broker intervened and asked me if we would be willing to sell to the same buyer at a lower price. At this point, I felt like we just needed to be done with the stress. A few thousand dollars difference was not worth the emotional price we were all paying. The buyer agreed to the reduced price. With this major obstacle removed, we could all move on to the next stage of our lives.

My job in California required me to get there right away. In fact, I was already a month overdue, but there was no way I could leave until everything was stable. It was now the first week of August. The family would follow me in three weeks. I worried about Ruth having to deal with finishing up all the odds and ends and getting the family out the door and on the road. Thank goodness we had a moving company taking care of a lot of that burden. The previous few months had taken a heavy toll on all of us, but especially on her.

One of the hardest things I have ever had to do was to leave Twin Falls. To physically pack up my things and load them in the pickup came with a stark realization that we were really doing this, and there was no turning back. I was leaving everything and everyone, not knowing what lay ahead, going completely on faith. The stress I felt leaving Ruth with the necessary burden of completing the move, bidding my family an emotional goodbye, and then finally driving away from the place and people I had come to love with all my heart, was nearly too much for me. I have moved many times, but this was the hardest move of my life.

My most vivid memory of that drive to California was being several miles down the road and having all my pent-up emotions finally break the surface. I cried out to God through hot and abundant tears, "Father, this is so hard! How can I do this?! I pray we are doing the right thing! The *only* reason I am going to California is because I believe it is thy will. I am putting all my trust in thee. Please bless me with strength to do this. And please bless Ruth, bless my family!" My feelings were intense. There, in the privacy of my vehicle – and because of the privacy of my vehicle – I sobbed and sobbed. My body was racked with emotion as I let out all the pain and longing and fear and frustration that were in my soul. I had a good hard cry. And finally, in humility and faith, I gave my personal desires and my will completely over to Him.

I learned something about myself that day. I learned that I was indeed willing to do whatever God asked of me, no matter how hard it was. I thought I had already been tested on this issue with Zion, but here was another test that took me even further down this road of commitment and humble submission. I have been left with a deep feeling of gratitude and humble satisfaction for the knowledge I gained about myself, that I am willing to pay a heavy price to do God's will, and that I have the ability, with His help, to do really hard things.

It has only just now occurred to me as I write this, that this was the same stretch of road where a year and a half earlier, while bringing Zion home from the hospital, I had asked Ruth, "How can we do this thing? How can we bring our baby home to die?" Isn't it ironic that these two significant events crossed paths going opposite directions? The highway of submission!

I wish I could say the problems ended there, but that is far from the truth. We were to be tested right up to the end. Just when I thought I was beyond the hardest part, there were still more challenges to come. Through a combination of hard work, divine guidance, and tender mercies, we finally found a nice affordable home in Moorpark.

In our last few months in Twin Falls, we had watched the ongoing construction of the nearby temple. It was now complete, and an open house had been held prior to its dedication. We had very much looked forward to having a temple so close to our home. This was not to be. The day before it was dedicated, the moving company finished loading our belongings, and Ruth and the kids packed up the Suburban and got a hotel room. The next morning, they attended the temple dedication, then started on their journey west.

Both Ruth and I have pioneer ancestors. We have likened our experience to theirs because of similarities we have seen. Our ancestors had been building a temple in Nauvoo, Illinois, and were looking forward to its completion. They barely got to enjoy the blessing of the near-completed temple when they were driven from their homes. They headed west, not knowing what lay ahead of them, or where they would wind up, but they trusted in God to guide them and care for their needs. Some of them lost loved ones along the way. They buried their dead and moved on with faith in every footstep. Through trials and difficulties, they wound up in the Salt Lake Valley and built a new life and legacy. Some of those pioneers were even asked to move yet again to settle new communities elsewhere for "the cause of Zion." And all this they did with only faith lighting their way. A collective term for these new communities in the west, where they intended to build a society of saints and live in peace and harmony, was Zion.

We too have felt like modern pioneers in our own right. This was our "Nauvoo experience," our personal pioneer trek. We left a temple behind that we barely got to enjoy, and headed west, not knowing what lay ahead of us. We had buried our dead and were moving on with life. There was still so much to live. We took with us our dreams and all the lessons God had taught us, with the intent to implement them to make a better life. We feel like we have achieved a balanced perspective of our experience with Zion. There is no longer a preoccupation with her life, but she is not forgotten. Her influence lives on. Zion's Garden in Twin Falls was never completed, but we did take with us a couple of stones intended for that garden to be used in future gardens.

Sometimes we do not know the reasons for the challenges we are called to endure, or for the path God has asked us to walk. Our lives are like a tapestry that is being woven, and we are in the midst of the weaving and cannot see the pattern. It may be years before we can see enough of the tapestry to discern the picture and pattern God is weaving with all our experiences. I have recently heard it said that we cannot connect the dots looking forward. It is only in looking back that we can connect the dots and see God's divine design in our lives.

I often wondered, "Why California?" It was a big question initially, though I eventually came to trust that God knows best, and that was sufficient. Now, many years have passed, and I am able to look back on the effects of the move. A couple of years after we moved, I remembered a night back in Twin Falls when there was an eruption between Adam, then a teenager, and Ruth over a big disagreement. It became ugly to the point I had to intervene. I had to physically restrain Adam and hold him in a bear hug until the situation de-escalated. That night I had offered a fervent private prayer, "Heavenly Father – please help us! Please save this family! Whatever we need to do, I will do it!" It was only a few weeks after this prayer when Richard Hawks called me about moving to a new assignment. I did not really connect the dots until we had been gone for at least a couple of years. Looking back, what I thought was a perfect life was not perfect after all. Things were headed down a dark path I could not know the end of. Adam had a mixture of friends; some were very good. He had another set of friends who had begun to make some poor choices and were having a negative influence on him. We do not know what would have happened to Adam had we stayed, but I have sensed it would not have been good. This is not meant to say things were perfect in California, but the move has been a blessing for our family, perhaps even its salvation. At this point in time, I am very grateful for the results. There may yet be other purposes that will emerge as the tapestry continues to weave.

As we look back over the experiences we have shared in this book, we are grateful to our Father in Heaven for all He has done for our family. He has taught us to trust Him even when we could not see beyond the pain of the moment. He has given us a pure and precious daughter, who in her brief mortal life brought us a greater love than we had ever known. We know that Zion is and will forever be a part of our family. We look forward to the day when all of us will be reunited through the resurrection and atonement of Jesus Christ, never to be separated again.

We try to live each day with faith in God, the Master Weaver, and His Son Jesus Christ, trusting them to create with the threads of our lives and choices a divine design. As we submit our lives to their loving hands and let them do the weaving, in time wonderful patterns and clear purposes will become apparent, beautiful beyond imagination. We will see Zion. We will be Zion.

Zion's Garden

Epilogue

We are thankful to God and to all of those who have touched our lives through these experiences. We feel like we are better versions of ourselves because of all we have experienced and endured.

Ruth's Final Thoughts

I could not have gone through this experience without the companionship and direction of the Holy Ghost. He is the one who has helped me to understand and to feel God's love throughout not only Zion's journey but through many of life's experiences. Maybe some say I am a simpleton, but I know who I can lean on. And I know that the Godhead are mindful of each of us, and our Heavenly Father loves each and every one of His children. Jesus Christ sacrificed His life that He might mediate and redeem us from our weaknesses and sins, and the Holy Ghost testifies of these truths. He comforts us in our sorrows. I have felt His healing warmth, His witness of truth, His calming power and gentle guidance.

I continue to smile and pick up my pennies from heaven and recognize I have a little guardian angel who watches over our family from heaven. Sometimes she seems so close and near, even though life has continued on and my heart doesn't ache as much. I have chosen to surround our family and home with reminders of our Zion. We have her pictures on the walls in about every room in our home.

They remind us that she is part of our family. Her story continues to touch the hearts of those who hear of her life.

Paul's Concluding Thoughts
To Zion: I love you so much and I do look forward to seeing you again someday. I know this will happen. It is an assurance born of faith, as the apostle Paul says, it is "the assurance of things hoped for, the evidence of things not seen."[1] I thank you for watching over our family. For watching over your siblings and your parents. You have been a great blessing both in life and in death.

To God: Dear Heavenly Father, this miracle you have given us is so much greater than the one I initially sought. Thank you for Zion, for the short life she had with us. You knew the blessing and the effect this would have and be in our lives. Thank you for allowing us to share her story with all who can benefit from it. I feel to echo the words of David as my own heartfelt expression: "I have not concealed thy loving kindness, nor hid thy mercies."[2]

And so, we end where we began – trusting in God. We leave you with these assuring words of consolation, hope, and the promise of ultimate peace and joy:

"... Whosoever shall put their trust in God
shall be supported in their trials,
and their troubles,
and their afflictions,
and shall be lifted up at the last day."[3]

1. Hebrews 11:1.
2. Psalms 40:9-10.
3 Alma 36:3.

"This story is very enlightening, heartwarming, and healing for grieving parents like me, still seeking peace after losing a child. Through storytelling and shared experiences of loss and grief, the Manwarings share proof of how God is intricately involved with our individual lives. It is an honor to read their sacred family story of brokenness and healing. It is eye-opening how miracles of the heart still happen, even during life's most grievous moments. It is raw, and it is real. It is a story to Cherish."

—**Jen Keller**, Pocatello, ID

"I read your book. I thought you did a wonderful job. You have an amazing and inspiring heart. The timing of reading it was special. Whether Christian, Catholic, Buddhist... all who read it can benefit from the authentic heart you showed in this book."

—**Shelby Ward**, Moorpark, CA

"This is a remarkable story about a remarkable family. The story is life changing. The book is powerful and inspiring. Reading it strengthened my resolve, inspired my faith, and enriched my testimony of God as I added the tender mercies and miracles to those in my life. I shared your book with my son, who is struggling with his own challenge. His 15-year-old daughter has been in a coma now for a year next month. I know this book will strengthen his faith as he struggles with the challenge of resolving the mystery of purpose and wrestles with the "what ifs" that inevitably appear in the middle of the night. Your story will help him, I know. I also sent a copy to a friend who is a grief counselor, an "end of life" counselor, a sensitive, caring individual "called" and trained to help others who are in the middle of the "ultimate" struggle of the loss of their own future as well as the premature loss of the future life of loved ones."

—**Lawrence Blonquist**, Ph.D., Westlake, CA

Paul A. Manwaring and his wife, Ruth, are the parents of six children. They consider their family their first and most important profession. They met, married, and started their family while in college. Living around the world, Paul was raised in a military family and grew up with six brothers. He has a Ph.D. in educational leadership. His career has been in education as a teacher and administrator. Ruth grew up on a potato farm in eastern Idaho. She has a bachelor's degree in communications with an emphasis in public relations. The Manwarings currently live in Southern California.

CherishingZion.com

Email: CherishingZion@gmail.com

www.ingramcontent.com/pod-product-compliance
Lightning Source LLC
Chambersburg PA
CBHW062042080426
42734CB00012B/2537